The Functions of
Role-Playing Games

T0041065

The Functions of Role-Playing Games

How Participants Create Community, Solve Problems and Explore Identity

SARAH LYNNE BOWMAN

McFarland & Company, Inc., Publishers

Jefferson, North Carolina, and London

LIBRARY OF CONGRESS CATALOGUING-IN-PUBLICATION DATA

Bowman, Sarah Lynne.
    The functions of role-playing games : how participants create
community, solve problems and explore identity / Sarah Lynne Bowman.
        p.   cm.
    Includes bibliographical references and index.

    ISBN 978-0-7864-4710-7
    softcover : 50# alkaline paper ∞

    1. Fantasy games — Social aspects.   2. Role playing — Social aspects.
I. Title.
GV1202.F35B68   2010
793.93 — dc22   2010001187

British Library cataloguing data are available

©2010 Sarah Lynne Bowman. All rights reserved

*No part of this book may be reproduced or transmitted in any form
or by any means, electronic or mechanical, including photocopying
or recording, or by any information storage and retrieval system,
without permission in writing from the publisher.*

Cover images ©2010 Shutterstock

Manufactured in the United States of America

*McFarland & Company, Inc., Publishers
  Box 611, Jefferson, North Carolina 28640
  www.mcfarlandpub.com*

Acknowledgments

I would first like to thank my chair, Thomas Riccio, for his wonderful enthusiasm and advice on this project. I also would like to thank my amazing professors at the University of Texas at Dallas: Dean Kratz, Thomas Linehan, Dean Terry, Michael Wilson, Cynthia Haynes, David Channel, John Gooch, and Tim Redman. Thank you, also, to Sherry Clarkson for her remarkable ability to guide students through the labyrinthine bureaucratic process of the University. From the University of Texas at Austin, I would like to thank my two life-long mentors, Sandy Stone and Janet Staiger, who eternally serve as an inspiration to me as an educator and a scholar.

Also, this volume would not have been possible without the contributions of my respondents, for their willingness to share their stories and their thoughtful self-examination: Chris, John T., Guillermo, Darren, Matthew S., Henry, Alex, Desiree, "Elton," Omega, Josh S., Haley, Josh Z., Kevin, Erin, and Carley. Special, enormous thank you to Walter, who taught me everything I know about role-playing and more. In addition, I would like to thank my fellow players past and present for all the incredible in-game experiences: Andy, Ralph, Ron, Guy, Justin, Randy, Kirstyn and Chet, and Neya in the tabletop realm; Lucas and Chris for BOGYA; and especially our past and present Darkeport LARP players, who provide daily inspiration for me: Harrison, Anne, Russ, Sarah Jane, Kim, Ken, Drew, Stacy, Nick, Zimka, Thax, Karen and John, Laura, Danielle and Chris, Walter II, John F., Doni, Mike and Loren, Ryan, Val, Ari, Pokemike, etc., etc. I love you all in my way.

Finally, I would like to thank all of my beautiful family: Robert and

Judy, Pat and Jim, Ron and Grace, Andrea and Lans, Christopher, Laura and Charles, Harley Jr./Sr. and Sydney, Bryan and Cindy, Eric and Barb, Abe, Patrick, Leigh, Michelle, Joyce: how incredibly lucky I am to have you in my life! To the unbelievable support of my friends in Dallas past and present: Alex, Chris and Brandi, Greg, Kyle, Nick, Dan, Elicia, Ducado, Jason H., Jerome, Mark B., Donna, Julie, Jim B., Kim, Paul H., John S, George and Claire, and Sunny. The Austin contingent: Taira, Ana, Allison and Jason, Matty, Kevin, Jerry, Jim R., Magda and Gary, Mark J., Jason B. and Trudi, Jason K., Ty, Crystal, Brooke, Tasha, Harry, Courtney, Sara, Kadija, Patricia, Morrie, Brad, and everyone in the 5i2/Actual Reality group.

My fellow academicians: Adam Blatner, Bryce, Rez, Angela and Don, Laura M., Debbie, Adrian C., Michael J., Lisa B., Paula E., Hushul, Matt, Trish, Haven, James King, Avi. The Entire cast of *There is Never a Reference Point*: Jamie, Lori S., Casey, Lori M., Andrea, LeeAnn, Brittney, Jenni, Shawn, Mason, Austin, Frank. And all you scattered loves out there: Cinder, Paul M., Bill, Christiana, Matthew W., Sam, Eli and Steph, Barb, Loyal and Susie and all the Kents, Darryl, Glen, Chris O., etc. etc. Your love and support have fueled me throughout this process of life and work.

Table of Contents

Preface

The present work explores the various social and psychological functions of role-playing, with a specific emphasis on role-playing games. The activity of role-playing finds its roots in essential aspects of human social behavior, including childhood pretend play, storytelling, and ritual. The subcultural practice of role-playing games emerged from these age-old practices, but also from several cultural shifts inherent to American life in the latter half of the twentieth century. These shifts include culture-wide paradigm shifts regarding diversity, religion, and alternative lifestyles; an increased interest in the genres of fantasy, science fiction, and horror; a heightened sense of cynicism and self-awareness characteristic of Generation X; and the large-scale technological advances characteristic of the computer and information age.

While these cultural shifts specifically contributed to the popularity of role-playing games as a subculture, people also engage in the practice of role-playing in a variety of different contexts, including business, education, military training, improvisational theater, drama therapy, health care, and leisure. The practice of role-playing offers three basic functions. First, role-playing enhances a group's sense of communal cohesiveness by providing narrative enactment within a ritual framework. Second, role-playing encourages complex problem-solving and provides participants with the opportunity to learn an extensive array of skills through the enactment of scenarios. Third, role-playing offers participants a safe space to enact alternate personas through a process known as identity alteration. This volume explores these three concepts with regard to the various forms of role-playing.

The study also offers a detailed, participant-observer ethnography on role-playing games. This ethnography involves extensive, qualitative interviews. I have personally participated in various forms of role-playing for fifteen years, including tabletop, Live Action Role-Playing (LARP), and virtual gaming. The ethnographic chapters of this study incorporate the contributions of nineteen participants, including myself. Most interviews were conducted in-person and range between thirty minutes and two and a half hours. Six of the respondents, however, replied to the questions via email attachment. These responses resulted in several rounds of follow-up questions and answers, which were appended to the original interviews.

CAST OF PLAYERS:

Alex, a twenty-year-old psychology major.

Carley, an eighteen-year old office manager.

Chris, a twenty-five year old web designer, technical manager, and sales engineer.

Darren, a twenty-eight year old military propagandist.

Desiree, a thirty-six year old day spa owner and masseuse.

"Elton," a twenty-nine year old fiber network field technician and business owner.

Erin, a twenty-one year old retailer and college student.

Guillermo, a twenty-eight year old operations category specialist.

Haley, a twenty-five year old compliance specialist in a market security firm.

Henry, a twenty-two year old college student.

John, a thirty year old sales representative.

Josh S., a twenty-two year old chemistry major with a biology and physics minor.

Josh T., a twenty-four year old retailer and college student.

Kevin, a forty-six year old retailer.

Kirstyn, a twenty-six year old vocal music director.

Matthew, a twenty-three, apparel associate and sales consultant.

Omega, a twenty-eight year old customer service representative.

Sarah, a twenty-nine year old arts and humanities doctoral candidate.

Walter, a thirty-one year old history and paralegal major.

One respondent, "Elton," did not wish for his real name to be used.

Chapter 1, "Historical Evolution and Cultural Permutations" establishes a framework for understanding the development of role-playing games (RPGs) as a cultural phenomenon. First, the essential roots of role-playing are explained as a ritual form of archetypal enactment and storytelling. Next, the cultural shifts that contributed to the development of role-playing games as a subculture are detailed. The sixties brought a paradigm shift toward greater acceptance of diversity and experimentation with alternative lifestyles. In addition, the publication of J.R.R. Tolkien's *Lord of the Rings* in paperback in 1965 increased people's interest in the fantasy genre and medieval reenactment societies. As a result, a group of war gaming enthusiasts utilized concepts from Tolkien's work to create the first official role-playing game in 1974, *Dungeons & Dragons*. Though many game companies attempted to rival *D&D* in the next twenty years, the publication of White Wolf's *Vampire: The Masquerade* in 1991 signaled the first major thematic shift genre-wise in the history of role-playing games. The games in White Wolf's World of Darkness encouraged players to challenge their paradigms of reality, morality, and community, fueled by the larger cultural concerns held by members of Generation X. Advances in video game technology offered additional platforms for RPGs to manifest. Virtual role-playing now exceeds in-person role-playing due to popular games such as *World of Warcraft*. Chapter 1 concludes with a delineation of types of RPGs, including tabletop games, LARP, and virtual role-playing.

Chapter 2, "Role-Playing in Communal Contexts," explains the many environments that utilize role-playing as a practice. This chapter offers a brief history of the development of improvisational drama, drama therapy, educational role-playing, and reenactment societies. The function of ritual is explained, which often involves the enactment of dramatic, archetypal concepts in order to form a greater sense of communal cohesion. The chapter concludes by suggesting that role-playing games serve as a modern-day ritual.

Chapter 3, "Interactional Dynamics in Role-Playing Games," begins the ethnographic section of the volume, addressing the potential for RPGs to provide a heightened sense of community. Fantasy reveals obfuscated elements of reality by encouraging people to see beyond the mundane. The enactment of roles allows for individuals to adopt a theory of mind for others and a greater sense of empathy toward them. Many of the role-players in my ethnography report feelings of childhood isolation, and role-playing games provide an outlet for social interaction. RPGs encourage individuals to enact archetypes and establish social cooperation in order to achieve a particular goal. Both the content and practice of RPGs reflect a ritual type of performance, as both players and characters must establish a sense of group cohesion to succeed.

Chapter 4, "Role-Playing as Scenario Building and Problem Solving," explores the variety of different skills acquired through role-playing scenarios. These skills fall under several dimensions: personal, interpersonal, cultural, cognitive, and professional. The chapter details the variety of societal locations that utilize role-playing for training purposes, including military, governmental, educational, corporate, and healthcare applications.

Chapter 5, "Tactical and Social Problem Solving in Role-Playing Games" explains how role-playing games, though entertaining in nature, also offer the potential for participants to develop these aforementioned skills. The game system provides an elaborate structure that encourages gamers to evaluate the world in terms of a complex set of rules. RPGs offer extensive scenarios that involve complex puzzles, tactics, and social maneuvering. These scenarios require the players to develop problem-solving capabilities in order to succeed. This chapter utilizes ethnographic data to explicate the different challenges role-playing games present to players.

Chapter 6, "Role-Playing as Alteration of Identity," examines the roots of identity alteration, in which an individual creates an alternate sense of self. The section explains forms of childhood play that indicate early examples of world-building and identity shifting, including pretend play, paracosms, and Imaginary Friends. The chapter then explains how, even as adults, people enact a variety of different roles in daily life and further suggests that every person contains a multiplicity of identities. The theory of Dissociative Identity Disorder, which emerges out of studies on psychological trauma, provides insight into the desire to create multiple selves. Though many of the concepts of dissociative theory are useful for understanding role-playing, ultimately, the creation of multiple selves does not necessarily result from trauma. The content of these personalities often arises from current cultural symbols and inherent psychological archetypes. By way of example, the chapter details the many "classes" and "races" of *Dungeons & Dragons* and traces them to earlier roots in cultural history.

Chapter 7, "Character Evolution and Types of Identity Alteration" offers an ethnography in which individuals attempt to explain the relationship between their primary selves and their characters. The chapter describes the moment in which a character is "born" and how role-players develop the character concept through various character-building activities, including back story writing, costuming, and co-creation with other role-players. This section also explains how role-playing characters evolve over time, offering four distinct stages of character development. The chapter then establishes a typography of role-playing characters. These types correlate less to inherent archetypes, and more to the relationship between character and player. These categories also offer potential motivations for the creation of particular types of personas. The nine types I describe are the Doppelganger Self, the Devoid Self, the Augmented Self, the Fragmented Self, the Repressed Self, the Idealized Self, the Oppositional Self, the Experimental Self, and the Taboo Self. The enactment of these personas changes the role-players' understanding of themselves and the world around them. Role-playing characters sometimes live on in the minds of the players long after the game has ended and players can utilize these experiences and personas in "real world" situations.

The volume concludes with the thought that the benefits offered by role-playing in more traditional environments are also offered through the leisure activity of role-playing games. Though mainstream American media channels often dismiss involvement in role-playing games as escapist and potentially dangerous, role-playing encourages creativity, self-awareness, empathy, group cohesion, and "out-of-the-box" thinking. The role-playing game platform facilitates the development of various cognitive and social skills that remain useful in the "real world." Thus, participation in role-playing games should incur a lesser amount of stigma from the larger culture.

Introduction

Human beings need fantasy for healthy psychic and social life. Regardless of time, space, or cultural background, the constraints of everyday society offer limited roles for people to inhabit. Each of us is expected to fulfill our assigned duties without complaint or conflict. We experience the psychic strain of trying to portray these socially-imposed identity roles, which invariably fall short of who we originally thought we would become. Children often state their dreams for the future at a young age: their desire to become a fireman, a famous singer, a cowboy, etc. If we become lucky, our adult lives will mirror our childhood dreams in some fulfilling way. More often than not, however, we find ourselves forced to make certain compromises as we shift from the fantasy realm of our childhood dreams to the reality of the cultural consciousness to which we all must adapt.

Certain cultural expressions give rise to a relaxation of these social roles, providing a needed release from the expectations of the outside world. The pressure of role conformity can diffuse when experiencing cultural forms, such as visual art, novels, theatre, film, music, video games, etc. Many of these art forms feature the journey of characters as they adventure through the fictional world expressed by the author. Art provides people with a space where they can temporarily suspend their ego-identification in a culturally-tolerated — if not always fully embraced — mode of expression. Some cultural critics proclaim art forms as liberating to the constrained consciousness of the human mind. Others find such "escapes" from reality potentially dangerous to the ego and threatening to the fabric of society. Still others worry that excessive indulgence in fantasy will blind people from the problems of the everyday world, problems which should be immediately addressed. Regardless of one's perspective, fantasy remains a strong element in culture, one worthy of study and important for understanding the way people process their experience of reality.

Cultural forms of art and expressive theater exist cross-culturally. While most of these artistic expressions encourage the artist to present their work to a passive audience, some forms of interactive creativity do exist. One such form has grown in popularity in the last forty years — the practice of role-playing games (RPGs). Role-playing games offer people the chance to actively take part in their own alternate expressions of identity, exploring parts of themselves that were previously submerged or repressed by the dominant culture and the requirements of daily roles. Role-playing games exist in many forms, from virtual role-playing to tabletop to "live action." While each type of role-playing offers a unique experience, these games provide a compelling escape from the mundane reality, attracting millions of players worldwide. Unlike the passive experience of watching a film or reading a book, these games encourage players to actively take part in the adventure, sometimes even developing their own stories and characters.

RPGs also offer a safe, relatively consequence-free space where players can develop certain aspects of themselves. Through role-playing, players learn how to inhabit the headspace of someone other than their primary ego identity, offering them the chance to develop a stronger sense of empathy. The shared, performative experience of RPGs provides a ritual atmosphere for players to enact compelling stories or perform unusual, extraordinary deeds. In this way, RPGs help encourage a sense of community, by teaching individuals to function as a group. Experiences transpiring in RPGs allow players to develop a deeper understanding about themselves and one another during the course of the adventure.

In addition, RPGs provide a space for players to practice certain abilities, including personal, interpersonal, cognitive, and even occupational skills. Gamers role-play out specific scenarios, guided by the game system and often a referee, known as the Storyteller or Gamemaster. Within the safe framework of the game, players have the chance to perform certain tasks and learn key skills that can actually translate to "real world" success in day-to-day life. For example, a player who considers himself shy or awkward in "real life" may learn how to approach social situations with more confidence through RPGs. The game may force a player to adopt a leadership position within the story and that player must learn those characteristics accordingly. RPGs also provide situations requiring puzzle-mastery and systemic thinking, encouraging players to think "outside-the-box" and develop new strategies for problem solving. For this reason, role-playing is considered a worthy practice in several important social arenas aside from leisure, including business, education, military training, psychotherapy, etc.

Finally, role-playing games offer individuals the chance to explore new aspects of themselves and others through a process known as identity alteration. In daily life, we must adopt several social roles in order to fully integrate with society, including: spouse, worker, child, parent, lover, friend, etc. While people may find fulfillment in these roles, many aspects of the psyche remain suppressed and underdeveloped as we strive to adapt to the demands of the external social world. Fantasy provides an outlet for these elements of the psyche to find expression, establishing a venue for players to develop alternate identities in a safe, controlled space. While some critics consider such behavior "dangerous" to the psyche, many players report developing a better understanding of themselves and others as a result of experiences within role-playing games.

In conclusion, people use fantasy as a means of self-expression and escape from the mundane in all parts of the world. Role-playing games represent both a new development in culture — with the advent of advanced, mass-mediated technologies — but also an age-old form of ritual performance. While many non-gamers may view participation in RPGs as potentially psychically damaging, this volume offers a myriad of examples to support the notion that these games provide a healthy, useful outlet for creativity, self-expression, communal connection, and the development of important skills over time.

1

Historical Evolution and Cultural Permutations

The subcultural phenomenon of role-playing games (RPGs) is a relatively recent development in popular culture. Most gaming historians indicate 1974 as the pivotal year for the inception of RPGs, marking the release date of the first coherent game system, *Dungeons & Dragons* (*D&D*). The rise in popularity of *D&D* led to an explosion of different styles of role-playing games, including tabletop, Live Action Role-playing (LARP), and virtual gaming. RPGs reflect a variety of different genres with regard to mood and setting, most notably fantasy, science fiction, and horror. Despite the magnitude and variety of these proliferate game systems, a few core cultural threads are responsible for providing the original seed for RPGs, as well as their evolution over time. This chapter will attempt to detail these roots, in both their ancient and more recent cultural manifestations.

The term "RPG" is used to describe a multitude of practices, ranging from pen-and-paper gaming to collectible card games to video game narratives. However, I believe that a true "role-playing game" must involve some combination of the following three major elements. First, a role-playing game should establish some sense of community through a ritualized, shared storytelling experience amongst multiple players. RPGs also should involve some form of game system, which provides the framework for the enactment of specific scenarios and the solving of problems within them. Finally, for a game to be considered "role-playing," the players must, on some level, alter their primary sense of identity and develop an alternate

Self through a process known as identity alteration. The players enact these secondary Selves in a co-created story space, imagined by both the players and their guide. This guide — also known as the Storyteller, Gamemaster, Dungeonmaster, or Referee — weaves the narrative into a coherent whole and provides final arbitration with regard to conflict resolution and rules.

This chapter explains how role-playing games came to develop. First, it delineates the universal components of RPGs, including role shifting, ritual enactment, narrative construction, and the utilization of archetypal imagery. Next, the chapter describes several cultural threads emerging in American in the last fifty years, including the rise in interest in medieval culture, Neo-paganism, and fantasy fiction; the desire to seek new frontiers; the growing disillusionment present in Generation X; and how Generation Y's comfort with technology allows them to immerse themselves in mass numbers in online role-playing worlds. Finally, chapter one delineates the three major types of RPGs: tabletop, live action, and virtual gaming and explains several related permutations, providing a brief explanation of common vocabulary amongst gamers.

Essential Roots

While the modern formulations of RPGs reflect these specific aspects, role-playing as a practice is, at its root, a fundamental aspect of human social interaction. As Erving Goffman describes in his *Presentation of Self in Everyday Life*, each social interaction remains, in and of itself, a type of performance. We enact our prescribed roles on the stage of social expectation, shifting our sense of identity as demanded by circumstance. We may be asked to embody the roles of child, parent, teacher, or student depending on necessity, and we unconsciously shift our behavior to suit these requirements in order to establish social cohesion. These roles form points of identification for the individual. Sociologist Gary Alan Fine explains the negotiation of these identities in his foundational study *Shared Fantasy: Role-Playing Games as Social Worlds*:

> The person consists of a bundle of identities that are more or less compatible, but which when enacted must presume a lack of awareness that the other identities are possible. The identity enacted is grounded in the assumption that this is the "real" identity, although often the enactor is well aware that this identity is chosen for purposes of impression management. The task of self-presentation does not merely involve manifesting an appropriate and coherent identity, but also involves concealing those other identities that are either incompatible or inappropriately keyed.[1]

Though this process of managing social roles in daily life often transpires on an unconscious level, certain cultural manifestations reflect a more conscious shift in identification. Many art forms involve the playful alteration of identity on the part of the artists and performers, particularly creative writing and theatrical dramatization. Role-playing represents a recent permutation in the evolution of such artistic representations and, thus, scholars should place it on a continuum with other forms of cultural expression.

The desire to construct narratives is also inherent to the human experience. We formulate stories in order to make sense of our reality, designing narrative arcs in a linear fashion. Though we experience an infinite amount of stimuli throughout our day-to-day lives, the mind is incapable of perceiving this data all at once. Thus, what we define as the conscious Self is produced through a complex method of filtration and narratization. We highlight key moments of significance and attempt to string them together in terms of some sense of causal logic. These narratives teach us where we have been and indicate where we might be headed.

We also learn about ourselves by vicariously experiencing the narratives of others, both fictional and non-fictional. Cultural products manifest as the creation of such narratives in various formats, including theatrical scripts, poetry, novels, screenplays, and other forms of story-driven art. We enact these stories in an attempt to understand the intricacies of human experience through the examination of constructed sequences of events and emotional interactions. These narratives aid us in making meaning of our own lives and instruct us on the complexities and potentialities of life. They also provide models for us to either embody or avoid, depending on our reaction to the personalities and events presented by the storyline.

RPGs allow individuals to participate in the construction of their own narratives in a group practice of co-creation. In a traditional play, novel, or film, the author uses the medium to communicate a story to the members of an audience, who experience the narrative in a state of passive observation and are allowed only momentary expressions of affect. In role-playing, though an author might have created the original world in which the action takes place, the majority of the story develops through a continual process of involved interaction and creativity on the part of participants. Thus, the "audience" of a role-playing game invents the narrative as well as experiences it.

The content of these narratives often emerges from deep, archetypal symbols cultivated from the wells of collective human experience. Myths, epics, and fairy tales often tell recurring types of stories that appeal to universal aspects of the human condition. As analytical psychologists such as Carl Jung, Erich Neumann, and Joseph Campbell have suggested, particular narratives tend to emerge cross-culturally, stories that resonate with the struggles inherent to the nascent development of human consciousness. In *The Hero with a Thousand Faces,* Campbell states,

> Throughout the inhabited world, in all times and under every circumstance, the myths of man have flourished; and they have been the living inspiration of whatever else may have appeared out of the activities of the human body and mind. It would not be too much to say that myth is the secret opening through which in inexhaustible energies of the cosmos pour into human cultural manifestation. Religions, philosophies, arts, the social forms of primitive and historic man, prime discoveries in science and technology, the very dreams that blister sleep, boil up from the basic, magic ring of myth.[2]

The universal plots of myths deal specifically with threshold moments in which the characters must face their own fears and weakness, transcend the folly of youth, and reemerge into the society with newly developed skills and a sense of responsibility. Each of us must face challenges throughout our lives, moments in which our deeper mettle is tested by environmental and internal pressures. These stories represent those challenges symbolically through recurring archetypes and narrative structures.

Rituals involve the enactment of age-old narratives, drawn from myth and other cultural sources. These stories provide necessary models for the comprehension of the gravity of these newfound social roles. For example, in Joseph Campbell's description of the *hero's journey,* or *monomyth,* the individual must depart the land of the familiar and confront a set of difficult challenges. In some myths, the hero must defeat a dangerous adversary, often expressed as a dragon or some other embodiment of evil. By defeating such a foe, the individual is proven worthy to lead the people, creating a sense of hope and communal connection through the trials of the rite of passage undergone by the "hero."

On a personal level, the symbol of the Dragon represents the Shadow side, the repressed aspects of the psyche that the individual finds fearful or disdainful or frightening. As Jungian theorist Joseph Henderson explains,

> The battle between the hero and the dragon ... shows more clearly the archetypal theme of the ego's triumph over regressive trends. For more people the dark or negative side of the personality remains unconscious. The hero, on the contrary, must realize that the shadow exists and that he can draw strength from it. He must come to terms with its destructive powers if he is to become sufficiently terrible to overcome the dragon. I.e., before the ego can triumph, it must master and assimilate the shadow.[3]

The hero must defeat and absorb these dark, repressed aspects of his or her psyche in order to ascend to a new level of consciousness and social responsibility.

These age-old crises are enacted through complex social rituals involving communities of people. Groups of individuals set aside their individuality in momentary expressions of solidarity, performing roles necessitated by the ritual in order to usher one another from one stage of life to the next. Arnold Van Gennep refers to this process of separation from the social order, immersion into a threshold role, and subsequent reintegration into the hierarchies of daily life as *liminality*.[4] The goal of such liminal experiences is the creation of a greater sense of social cohesion, a process that Victor Turner labels *communitas*.[5] These rituals — also known as rites of passage — allow the group to collectively acknowledge the transition of individual members from one set of social roles to the next.

Though role-playing games in their current formulation are relatively new forms of emerging cultural expression, they fall into the category of ritual at their essence. They provide enactments of epic stories in a communal context, promoting social cohesion and providing an imaginary space of testing and learning for the individuals within a group. As our society becomes increasingly secularized, fragmented, and globalized, the traditional, established rituals of the past are diminishing in universality. Though we still standardize ritualized rites of passage such as graduation, marriage, and funerals, Western society fails to establish a strong sense of universal community, particularly in an urban context. The modern world provides a multitude of different forms of social identifications, but our communal activities are relegated mainly to subcultural behavior, either in virtual environments or so-called "real world" groups. Because the need for ritual remains central to the development of social cohesion, we often now seek out these threshold experiences in smaller, more specified groups based on mutual interest rather than physical location, ethnicity, or other demographic identifications.

Role-playing games fulfill the need for modern-day ritual, cultivating the archetypal symbols of myth and providing a co-created social activity for the enactment of meaningful narratives. By descending into "dungeons" and facing "dragons," players experience a collective heroic journey. According to Daniel MacKay, popular culture "fails in its essential ritual function" in that the passive consumption of texts provides no space for the reintegration of the audience back into society after the liminal moment.[6] "The role-playing game process," MacKay insists, "is a redirection, a reapplication of the energy to *possess* the *creation* of the aesthetic object, a performance, that the players embody."[7] By actively enacting the roles within the framework of the game in groups, role-players experience the establishment of a sense of *communitas*, a much-needed experience in our fragmented, modern world.

Cultural Emergence

Though role-playing games are a form of cultural ritual, they have also emerged from socio-historic specificities present in the last forty years of Western society. As I described, the content of popular role-playing games, such as *Dungeons & Dragons*, is often rooted in fundamental symbols recurrent throughout human cultural expression. However, the explosion of certain generic themes also represents important shifts in modern culture as a whole, and thus, must be placed in its proper context. Mainstream society often marginalizes role-players, but this practice, which many view as a fringe activity, taps both into the fundamental need for humans to enact narratives but also into important threads emerging from Western cultural identity.

The chronological development of the major themes inherent in modern role-playing games reflects important shifts in Western society and the modern psyche. *Dungeons & Dragons* allows a group of adventurers to collectively experience the hero's journey, providing a ritualized space for a new manifestation of traditional rites of passage. The popularity of such stories, however, also emerged as a result of the mainstreaming of the work of J.R.R. Tolkien. *The Lord of the Rings* enjoyed widespread paperback release in 1965, sparking a revival of interest in mythological, heroic, and chivalric themes. As MacKay explains, "After its publication in paperback, Tolkien's work became tremendously popular, especially on college campuses in America during the late 1960s and early 1970s. The paperback ... went through twenty-five successive printings by 1969!"[8] The success of Tolkien's work inspired a surge in demand for other works of fantasy fiction and the genre flourished.

The creators of the original *Dungeons & Dragons*, E. Gary Gygax and Dave Arneson, drew heavily from Tolkien when developing the standardized character races and classes. However, *D&D* represents what MacKay refers to as a "pastiche" of several works of fantasy literature.[9] Released nearly a decade after the paperback version of *The Lord of the Rings*, the authors drew from a multitude of popular sources. Gygax details other "immediate influences ... [that] certainly helped to shape the form of the game," such as various war histories and the fantasy work of L. Sprague de Camp, Fletcher Pratt, Robert E. Howard, Fritz Leiber, Jack Vance, H.P. Lovecraft, and A. Meritt.[10] As MacKay suggests, "The trend was to create role-playing games based on works of literature ... this trend also applies to the comic book influence." The RPG *Pendragon* (1985), for example, found influences in the works of Chretien de Troyes, Sir Thomas Malory, and Lord Alfred Tennyson. William Gibson's fiction inspired certain science fiction RPGs, such as *Cyberpunk* (1988).[11] *Call of Cthulhu*, a horror genre RPG, replicated several of H.P. Lovecraft's stories and cast players as intrepid investigators, enacting scenarios based on that universe.[12]

Concurrent to the rise in popularity of fantasy fiction, new paradigms were spreading throughout America in the sixties. Hippie culture inspired a revision of traditional forms of ideology, including the critique of what some considered oppressive religious practices. Neo-paganism emerged, ushering forth a renewed interest in tribal communities, pre–Christian religions, and the potentialities of so-called "magic." In her discussion regarding the work of influential author Marion Zimmer Bradley, Carrol Fry describes the overall relationship between Neo-paganism and the development of the fantasy genre:

> Neo-paganism has quickly become the grist for the popular fiction mill.... In fact, the use of Neo-pagan ideas in myth and fiction offers a fascinating study of the rapid adaptation of a cultural movement by writers. Perhaps because of the close tie between Neo-pagan beliefs and western and literary folk traditions — and perhaps because of Pagan's love of medievalism — writers of heroic fantasy have learned to use the Craft, as practitioners call it, as the frame for their works.[13]

Though not all fantasy authors from this period — including Bradley — would describe themselves as Neo-pagan, the "new religious movements" influenced the overall interest in alternate spiritual beliefs and acceptance of controversial concepts like magic.

The rebellion from the rigidity of fifties ideological structures inspired people to reinvent themselves in a variety of ways. Several subcultural groups erupted as a result. Scholarly manifestations dedicated to study of the works of Tolkien and other fantasy authors emerged, such as the Mythopoeic Society in 1967[14] and the Tolkien Society in 1969.[15] Re-enactment groups also rose in popularity, including Renaissance Faires, historical war simulations, and medieval recreation groups like the Society for Creative Anachronism (SCA). Founded in 1966, the SCA originated amongst friends "as a medieval-style going-away party," eventually growing into a non-profit educational society. According to Thomas Stallone, as of 2003, the SCA boasted 29,600 paying members and 50,000 total participating members worldwide.[16] Stallone describes the overall goal of participants in SCA in the following passage:

> This "modern" medieval world doesn't pretend to recreate the Middle Ages as they were — a life often laced with elements of squalor — but rather, these groups strive to create an idealized version of medieval life emulating chivalry, honor, courtesy, beauty, and grace without such inconveniences as the Black Plague, Inquisitions, and intercultural strife. Participation allows people to enjoy an alternative world, experienced fully (in contrast to living semi-vicariously through video games).[17]

Stallone further explains that SCA members develop an "alter-ego that gradually evolves, much as a child would develop into adulthood, wrought from the social and historical influences of living within this shared alternate reality."[18] This statement also describes the process involved in the development of a character in a RPG, though, technically, the first RPG was published eight years after the foundation of the SCA. Though the SCA remains more of a subcultural social group than a structured "game," the experimental nature of reenactment societies did contribute to the development of RPGs.

One form of reenactment group that grew popular during this time was the war game. Military groups have utilized games such as chess in order to train soldiers in strategy for centuries. According to David Pringle, aside from chess, the first recorded military simulation game, *Kriegspiel*, was written in 1824 Prussia.[19] These battle scenarios eventually developed into two civilian subcultural activities: miniature war games and board war games. In both styles of gaming, individuals pitted armies against one another, playing out potential outcomes.[20]

Dungeons & Dragons sprouted as a collision of Tolkien-inspired themes and tactical simulation games. A group of gamers from the Minneapolis/St. Paul area sought to complexify the original miniature reenactments, influenced by concepts arising from game theory. These players innovated strategy games in four specific ways: they introduced the role of an impartial referee; they began to identify their sense of self within the role of one specific miniature rather than an entire army; they charted a storyline over time, creating a "campaign" rather than a single battle; and they established an open setting, in which characters could perform a multitude of actions beyond fighting. One of the most dedicated Twin Cities referees, Dave Arneson, devised a heroic fantasy setting for his players called Blackmoor. According to RPG historian Lawrence Schick, the characters in Blackmoor "were hurled into the distant past where monsters roamed and magic worked."[21] The characters could improve over time as they practiced their skills and adventured in vast labyrinths, also known as dungeons.

The players eventually demanded a greater sense of consistency in combat and event resolution, desiring a standardized system of rules. Arneson enlisted the help of Wisconson-based gamer E. Gary Gygax. Gygax had co-created a miniature system called *Chainmail.* Drawing heavily from the thematic content of Tolkien, *Chainmail* included hobbits, dwarves, goblins, orcs, and other races. The characters in *Chainmail* could also use magic, a new innovation to typical war game scenarios. Gygax and Arneson formed the publishing company Tactical Studies Rules (TSR), and, blending the *Chainmail* rules with the Blackmoor setting, *Dungeons & Dragons* was born in January 1974. Many imitators have subsequently released competing RPGs, but *Dungeons & Dragons* in its various editions remains dominant in popularity. White Wolf Games established their World of Darkness in the early nineties, however, and their RPGs have rivaled *D&D* in popularity for almost two decades.[22]

Though the fantasy genre remains the popular theme for RPGs to date, the eighties ushered forth the development of science fiction role-playing games. The growing interest in the relationship between human beings and technology paralleled the popularization of the use of personal computers and telecommunications. As advanced forms of technology became more available in modern society, humans began to integrate these new means of media and expression into daily life. The science fiction setting of games such as *Traveller, Shadowrun,* and *Star Trek* provided an outlet for players to explore the complexity of the relationship between technology and human experience. Though science fiction narratives often vary in theme and content, they tend to deal most specifically with the impending issues created by modern technology. The genre investigates the degree to which the consistent integration of machines and the alteration of the self through technological means might distance us from the essence of humanity. Thus, science fiction as genre reflects the ambivalence of the modern condition with regard to the supposed progress of rapid technological advance.

Science fiction also offers an exploration of potential worlds beyond our own. The moon landing in 1969 proved that space travel was tenable and colonization of other worlds possible. Contemporary science fiction texts such as the television show *Star Trek* attempted to conceptualize the potentialities of interactions with other planets in the universe, famously referring to space as "the final frontier" in the opening credits. The twentieth century brought the rise of globalization, cultural cross-pollination, technological advancement, and ease of transportation. Previously uncharted territories on the globe were discovered, infiltrated, and in many cases, consumerized. The mysteries of the world became less mysterious, yet human imagination still craved adventure: "to boldly go where no one has gone before."

Science fiction scholar Garyn Roberts suggests, "As human beings, our frontiers have shifted continuously, and so have our mindsets regarding who and what we are in the greater scheme of the universe."[23] Role-playing provides an outlet for this desire to explore new frontiers, using the imagination, the ritual of communal play, and the settings of the game system as a conduit. As *D&D* creator Gygax explains:

> Our modern world has few, if any, frontiers. We can no longer escape to the frontier of the West, explore Darkest Africa, sail to the South Seas. Even Alaska and the Amazon Jungles will soon be lost as wild frontier areas. Furthermore, adventures are not generally possible anymore.... It is therefore scarcely surprising that a game which directly involves participants in a make-believe world of just such nature should prove popular.[24]

Science fiction and fantasy as genres emphasize the thrill of adventure and exploration, situations that afford the characters the chance to act in heroic or at least extraordinary ways and make an impact on the world around them. The investigation of the "dungeon" and the exploration of new planets and life forms serve as metaphors for this concept of the new frontier, as does traversing the very bounds of the human imagination in the safe space of the game.

One innovation arising from the science fiction theme in RPGs was the development of "skill-based" game systems as opposed to so-called "class-and-level" systems. Essentially, modern characterizations of identity resist the cookie cutter archetypes of the fantasy genre. Instead, science fiction characters were offered a variety of skills and could customize their specialties according to the demands of the story and their character background.[25] This skill-based format inspired players to achieve new levels of creativity and to develop more complex stories with regard to character development. Skill-based character creation also reflected a more modern conceptualization of personality. Rather than relegated to predefined social roles based on profession and social status, modern society allows for more varied interests, identities, and personality characteristics, reflected in this enhanced form of customization that later game systems provided.

The late eighties and nineties ushered in a new era of games reflecting many of the motifs present in so-called Generation X. These hyperconscious individuals perceived the degradation of the world around them in terms of the greed, corruption, and destruction of the environment brought on by the "mentality of excess" of the Baby Boomers. Douglas Coupland's character Andy details this critique of excess in his definitive novel, *Generation X*:

> "'God, Margaret. You really have to wonder why we even bother to get *up* in the morning. I mean, really: *Why work?* Simply to buy more *stuff?* That's just not enough. Look at us all. What's the common assumption that got us all from here to there? What makes us *deserve* the ice cream and running shoes and wool Italian suits we have? I mean, I see all of us working so hard to acquire so much *stuff*, but I can't help feeling that we didn't merit it....'"[26]

Gen Xers also became painfully aware of their own participation in the negative developments of the modern world, such as the exploitation and oppression of marginalized social groups. The guilt inspired by such awareness found outlets in popular culture, as Gen Xers felt compelled to expose their deeper issues in a confessional manner.

Coupland delineates Gen Xers as those born "in the late 1950s and 1960s," which would adequately describe many of the individuals participating in role-playing games throughout the seventies and eighties. According to Catherine Martin:

> The youth of Generation X were exposed to crass consumerism in the marketing of expensive action figures; preestablished hierarchies; machine culture; and an emphasis on masculine characteristics, aggression, the importance of power and wealth, and human powerlessness. The boys were not merely passive recipients of these messages, however, but learned to manipulate and reject them.... As adolescents, they reacquired some of their power and creativity as human beings through their role games, played among themselves with rules manipulated by them and a Dungeonmaster chosen by them.[27]

While fantasy and science fiction allowed players to reclaim this sense of personal power and creativity, the horror/gothic-punk genre served as a more direct thematic response to the concerns of Generation X. Role-playing games such as White Wolf 's *Vampire: The Masquerade* (1991) surged in popularity during the nineties and in the early part of the twenty-first century, thematically exploring this sense of hyperawareness and critique of power, consumption, and greed. *Vampire*, along with the other games in the World of Darkness, presented a fight against the overwhelming sense of "evil" and self-interest that have become prevalent in the modern world. However, these qualities are not simply embodied in an external "dragon" to be slain, but are specifically present within the self. Unlike games such as *Dungeons & Dragons*, in which characters tend to face external manifestations of absolute forms of evil, the World of Darkness focuses on both inner and outer struggles. While characters vie for dominance amongst each other, responding to the deterioration of the moral and spiritual values of the world, they also must battle their own cynical and exploitative natures, attempting to regain some sense of moral conscience. Thus, *Vampire* represents a more introspective form of role-playing when compared to previous RPG offerings.

The creators of *Vampire: The Masquerade* subtitle their RPG "A Storytelling Game of Personal Horror."[28] The horror genre, though fantastic in nature, as it often deals with the supernatural, taps into the darker aspects of our own unconscious. Horror forces us to encounter the symbolic content of nightmares made manifest, such as vampires, werewolves, wraiths, zombies, etc. However, White Wolf more specifically describes its World of Darkness as "gothic-punk," merging the conventions of Gothic Romanticism with a modern punk aesthetic. The game designers describe the setting in the following manner:

> The world of *Vampire* is not our world — at least not quite. It is a Gothic-Punk vision of our world, a place of extremes — monolithic, majestic and altogether twisted. The government is corrupt, the culture is bankrupt, and the decadent mortals revel in the flames of the final days. It is a world where the forces of evil and entropy are even more powerful than they are in our world. It is a world of darkness.[29]

Thus, White Wolf presents a narrative of personal horror, but not in the mindless "slasher" variety of the genre.

While the hero's journey often portrays a clear cut Good versus Evil scenario, in which the hero triumphs over the externalized Evil foe, the horror genre often forces the individual to confront Evil within the Self and the paralysis caused by terror. Werewolves, for example, face the challenge of shifting from the human to the bestial, often losing control of their conscience and consciousness in the process. Similarly, vampires must negotiate their predatory nature with their sense of compassion; forced to subsist on the life force of humans, they remain covetous of human innocence and face serious moral quandaries with regard to their own behavior. The popularity of White Wolf's World of Darkness, therefore, can be attributed to the themes inherent to the horror genre resonating strongly with the moral concerns and sense of guilt experienced by Gen Xers.

Since their inception in the early seventies, RPGs have emphasized three major generic themes: fantasy, science fiction, and horror. Each of these genres activates particularly powerful aspects of the human psyche. Fantasy taps into the deep well of the collective unconscious, calling forth the age-old archetypes and myths inherent in ancient storytelling practices. The content of fantasy will always find relevance to human beings because these mythological symbols represent, in Erich Neumann's terms, the three most important and eternal threshold experiences of human existence: the processes of birth, maturation, and death. Science fiction offers an exploration of the relationship between human beings and technology in an age of increasing reliance upon machines. Horror allows people to confront the monstrous, both internally and externally. Thus, the history of role-playing games with regard to thematic popularity reflects both universal aspects of the human psyche and culturally specific ones. Regardless of the content of RPGs, however, the practice provides a much needed outlet for shared, performative exploration and lends to the potential for enhanced communal cohesion.

RPGs have exploded in popularity in online environments in recent years. These games are particularly appealing to individuals from Generation Y— individuals born in the early eighties and later— who fluidly integrate technology into their lives. As Rebecca Huntley describes in *The World According to Generation Y: Inside the New Adult Generation*:

> [Generation Y] is clearly the most technologically savvy generation yet, a group that has never known a world without remote controls, CDs, cable TV and computers.... Gen Y's understanding and early adoption of new technologies goes beyond its seemingly unique capacity to program the household DVD. Generation Y's mastery of and reliance on technology has altered the way it views time and space.[30]

This shift in perception of time and space mixed with immersion into technology attracts Gen Yers to online role-playing environments.

Online games like *Everquest* and *World of Warcraft* tend to focus less on in-depth character development and more on the instant gratification of conquest and reward. The perception of many gamers who prefer person-to-person role-playing is that virtual environments can reduce the complexity and community building aspects of the experience. In an interview for *Uber Goober*, a 2004 documentary on RPGs, Gygax claims:

> The modern hobby gaming industry is not going much of any place because of the severe competition from electronic games. Home computer games are going to be like the feature film industry in their popularity. Lots of people play. Even more popular are going to be the online games; that's the television of gaming. And then, I'm afraid, that the Broadway theater is the in-person, paper-and-pencil gaming. The finest experience, but relatively small.[31]

The first computer-based RPGs emerged in the 1970s, around the same time as the pen-and-paper games.[32] However, recent technological advances in graphical realism and game engine streamlining have increased player interest in these forms of RPGs. As Gygax rightly asserts, the majority of gaming designated as "role-playing" now transpires in online environments. According to Blizzard Entertainment, the design team responsible for *World of Warcraft* (*WoW*), paid subscriptions to the game exceeded ten million in January of 2008. This number does not reflect players who utilize each other's accounts. Blizzard reports, "Since debuting in North America on November 23, 2004, *World of Warcraft* has become the most popular MMORPG around the world. It was the best-selling PC game of 2005 and 2006 worldwide, and finished behind only *World of Warcraft: The Burning Crusade*, the first expansion pack for the game, in 2007."[33] According to these statistics, more users purchased *WoW*, a *Dungeons & Dragons*–based Massively Multi-Player Online RPG (MMORPG), than any other style of computer game. Comparable statistics for in-person RPGs are more difficult to acquire, as player often share materials and rarely systemize records of their gaming behavior on any sort of centralized computer database. Regardless, the assumption remains that the majority of RPG activity currently takes place in online environments.

Other influences, such as improvisational theater troupes and the inception of psychodrama, led to the creation of role-playing games. I will detail these factors more extensively in Chapter 2.

Form and Structure

Role-playing games take place in a variety of different formats both in-person and online. The following descriptions provide a basic vocabulary and outline the structure within which most RPGs fall. I delineate three major areas of gaming — tabletop, live action, and virtual.

Tabletop Role-Playing

Tabletop role-playing refers to any number of games played, generally, in groups of less than twelve. Tabletop RPGs resemble board games, where players sit and relax while maneuvering pieces on a board. Tabletop war games, such as *Warhammer*, involve the strategic placement of small figurines on an imagined battlefield. *Warhammer* players rarely wear costumes, though they often paint their battle figurines with a painstaking amount of detail. Though war gamers do not consistently enact individual roles, they may invent extensive back stories to explain the history of the battles and the heroic characters within them.

Most tabletop gaming, though, refers to the role-play format popularized by *Dungeons & Dragons*, which involves one player officiating the process for a group of participants. This individual was originally dubbed the Dungeonmaster (DM), though gamers often prefer using the terms Gamemaster (GM), Storyteller (ST), or Referee. The Storyteller oversees the world of the game and is often responsible for inventing the *metaplot* that ties the universe together. This metaplot is also known as the *Campaign* or *Chronicle.*

Some Storytellers rely primarily on *stock characters* and *modules* as the source of the metaplot: pre-formulated personalities and story lines originally published by game designers. *Stock characters* flesh out the social world of the game and are called Non-player Characters (NPCs), meaning that the Storyteller enacts them. Storytellers also commonly invent their own NPCs to serve as villains, allies, mentors, family members, and retainers. However, NPCs can also remain neutral or apathetic to the desires of the Player Characters (PCs). *Modules* are self-contained scenarios offered by the game designers as suggested adventures for the Storyteller to run. Many new Storytellers cut their teeth on modules and then expand the plot with their own creations; others never need these tools.

Regardless of the extent to which the Storyteller relies on the game developers for inspiration, the players must agree to a *game system* of some sort. The game system provides a set of rules that all performed actions in the world must obey. Many RPGs integrate some form of magic or advanced technology that allows the characters to perform remarkable actions. The game system establishes how such feats are possible within a set of governing laws called *mechanics.* Mechanics are often mathematical in nature, delineating the structure of the game through an elaborate, numerical *point system.* Players utilize this point system during *character creation* and when attempting to succeed at particular actions. The points alone, however, do not generally dictate the results of a player's actions. Most role-playing systems also involve a complex method of action-resolution called *fortune.* In most tabletop systems, like *Dungeons & Dragons* and *Vampire: the Masquerade,* the Storyteller and the players roll many-sided dice in order to reflect fortune. The game system establishes which numbers on the dice represent "success" at any given action. Recent versions of *Dungeons & Dragons,* for example, rely almost exclusively on d20s, or twenty-sided dice. On the other hand, games designed by White Wolf Studios, like *Vampire,* only use d10s — ten-sided dice — for fortune resolution. The amount of dice allowed to attempt an action is called the *dice pool;* the player rolls the amount of dice in the pool and the Storyteller interprets the results.

The game system is the major element separating an RPG from the general practice of *pretend play*. Children often engage in pretend play without adhering to any set list of rules, changing the laws of reality as they go along. Older gamers, though, tend to desire an established system in order to prove whether they succeed or fail at a task and by what measurement. Many players become emotionally invested in their characters, dedicating large amounts of time to the background, characterization, and evolution of their persona. The game system provides a source of security for gamers; if the villain in the story wins a battle and a character dies, the player may need established verification that they, indeed, failed. The game system provides that verification and represents a social contract of sorts. The Storyteller is considered god-like in the game world — omniscient and all-powerful. However, the ST should never alter this social contract without first informing the players, as the literal life-and-death of their characters may depend upon an agreement and understanding of the rules. Thus, gamers will often pour countless hours into memorizing the rules of that particular universe.

In most RPGs, the next step of the process is compiling a *character sheet*, which delineates the *statistics* (or *stats*) of the character. Stats are generally based on a complex method of point allocation detailed by the game system.[34] The *Vampire* character sheet provides numerical values for Attributes and Abilities. Attributes describe a character's inherent stats: physical-based characters allocate their points primarily into Strength, Dexterity, and Stamina; social-based characters favor skills such as Manipulation, Charisma, and Appearance; and mental-based characters focus on Perception, Intelligence, and Wits. Abilities refer to the Skills, Talents, and Knowledges a character has obtained. Sample abilities include: Melee, Dodge, Stealth, Etiquette, Investigation, Academics, Empathy, and Subterfuge.[35]

The *Vampire* character sheet also includes other important personality aspects. The *clan* indicates the type of bloodline from which the vampire originates; I primarily play Toreador vampires, a clan oriented toward the creation and preservation of art. Though some players do "play against type," one's clan generally offers important role-play direction. Toreador characters, for example, tend to act effete and snobbish regardless of their personal artistic ability. Thus, the clan represents an established archetype for the character to either adopt or reject. Each clan also possesses inherent supernatural abilities with ascending levels of power, or *ranks*. Members of the Toreador clan are inherently capable to move at supernatural speed (Celerity), perceive beyond the material plane (Auspex), and inspire strong emotions in others (Presence).[36]

The *Vampire* system also offers archetypes more specific to the individual character, described as one's Nature and Demeanor. A character's Nature is their true self, the personality aspects that describe their inner subjectivity. One's Demeanor, however, is the face the character presents to the outside world.[37] Thus, *Vampire* specifically — and games created by White Wolf in general — immediately force players to begin to think about their character as a layered, multi-faceted being upon character creation. Role-playing characters, like real-life personas, are often complex and even contradictory, as differing aspects of self emerge depending on the requirements of particular social and personal situations.

When players are *in-character* (IC), they are actively portraying their character's persona. In tabletop, a person can perform an action IC simply by describing that action in the first or third person. For example, I, as a player, can describe my character's actions in two ways: "I'm going to attempt to seduce the waiter so he'll allow me to drink his blood" or "Viviane seduces the waiter." The Storyteller will then ask, "How will you attempt to do this?" My response would be, "I will use the third rank of Presence, Entrancement, to enthrall him for hours" or "She uses Entrancement." The Storyteller will then ask me to roll a certain number of dice, in this case equal to the die pools necessary for Entrancement: my character's Appearance score added to her Empathy score.[38] If my character has four ranks in Appearance and three ranks in Empathy, I would roll 7d10, or seven ten-sided dice. A "success" in *Vampire* is usually indicated by rolling a six or above on a d10. Simplistically speaking, if I roll seven dice, and four of those dice read six or above, I made four successes on my roll, which translates to performing well in this circumstance.

While some players simply describe their IC actions to the Storyteller, they may also "act out" their scenes in tabletop, at least verbally. In the tabletop *Vampire* Chronicle in which I participated for over seven years, characters would often engage in lengthy IC conversations with the Storyteller's NPCs. If, during the course of this role-play, the player wishes to use a specific ability, the Storyteller may "break character" to ask for a roll, but this rolling does not disturb the flow of the interaction. Other players may talk to each other in- or out-of-character while such role-play transpires, but the Storyteller must keep tight rein over completely OOC conversation in order to avoid derailing the game.

Live Action Role-Playing

Live Action Role-playing (LARP) refers to a more physical form of performance, often involving the donning of elaborate costuming and moving around in the designated game space. I will designate three major types of LARP: Renaissance Faires, reenactment societies, and theatrical RPGs.

The character enactment at Renaissance Faires can only be loosely affiliated with role-playing, as it tends to require no game system for participation. The Faire itself hires actors to enact staged performances and adopt improvised roles, which is more akin to theater than the more loose creativity of a RPG. Other performers will play the roles of psychics, astrologers, and merchants, though to what degree these participants associate their primary sense of selves with their performed personas varies. Attendees of the Faire often don costumes and sometimes refer to themselves by an alias, though to what degree they "act out" their role also varies.

Renaissance Faires, though, are important to include in the role-playing continuum. Not only do many role-players avidly attend them, but Renfaires also resemble *reenactment societies.* Re-enactment societies take many forms. Some of these groups attempt to recreate history with a high level of verisimilitude, like acting out battles from the Civil War. Other groups, such as the Society for Creative Anachronism (SCA) provide a space for participants to re-imagine the past and transport themselves to an idealized version of the European Renaissance or the Middle Ages. Activities in the SCA range from full-armored battle with rattan weapons to crafting to costuming to vocal and theatrical performance.[39] Similar groups, such as Amtgard[40] and the High Fantasy Society,[41] focus primarily on the enactment of fighting in a fantasy context. Unlike SCA role-players, Amtgarders use foam bats rather than rattan and do not generally don extensive armor.[42]

Regardless of the manifestation, reenactment societies tend to emphasize the physical performance of imagined battles within a particular rule set. Though participants often adopt character names and associate these personas with archetypes, the distinction between their primary selves and the character is often blurry. However, many LARPs establish an elaborate social hierarchy, including the nomination of Kings/Queens of the Kingdom and a long apprenticeship progression from Squirehood to Knighthood in a number of skills.[43]

The third style of LARP is theatrical in nature and emphasizes character development over combat reenactment. White Wolf converted their tabletop games into a more workable system for a Live Action setting in a series of books called *Mind's Eye Theatre.*[44] The specific use of the word "theatre" in this style of LARP encourages players to understand their action as performance and more fully play the role of their character. Players in *Mind's Eye Theatre* are less likely to describe their characters' actions in the third person and more likely to literally "act out" their role. However, any use of weapons or violence is strictly prohibited by the game system, so some actions are relegated to description. The game world is similar to the tabletop versions, except the mechanics are slightly different. For example, instead of rolling dice, which can be cumbersome and easy to lose in a live action setting, conflict resolution is simplified by the use of rock-paper-scissors.

Not all theatrical LARPs thematically reflect the gothic genre, but due to the huge popularity of *Mind's Eye Theatre*, the majority of popular games are based in the World of Darkness. Access to White Wolf gaming materials is easy and gaming shops tend to carry, and subsequently sell, large amounts of them. Theatrical LARPs can take place in any dwelling, though I do think the OOC setting of the game slightly influences the mood and capacity for immersion. I myself have attended LARPs in residential homes, parking lots, and college campuses. The environment that worked best for the *Vampire* theme was the Student Union at the University of Texas at Austin, which offered wood-paneled walls and wrought-iron chandeliers, adding to the ambiance of the genre.

Another form of theatrical LARP is *cosplay*, in which players perform characters from Japanese animation (anime). Central to the activity of cosplay is elaborate costuming, though some cosplays are enacted using a game system. Costuming also takes place at *conventions* (cons). Cons are similar to Renfaires in that they tend to be consumer-oriented. At conventions, fans of a particular genre or popular culture text gather together in order to share their interests. Merchants sell related goods and special guest stars are often hired to perform or sign autographs. Though attendees may don elaborate costumes and adopt alternate names, full role-play tends to be limited at cons, unless the gathering is specific to gaming. However, these activities *can* allow for a shift in identity and the establishment of a sense of community, even without the boundaries of a game system.

Virtual Role-Playing

The following section delineates the variety of formats of role-playing in virtual environments. As with the sections regarding person-to-person RP, this list is intended to provide overarching generalizations rather than a comprehensive survey. Video gaming is hugely popular and the market balloons daily, offering a myriad of titles with various settings, themes, and styles of play.

When some gamers hear the term RPG, they more readily think of virtual games than those performed person-to-person. In the video game world, a RPG refers to a style of game based on specific elements of *Dungeons & Dragons*. Characters adventure through a virtual universe fighting monsters, gaining experience, improving their stats, gaining levels, and acquiring special items that either enhance their power or increase their wealth. For both in-person and virtual games, this model is referred to as *hack-and-slash*, or *leveling*.

Video game RPGs manifest in a variety of formats but the most popular ones include some element of hack-and-slash. Single-player RPGs for consoles or the computer tend to run the characters through a predetermined storyline. These games include one or several protagonists, and though the player's perspective may shift between characters, the player has little-to-no control over the progression of the story. The popular *Final Fantasy* series follows this structure. Most *Final Fantasy* adventures present a hybrid fantasy/science fiction narrative, though the main character is almost always male and the storyline roughly follows some version of the mythic hero's journey. The recent *Fable* offers more variety in the story, as the main character, still male, is offered the chance to perform a multitude of actions, each of which mark him on a continuum between good and evil. Thus, player decisions directly affect some aspects of the story progression. Also, unlike *Final Fantasy*, players can physically alter the *Fable* character, changing his hairstyle and marking him with tattoos of their choosing. Despite this enhanced flexibility, the game still follows the typical hack-and-slash style and is focused on single-player immersion.

Online virtual gaming environments fall into two major categories: text-based and visual-based, also called "graphical." Similar to the general progression of Western culture from a print culture to a visual culture, the emphasis of online role-playing games has shifted from a primarily text-based medium to a graphical one. As technology advances, media artists can more accurately depict alternate realities utilizing a digital format. Game designers can now render magic and advanced technologies visually rather than merely textually, offering some level of imagined mimesis. Thus, many gamers have abandoned the previously popular text-based worlds in favor of newer, more visually evocative ones.

Online role-playing games typically follow the quest-based, hack-and-slash model. The text-based model of this style of RPG is the Multi-User Dungeons (MUD). Multiple players log into a MUD and level alone or in groups. On most MUDs, players can create a description for their characters, but otherwise have little role in shaping the game universe.

The game world is preprogrammed with monsters, rooms, and items. However, if a player is given *Immortal*, or Wizard status, they gain the ability to create items, run quests, etc. In virtual worlds, Immortals serve the function of Storyteller, though the MUD code allows players to level without facilitation by another person.

A MOO (MUD Object Oriented) removes the leveling element from online role-playing and allows the players greater freedom in the shared creation of the world. MOOs permit players to make rooms, items, and *robots.* Robots are primitive, programmable AI machines that, at least superficially, can appear and respond like "real" players. On MUDs, robots are preprogrammed and are referred to as *mobs* (mobile objects) or "monsters." Players can barter with some mobs for goods and services, though most monsters exist specifically for players to kill in order to gain experience. Occasionally, an Immortal will inhabit a mob in order to run a quest or otherwise communicate with a player, but generally these creatures are limited in interaction and movement. A MOO, however, allows the player to sculpt the robot, offering more flexibility in their own creation of virtual representation. In a sense, mobs and robots are the NPCs of the virtual world. Another user-generated variant is called a Multi-User Shared Hallucination (MUSH). A MUSH provides even greater flexibility in object-creation than a MOO. MOOs and MUSHs allow for intensive customization of the virtual space, adding to the potential experience of immersion.

These two basic text-based formats for online role-playing later evolved into graphical counterparts. MUDs developed into Massively Multi-User Online Role-playing Games (MMORPGs) such as the hugely popular *Everquest* and *World of Warcraft.* Like their MUD brethren, MMORPGs favor hack-and-slash, quest-based scenarios and are played either alone or in a group. Also like MUDs, MMORPGs tend to downplay character development, even on game servers specifically created to encourage role-playing. MOOs evolved into MMOs, which aesthetically appear similar to MMORPGs but contain no pre-programmed game system per se.

One advantage virtual environments have over person-to-person role-playing is that they offer players the opportunity to alternately represent their physical self beyond the realm of costuming. Even if online gamers do not always develop elaborate storylines for their characters, they still create a virtual Self that appears fundamentally different from their physical Self by virtue of its digitally rendering. This virtual Self is referred to as an *avatar.* Through the use of avatars, a participant in an online environment can represent the self as an alternate gender, race, ethnicity, or even species. Avatars on fantasy games such as *World of Warcraft* tend to fall into mythic archetypal representations such as elves, dwarves, etc. The MMO *Second Life* offers far greater customization of avatars. *Second Life* is similar to a MOO in that players can take part in the creation of an alternate universe without the hack-and-slash gaming element.

Some gamers role-play in simple chat rooms, instant messaging programs, or over email. Others prefer online *bulletin-boards* (or *forums*). Bulletin boards allow picture and file attachments, as well as the manipulation of the font, color, and size of the text. Role-play in these environments is also called *play-by-post*, where the other players need not respond immediately. Forum role-play and discussion sometimes accompanies other forms of role-playing. For example, a LARP that only meets once or twice a month can utilize an online forum to fill in story gaps and enact scenes in between game sessions. Bulletin boards offer the chance for relationships to be cemented, drama to unfold, and pieces of story to be exposed that players never would have explored in the live action format due to time constraints. The presentation of an avatar allows for enhanced immersion. The reference point for the characters is no longer the physical manifestation of the players themselves but the iconic representation of the avatar. The format forces the players to describe their actions, enhancing the experience by emphasizing the creative expression of language, an aspect that often gets lost in graphical representations.

Psychological Pleasures

This plethora of role-playing formats leads me to believe that gaming has the potential to fulfill a multitude of enjoyments. For some, the pleasure of role-play lies primarily in the development of story and character. For others, the strategic elements of problem solving, scenario building, and skill acquisition provide a challenge and subsequent sense of accomplishment upon success. Others primarily value the IC and OOC social interactions and feel that gaming is a relaxing way to cement friendships and feel connected to others. Some gamers enjoy the release role-playing affords them from the constraints of their primary social identity. Still others view gaming as a psychological tool to examine themselves and others within shifting contexts and situations. Ultimately, gamers enjoy each of these aspects to varying degrees. The remainder of this study seeks to explore the social and psychological aspects of role-playing and to establish three major functions that role-playing games serve: community building, problem-solving, and identity alteration.

2

Role-Playing in
Communal Contexts

Role-playing as a practice is utilized in a variety of different contexts. Theater instructors use role-playing and improvisation as a means to tap into creativity and allow actors to experience an immediate flexibility of identity. Business practitioners find unscripted, improvisational drama to be an important tool in developing a wide range of essential skills. Psychotherapists use role-playing techniques as a means to work through personal and interpersonal issues. The military puts its members through "role training," immersing soldiers in tough scenarios in order to build problem-solving skills. Educators use role-playing techniques to teach social skills. Drama therapists work with patients both young and old; these specialists can even assist the elderly, using interactive drama as a way to share experiences with later generations and relive/retrieve lost memories. In addition, a growing number of social action groups encourage people to engage in improvisational drama as a means to develop awareness, coping skills, and compassion. Finally, role-playing remains a hugely popular entertainment practice, in both in-person contexts and online.

This myriad of applications of role-playing and improvisation indicates that the practice is, in fact, an inherent impulse in humanity. Young children engage in the shifting of roles unconsciously and un-*self*-consciously. Our older selves, forced by the necessities of society into more rigid patterns of behavior, experience the permeability of childhood identity through a multitude of these role-playing practices. Adam and Allee Blatner have created an approach called *The Art of Play*, in which they lead adults through a number of dramatic exercises in order to help them reclaim their inner spontaneity and imagination.[1] They explain that "play" is a "natural and easy realm children continually pursue" and that "playing monsters, kittens, warriors, and princesses is so easy and refreshing in childhood."[2]

They also maintain that adult forms of play and role-taking provide participants with inherent advantages:

> When children play, they tend to improvise from the viewpoint of themselves and their chosen role or character. It requires a bit of adult thinking to relinquish one's tendencies to be egocentric and instead to offer one's own imagination mixed with mature judgment in the service of either acting as a directive facilitator or as a true supporting actor who, for the duration of the enactment, strives to become what is most needed by the protagonist of main player.
>
> Children at play cannot achieve this level of focus. They unconsciously compete even as they cooperate. The understanding that people will take turns in the various roles demands a capacity for mature time-binding and a temporary relinquishment of egocentricity.[3]

While I think that some adult forms of role-playing — particularly role-playing games (RPGs) and improv comedy groups — still encourage competition among participants, I do agree with the concept that the adult consciousness possesses the inherent advantage of distance from its narcissistic viewpoint. Even in competitive RPGs, adults are capable of forming a "theory of mind" regarding the other players, affording them the opportunity to anticipate, respond to, and sometimes counter potential future actions. In this regard, adult role-playing — and by "adult," I mean adolescent-age and older — encourages problem-solving on a level that child pretend play cannot.

According to historian Lawrence Schick, the original concept fueling the inception of RPGs was the desire to create a war game-like scenario encouraging players to work together as a team rather than battle each other. Game theory refers to this model as a *nonzero-sum* game, meaning that the "players can get ahead without cutting each other down."[4] Later chapters in this volume will explore the extent to which players cooperate versus compete in RPGs. Regardless, in each of their therapeutic, educational, and leisure contexts, role-playing activities and other forms of interactional drama work to build an overall sense of connection and community amongst participants. This chapter will detail a variety of general role-playing activities and explore their relationship to community and ritual; then, Chapter 3 will explore how these principles apply to the specific form of RPGs.

Examples of Interactive Drama Through Time

Improvisational Theater

If the roots of role-playing emerge in childhood, then evidence of improvisational play should be evident both cross-culturally and historically. As David L. Young suggests, "Improvisational drama was an extension of storytelling and enacting and is part of many tribal cultures."[5] The impulse to share history through narrative and play-acting appears throughout time and space, regardless of a society's level of cultural or technological sophistication. Young states, "As writing entered civilization, the reading and then memorization of lines began, but many theatrical forms continued to include various degrees of improvisation — including Shakespeare's productions!"[6] This communal sharing of emotion and story operates on a ritual level; often, these enactments require no established script, instead relying on a complex system of symbology and psychic transformation, as described later in this chapter in the section on ritual.

Interactive drama theorist Brian David Phillips locates the Western roots of the improvisation in the parlor drama games of the fourteenth century.[7] The Master of the Masque would assign roles to guests at costume parties, which they would then role-play and improvise for the rest of the night. This original format later developed into masquerade balls, where participants wear costumes but are not required to act out roles. "While it is not currently clear whether or not the players were expected to accomplish goals during the evening or if the role-play was completely freeform," Phillips explains, "there are contemporary forms of Interactive Drama which incorporate either strategy."[8] One such form is the yearly ritual of Halloween.

Young describes the *commedia dell'arte*, a type of theater originating in Italy and popular between the fourteenth and eighteenth centuries, which was "also was mainly improvised."[9] Martha Fletcher Bellinger insists that despite the supposed unscripted nature of the *commedia dell'arte*, the result was not, "in any sense, the result of the moment's inspiration":

> The subject was chosen, the characters conceived and named, their relations to one another determined, and the situations clearly outlined, all beforehand. The material was divided into acts and scenes, with a prologue. The situations were made clear, together with the turn of action and the outcome of each scene. When this general outline (called also scenario or canvas) was satisfactorily filled out there was left an opportunity for actors to heighten, vary, and embellish their parts as their genius might suggest.[10]

Regardless of the constructed nature of the form, the *commedia dell'arte* offered a conceptual framework for improvisation in its original Western context. Phillips claims that though the *commedia dell'arte* faded into obscurity, our modern form of improvisational theater reemerged as a result of the separate but simultaneous efforts of Keith Johnstone and Viola Spolin, who shaped the craft as it exists today.[11] Johnstone created an improv company in the 1960s called the Theatre Machine at London's Royal Court Theatre. Inspired by the "working class theater" of professional wrestling, he replaced wrestlers with improvisers.[12] At the University of Calgary in the mid–1970s, he and his students developed a competitive improv acting program that played as much for audience reaction as for their final score. Young states:

> This type of off-the-wall entertainment was an immediate success, and with success came the evolution of increased organization, newly developed games, and a more formalized format utilizing more recognizable theatre structures like props, costumes, sound and lighting effects, and a master of ceremonies to facilitate the show.[13]

These enhancements led to Johnstone's creation of the Loose Moose Theatre Company and the TheatreSports format.[14]

Viola Spolin began developing her Theater Games in the early 1940s, though her approaches only became readily available in 1975 with the publication of *Theater Game File*.[15] Spolin originated Theater Games as a tool for crossing cultural and ethnic barriers amongst inner-city and immigrant children. The new approach of Theater Games focused and adapted the concept of play to unlock the individual's capacity for creative self-expression. Spolin's games emphasize physicality over verbalization, as well as spontaneity, intuition, audience participation, and transformation.[16] Spolin's son, Paul Stills, collaborated with David Shepherd to found the first improvisational theater group in America, Compass Theatre, in Chicago in the early 1950s. Compass Theatre led to the related troupe of Second City, famous for helping several modern celebrities get their start in the acting business. Shepherd then created the Improv Olympics in 1974, incorporating a mixture of professional actors and high school students into the production of a high-energy, improvisational festival.[17]

From these formalized roots emerged our modern conceptions of improvisational theater and interactive drama. Though historians focus more on the influence of war games and fantasy fiction when explaining the development of RPGs, the loose format of improvisational theater had already begun to spread in popularity. Therefore, the concept of improv more than likely provided a model for the burgeoning new art form emerging at the time: role-playing games.

Psychodrama and Other Forms of Drama Therapy

Improv theory in the twentieth century found a pioneer in the work of J. L. Moreno. Moreno developed the practice of psychodrama in the 1930s,[18] a process of working through a problem "by improvising an enactment as if it were a series of scenes in an unfolding play."[19] Moreno possessed an exceptional interest in the applications of group therapy and with the "dynamics of rapport, [meaning] how people felt attracted to or repelled by one another in a group setting."[20] He also founded one of the first improvisational social theater troupes in Vienna in 1921, setting the trend for many later groups that use improvisational theater as a method for exploring social dynamics. Moreno delineated "role theory," an idea focused upon exploring the psychosocial expectations placed on each of us to perform particular roles, a concept later embraced by Erving Goffman.[21] Blatner asserts that one of Moreno's main insights was the belief "that the most useful way to cultivate creativity is through promoting spontaneity." Blatner continues,

> Another important related idea is that in general the setting needs to be experienced as safe for spontaneity and improvisation to emerge, because it is a subtle observation of the nervous system that is inhibited in states of anxiety. Therefore, activities that lower anxiety, such as the context of play and the development of trust in a group, supports improvisation, which then increases the likelihood of the discovery of more creative solutions to problems.[22]

This emphasis on the development of trust and relaxation in a safe atmosphere is important in all forms of improv, including role-playing. Though gamers often take their participation in role-playing extremely seriously, the emotional space provided by the game format itself offers a relatively consequence-free environment. Players must feel comfortable expressing themselves and realize, on some level, that no matter how intense in-game events become, ultimately "it's just a game" that they play "to have fun."

Critics of gaming and of other forms of dramatic play often dismiss this concept of "fun," deeming fun activities as escapist. Escapism is commonly seen as frivolous or even damaging to real-world interactions. However, as Blatner mentions above, one of the most important aspects of role-playing is utilizing the form in order to practice problem-solving skills through the enactment of in-game scenarios. These scenarios become learning platforms for complex decision making. As psychotherapist Daniel

Weiner insists, "In order to experiment and explore other choices we all need safety, meaning immunity from such real-life consequences as being judged or punished."[23] Moreno's emphasis on group work and interactive drama highlighted the importance of establishing a safe mental, physical, and emotional space for the exploration of the self and its relationships with others.

Drama therapy has since blossomed as a method for encouraging holistic healing through the performance of new roles. As an alternative to psychotherapy, which emphasizes one-on-one verbal communication as the primary source of expression, drama therapy uses role-playing, story-telling, psychodrama, and theater games. Drama therapy also employs puppets, masks, and other types of performance to aid in patient rehabilitation.[24] Renee Emunah defines five stages inherent to most drama therapy procedures:

1. *Dramatic Play*, in which the group gets to know each other and the therapist through play, developing trust, group cohesion, and basic relationship skills.
2. *Scenework Stage*, in which the group recovers dramatic skills, tapping into abilities developed in ages 3–5, when children learn about the world through imitation and dramatic play. The abstract reasoning skills developed in school often preclude hands-on forms of learning, but we can recover our ability to perform through various dramatic exercises.
3. *Role Play*, in which the players act out issues fictionally, such as enacting a familiar family conflict or using a fairy tale as metaphor for a larger psychological complexes.
4. *Culminating Enactments*, in which players work through personal issues directly through psychodrama or autobiographical performance.
5. *Dramatic Ritual*, in which the group provides a sense of closure by engaging in a final ritual performance or evaluation either publicly or privately. During this session, the clients can review what the process has taught them.[25]

According to therapist Susan Bailey, despite the variability of drama therapy techniques, certain universal themes remain constant. Drama therapy utilizes *metaphor through action*, in which a set of behaviors is embodied in an archetypal role, such as victim, mother, or hero. Emotions are represented as metaphoric images, such as anger displayed as a volcano. These images allow insight into the qualities of roles and emotions and how they affect people's lives.[26] *Concrete Embodiment* allows players to act out abstract thoughts in a concrete fashion through the use of the body. Clients can "experience" or "re-experience" events psychophysically, offering them the possibility to learn coping strategies, practice new behaviors, and experiment with change.[27] *Distancing* is a method by which the therapist can alter the level of involvement that the player has with the role. Playing a character "like" the client but not associated with the client's real-world identity diminishes the potential for shame; the individual embodies the experience more symbolically than literally. The utilization of puppets or fairy tales aids in this process. Alternately, some clients need less distancing, and should play a more direct role in order to get more in touch with and be able to express their issues.[28]

Another universal aspect of drama therapy is *Dramatic Projection*, the process of accessing an emotion within a client and portraying it outwardly, allowing for a physical examination of the problem.[29] Drama therapists also must establish a *Transitional Space*, "the imaginary world that is created when we play or imagine together in a safe, trusting situation. It is a timeless space in which anything we can imagine can exist, a place where change and healing can happen, created jointly by the therapist and client playing together."[30] This concept of the Transitional Space corresponds directly with the liminal space of ritual, described later in this chapter.

Many other forms of interactive drama have emerged with surprisingly similar goals and results. Daniel Weiner's group, entitled Rehearsals for Growth, employs theater games as a method of expanding the group's repertoire of roles and encouraging the participants to break free from habitual reaction patterns.[31] He cites several familiar advantages to improvisational play, including: expanding interpersonal trust; accessing playfulness; experiencing spontaneity; opening to creativity; broadening sensory, emotive, and movement expressiveness; and co-creating new realities with others.[32] He believes that these qualities — especially the active co-creation of new worlds — offer a practical benefit by enhancing the functionality of relationships:

> In life generally, and especially in relationships, we develop predictable roles and habitual responses, forgetting that we can make other choices. Established relationships (most especially dyadic ones) have a collusive quality, wherein each partner responds to the other's offers in predictable ways, setting in motion a predictable sequence (or "script"). The resulting relationship dynamics then cement the tradeoff of safety for novelty, often resulting in boredom and over-familiarity.... By staging improvised enactments, the

Director undoes the predictability, setting loose an adventure in spontaneity and provoking a challenge to the relationship's status quo.[33]

Some groups apply improvisational drama in the service of healing social ills, not just personal ones. One popular method, called Playback Theatre, is practiced in over fifty countries worldwide in a variety of settings, such as schools, social service organizations, prisons, conferences, hospitals, and public theaters. Created by Jonathan Fox in 1973, Playback Theatre is widely used as a vehicle for social change.[34] Fox's method includes the sharing of stories by audience members of transformative or traumatic moments and the subsequent reenactment of particular moments in these stories by trained actors.[35]

Fox's inspiration for Playback arose from his dream "of a new kind of theatre that brought theatre back from the domain of entertainment to its earlier purpose of preserving memory and holding the tribe together."[36] Performance, according to Fox, should be a medium for personal and societal transformation. Hannah Fox explains,

> Anthropologists describe how theatrical performances of early societies often functioned as "ceremonial centers" at which groups would gather to exchange dances, songs, and dramas. These gatherings used performance to incite certain actions, such as dancing for rain, praying for a good harvest, healing the sick, or celebrating a birth or death. Fox wanted to find a way to "recapture that kind of ceremonial enactment in which there is no distinction between art and healing," and to "embody a transformational ritual that could be a source for hope without whitewashing what is wrong with the world."[37]

Jonathan Fox felt that interactive theater held the potential for group bonding and transformation and was particularly crucial to emphasize in a world that mainly utilizes only technology as a means for narrative transmission.[38]

One of the most influential groups internationally remains the Theatre of the Oppressed, invented in Brazil in the 1960s by Augusto Boal. The Theatre of the Oppressed seeks to help liberate communities and individuals from oppressive situations and beliefs by challenging existent power structures and inspiring people to take action, engage in dialogue, and work for liberation. This group "draws on the artistry of theatre to infuse social activism with vitality and aesthetic pleasure."[39] One of the most striking exercises developed by the Theatre of the Oppressed was labeled Invisible Theatre, where performers enacted "ostensibly unstaged, politically charged provocations in the streets and public places of Buenos Aires."[40] While these performances were actually carefully planned and rehearsed, the onlookers perceived them as real. In this case, the presence of the crowd offers the unknown element inherent in any improvisational drama; "Actors planted in the crowd as *agent provocateurs* emerge to vehemently take a side" in the unfolding scene "and thus galvanize onlookers to voice their own opinions on social issues like race or gender."[41]

Another important group, referred to as Healing the Wounds of History, works with nonparticipants originating from two cultures who share a common legacy of historical trauma and violent conflict.[42] Armand Volkas originated the process as a salve to heal the wounds between Nazis and the daughters of Holocaust survivors, but later expanded the techniques for application in a variety of "rival" cultures, including: French and Algerians; Palestinians and Israelis; Japanese, Chinese, and Koreans; Americans of both African and European descent; Blacks and Jews; Bosnian Serbs and Muslims; and Deaf and Hearing cultures. Healing the Wounds of History attempts to tackle issues surrounding identity, victimization, perpetration, meaning, and personal/collective grief.[43] The enactments help participants recognize cultural or national identity; open and enhance intercultural communication; experience grief and mourning; and create a culture of empathy.[44] Volkas leads participants through several phases: breaking the taboo against speaking to one another; humanizing one another through sharing personal stories; exploration of one's own perpetration; moving deeply into grief; creating performances *in memoriam*; and making commitments to acts of creation and acts of service.[45]

The sharing stories phase involves reenactment of a particular memory from childhood or adult life and later adds a short "History of My People." The facilitator asks participants from enemy cultures to step into the narrative of the original story, creating shared experience and empathy between individuals who have traditionally hated each other.[46] This phase incites a sense of role reversal, "a psychodramatic process in which one participant begins to experience in an embodied and affective way the reality of another."[47] In the third phase, a collection of historical photographs is presented then reenacted by the participants, who must take the roles of victims, perpetrators, and bystanders. Individuals must "confront their own complicity as well as their victimization" through this process.[48] In the fifth phase, the group enacts a ritual of commemoration, which includes elements of memory, celebration, and transcendence. This enactment represents the final performance element of the seminar, in which the group creates vignettes or images for each other and places important items onto a makeshift altar.[49] These interactive processes encourage participants previously estranged by cultural differences and traumatic memories to join together and form a common bond.

Other groups work specifically with individuals who reside in institutions or require special care due to age. LifeDrama works with the elderly, encouraging them to tell stories in order to uncover old memories. Through storytelling, these individuals can share with each other and with the younger generations the trials of their lives.[50] ActingOut is a teen drama program based in southwestern New Hampshire performed by and for young people between the ages of twelve and eighteen. The content of these performances focuses on contemporary issues, including AIDS prevention, sexual harassment, substance abuse, conflict resolution, and teen pregnancy.[51]

Other groups, such as Geese Theatre UK, work with prisons and probation services, using interactive drama techniques to help offenders develop self-esteem, empathy, and responsibility.[52] One powerful technique utilized by Geese Theatre is called *mask lifting*, in which audience members can ask masked or half-masked performers to remove their mask and question the feelings and thoughts underlying their outward attitudes and behaviors. Mask lifting creates awareness of the distinctions between our external front and our internal subjectivity through the use of metaphor. Geese Theatre also utilizes both personal and fictional role-playing, encouraging offenders to play the roles of all the people involved in the fallout of a crime, providing another step toward improving empathy skills and personal responsibility.[53] Role-playing also allows offenders to practice new skills in a safe environment where mistakes are acceptable, including: apologizing; cooperation; job interviews; question asking; interpersonal communication; saying and receiving "no"; expressing concern; compromising; handling jealousy; etc.[54] Role-play used successfully in this context may help an offender develop the skills necessary for living a successful life outside of incarceration.

These processes inherent to drama therapy are also present, if implicitly, in the RPG experience. Gamers also inhabit an imaginary, shared reality in which they take on roles that are "like" them but "not" them. Through the embodiment of archetypal and metaphorical imagery, gamers experience and, thus, have the opportunity to examine, essential human dramas, complexes, and emotions in a safe, low-stress environment. These experiences occur in a group setting and are ritualized, resulting in a feeling of connectivity among members who might normally feel estranged from each other due to cultural or ideological differences.

Educational Role-Play

Cognitive theory suggests that the capacity for creativity can be cultivated in arts education. Integrating the right and left cerebral hemispheric functions encourages intuition, imagination, straight reason, emotional sensitivity, and material practicality.[55] The dramatic arts aid in this integration process, and various forms of interactive drama are utilized to develop important skills. *Process Drama*, a term popularized by Cecily O'Neill, allows instructors to teach a subject matter or moral concept using drama as a vehicle. Instead of passively absorbing the sometimes dry content of school work, Process Drama allows students to enact the course material, making school work more relevant, alive, and unforgettable for students.[56] Process Drama instructors utilize improvisation to create fictional worlds where participants take on roles, answering the important questions of who, what, when, where, and why a character exists:

> The teacher and the students imagine a situation, and in many cases the teacher actually becomes one of the figures within that situation. If, in order to learn about ... astronomy, physics, and group-problem solving, they may play at being on a space ship, [and] while the teacher may not take the role of the pilot, she might "be" one of the engineers. The challenge is to allow the students to find themselves faced with making new decisions, and the teacher then becomes a combination of resource and fellow inquirer.[57]

Unlike production-centered theater work, actions and justifications are determined by the player's life experience rather than an external source.[58] Process Drama aids students in learning valuable critical thinking, problem-solving, and teamwork skills.

Process Drama is a specific form of role-playing, which remains a valuable tool for educators in general. Teachers use role-playing skills in the service of developing social and emotional learning, including helping students develop a greater understanding of situations and empathy for the feelings of those involved.[59] As Blatner suggests, "Role-playing also offers an experiential vehicle for developing skills in communication, problem-solving, and self-awareness."[60]

Role-playing techniques are also useful for instructing adults in the professional sphere. In business applications, improvisational drama aids organizations worldwide by teaching a wide range of skills, including: management and leadership; communication and presentation; diversity and ethical awareness; coaching and facilitation; and organizational development. Unscripted improvisational drama teaches "emotional intelligence" and encourages spontaneity, quick thinking, alternative solutions to old problems, acceptance of difference, flexibility, and listening.[61]

The military also values role-playing as a training tool. Improvisation and simulated situations have been utilized to assess performance in military officer and intelligence personnel training since the 1940s.[62] According to Mark Prensky, the U.S. military is the biggest spender in the world on training simulations games and regularly organizes conferences to promote conversation between instructors in the armed forces and game developers, film studios, theme park executives, and universities. Prensky states,

> The military uses games to train soldiers, sailors, pilots, and tank drivers to master their expensive and sensitive equipment ... it uses games to teach senior officers the art of strategy. It uses games for team work and team training of squads, fire teams, crews and other units; games for simulating responses to weapons of mass destruction, terrorist incidents, and threats; games for mastering the complex process of military logistics and even games for teaching how not to fight when helping to maintain peace.[63]

I elaborate more extensively on the use of role-playing scenarios to teach problem-solving skills in chapter four.

Reenactment Societies and Role-Playing Games

Though role-playing games (RPGs) and reenactment societies developed along parallel, separate trajectories, both strands reflect the relative freedom of expression offered in the sixties and seventies with regard to self-expression and exploration. As explained in Chapter 1, these freedoms emerged as a result of the breakdown of the conservative traditionalism and the widespread discovery of alternate forms of spirituality, as well as the emphasis on diversity championed by the Civil Rights movement. On a large scale, people questioned the ideological doctrines of the past and found new roles to inhabit, forming groups with similar sensibilities.

During this time period and beyond, creative self-expression blossomed in many forms, including the formation of reenactment societies. These groups attempt to recreate a particular period and/or event in history by replicating aspects of that time through costuming, behavior, and attempting to approximate past cultural paradigms. Several historical reenactment groups exist, representing a variety of time periods, including: the English Civil War, the American Revolutionary War, Black Powder groups portraying early American explorers and trappers, the American Civil War, the cowboys of the American West, and World Wars I and II.[64]

However, the most widespread and popular of these communities remain the medieval reenactment groups, such as the Renaissance Faires and the Society for Creative Anachronism (SCA). Offshoots such as Amtgard and the High Fantasy Society also emphasize a medieval or Renaissance theme, but add fantastical elements to the mix, an aspect that distances them from the more historically-focused reenactment groups. Because of the widespread belief in the explanatory power of magic during the medieval period, influenced in part by the lingering influence of pagan culture on European society, this time period allows for a certain flexibility in the rules of reality that players find pleasurable. Thomas Stallone suggests, "The allure of the medieval world inspires many to enter this magical world of reenactment where modern people create roles for themselves and live out their fantasies."[65]

This "magical world" is not meant to provide a direct representation of life during the Middle Ages or Renaissance. According to Stallone, two major types of groups exist: *reenactment* groups, which stringently seek a sense of verisimilitude, and *re-creation* groups, which tend to be more free-wheeling and casual. Reenactment groups impose strict restrictions on their members, regulating how costumes are made, what materials participants can use, which accessories participants can wear, and how participants must speak and behave in public.[66] Re-creation groups, on the other hand, emphasize freedom of creativity and allow members to push the boundaries of the imagination. The RPG format of the LARP most closely represents Stallone's description of re-creation societies, as does the less game-like format of the SCA.

SCA members perform mainly for each other in order to "enhance the quality of 'The Dream'—i.e., their shared culture."[67] According to Stallone, the Society serves two main functions, providing both a space for like-minded people to socialize and an avenue for them to research and explore the world they are trying to emulate.[68] However, one should not underestimate the performative elements of the SCA and other reenactment societies. For many members, these groups provide an important creative outlet for social bonding and exploration of identity. Stallone further insists, "The SCA is not your everyday social club," offering a detailed description of the endeavors and rationale of SCA members:

> [SCA members] hold events such as tournaments and feasts where members dress in clothing styles worn during the Middle Ages and Renaissance, and participate in activities based on the civil and martial skills of the period. These activities recreate aspects of the life and culture of the landed nobility in Europe, beginning with the fall of the Western Roman Empire

and ending in 1600 C.E..... The allure of this medieval world is such that members will drive an hour each week to strap on sixty pounds of leather and steel just to get whacked on the head and arms with weapons at fighter practice with friends. Some come to learn the latest medieval dances, practice calligraphy, or how to design and create that new costume they saw in a book.[69]

Many SCA members engage in "heavy combat," the use of real armor with rattan weapons. The masters-of-arms and knights are considered the "black belts" of this new, applied martial arts form and squires apprentice beneath them in order to rise in the social ranks.[70] The SCA also offers its members the opportunity to excel in other arts and sciences, including: costuming and period costume design; needlepoint and embroidery; medieval recipes and cooking; brewing and wine making; candle making; medieval music, instruments, poetry, and dance; calligraphy and illumination; heraldry; story-telling; juggling; ritual theater; carpentry; and metal-working practices, such as jewelry making; the coining of money; the creation of arrows and bows; the making and forging of armor and swords, and the sculpting of medieval utensils. Some SCA members pursue the equestrian arts, including tilting at the rings and jousting.[71] This large range of activities available to members of the SCA provides participants with greater opportunities for personal exploration and shared experience.

Renaissance Faires differ from the SCA and other groups in that they offer food, activities, and entertainment to paying customers. Theatrical performances are scheduled and performed on stages and a multitude of booths hawk various goods and provide services, such as astrological and psychic readings. The audience members sometimes arrive in costume or in-character, but are not required to do so. Thus, Renfaires operate more like period theme parks than reenactment societies, running for profit rather than non-profit. Renfaires also — as the name suggests — focus on the period of the Renaissance rather than the Middle Ages, another distinction from groups like SCA, though these distinctions ultimately remain rather blurry in both practices.

Each of these various applications promotes social cohesion through the use of interactive dramatic methods. As many of the above mentioned practitioners describe, play, role shifting, and dramatic enactment are essential aspects of young childhood and can be used strategically later in life to promote social cohesion. By understanding the nature of ritual, we can further see how interactive drama — and role-playing specifically — can become an important tool for communal interaction.

Role-Playing, Ritual, and Community Building

The practice of inhabiting roles is inherent to the human psyche. As young children, we consistently engage in forms of play that encourage us to move beyond our individual sense of identity and inhabit a new mental space. This mental space can manifest as the fantastic and whimsical or it can involve the known and familiar. Regardless of the psychic content of these diversions, we do not form a coherent sense of Self until adolescence and the playful negotiation of time, place, and identity remains a necessary and inherent component to the development of the mind.

These processes also exist on other levels beyond the personal. The creativity sparked by an individual imagination yearns to be shared with others, both to validate one's own existence and to establish cohesion with reality, even if that reality fails to correspond with the common cultural consciousness. This desire for personal expression and establishing a shared reality forms the basis of many of our creative endeavors, from writing to art to drama. Each of us experiences the world in a unique fashion and has a particular perspective to offer. Cultural art forms allow us to share these experiences and perspectives with one another, lending to the development of cooperation, compassion, sympathy, and empathy.

The act of taking on a role that one does not normally inhabit in the mundane world allows for the facilitation of self-expression and shared experience. Each of us unconsciously performs roles on a day-to-day basis, as Goffman suggests in his *The Presentation of Self in Everyday Life*. We implicitly agree to accept each other's performed roles in order to maintain our sense of comfort with the established reality. However, we can find ways to *play* with these notions of self through various actions and mediums and, thus, become more consciously aware of the process of role-taking. By enacting a drama, for example, we present a sense of hyper-reality, an acknowledgment of the fixity of the mundane versus the fluidity of our psychic experience. We experience a new version of reality through embodiment, narrative, and spectatorship. The suspension of the drama of everyday life and the enactment of staged narratives in tragedy, for example, provokes feelings of empathy, horror, and catharsis. We share these experiences together, either as directors, performers, or audience members; sometimes, we even inhabit all three roles.

The most common form of role-playing in this sense is the expression of narrative through a dramatic medium. These mediums include, but are not limited to: oral histories, songs, dances, plays, and poems. The act of "putting on" a performance engages the performers and the audience in sort of ritual, in which the participants understand the temporary and special nature of the enactment. *Ritual,* according to anthropologist Roy Rappaport, is "the performance of more or less invariant sequences of formal acts and utterances not entirely encoded by the performers."[72] His definition encompasses not only human, but also animal forms of ceremonial experience and spans multiple dimensions, both sacred and secular.

However, according to Emile Durkheim, ritual enactment emerged initially alongside the formation of human religions, offering a means of strengthening social bonds and establishing categories of classification. In his *Elementary Forms of Religious Life,* Durkheim put forth the notion that religion itself is the primary building block of social groups. He states, "At the basis of all systems of beliefs and all cults there must be a number of fundamental representations and ritual practices that, despite the diversity of forms they assume in various religions, have the same objective meanings and fulfill the same functions."[73] For Durkheim, understanding the most early and basic forms of religion illuminates the ways that even the most complex social structures function, despite any cultural specificity. If ritual is somehow inherent to the enactment and continual establishment of religious principles, then ritual must also exist in other forms of social organization. Ritual, therefore, remains central to group cohesion in both sacred and secular contexts.

The process of ritual takes place in three major phases, according to Arnold van Gennep. These phases involve crossing over a threshold of "magico-religious" significance through the performance of rites. These thresholds may exist symbolically on the physical plane, such as an actor's stage or a temple's altar; primarily, though, this crossing is experienced psychologically.[74] The first phase is one of *separation* from the previous world, which van Gennep refers to as the *pre-liminal.* The second phase involves a transitional stage of *liminal,* or *threshold,* rites, in which the individual and/or group experiences this sort of "crossing over" into an alternate psychosocial reality. After successfully completing this phase, the participants *return* to the world they left behind; in this *post-liminal* stage, they reincorporate themselves back into the mundane work with new knowledge and social standing.[75] These rites of passage generally induct participants into the major hallmarks of the life cycle: pregnancy, childbirth, puberty, betrothal, marriage, and death. While more secular forms of ritual need not mark major rites of passage, they do transport the participants to an alternate psychological — and sometimes physical — space, a space that provides the opportunity for a profound transformation to occur.

Victor Turner further elaborates on van Gennep's formulation in his book *The Ritual Process: Structure and Anti-Structure.* Turner's study of the Ndembu people of northwestern Rhodesia elucidates many of the principles of ritual through example, particularly focusing on the use of symbols, which he calls the "basic building-blocks, the 'molecules,' of ritual."[76] Turner writes, "In a Ndembu ritual context, almost every article used, every gesture employed, every song or prayer, every unit of space and time, by convention stands for something other than itself. It is more than it seems, and often a good deal more."[77] We can extend this description of the symbology utilized in sacred ritual practices to other ceremonies as well; each symbol represents a story or an idea that the practitioners wish to evoke. Ordinary objects take on special meanings and become otherworldly during the liminal state, heightening the emotional intensity of the experience. Furthermore, aspects of the "real world" that threaten to invade the reality of the ritual must be overlooked in order for the ritual to take place.

If we think of a traditional dramatic play as a ritual, then stage props take on a symbolic meaning beyond their everyday use value. No item is placed on the set by accident, no costume arranged arbitrarily. Indeed, for the performance to assume significance, certain agreements must be made between audience members and actors, observing the sanctity of the space and the process. To fully transform from one identity to another, to transport from one time and space to somewhere altogether different, each participant must respect the rules of engagement, agree to "suspend disbelief," and fully immerse themselves in the narrative.

Role-playing, when understood as ritual, contains these same defining elements. Role-playing as a practice tends to be more free-form and improvisational than a traditional stage play, but still follows the same principles of liminality. J. Tuomas Harviainen's article "Information, Immersion, Identity: The Interplay of Multiple Selves During Live-Action Role-Play" specifies the process necessary for the participants to fully engage in the *diegesis*, or "the sum of all that is true in the reality of the game."[78] Harviainen describes how Live-Action Role-players (or LARPers) must mentally prepare for the ritual:

> Live-action role-play takes place within a temporary reality definable as potential space ... it is essentially a spatial representation of an imaginary place that is imposed upon an actual place ... through a jointly agreed-upon social contract. A level of belief in this potential space is then created through a process consisting of two factors: Eidetic reduction (i.e. intentional ignorance of observed elements inconsistent with the intended "pure

experience"), and a semiotic re-signification process. The latter is used upon those real-world elements that are incompatible with the potential space but can be to a certain extent ... translated into interpretive forms that are compatible with the diegesis.[79]

Thus, performance spaces and objects take on new meanings in order to comply with the ritual intention of the role-play experience and participants must form a temporary belief in the liminal reality.

Tabletop role-playing requires less props and costuming than Live Action and less representational symbology, but still demands that players cross the imaginary threshold of the role-play universe despite the visual intrusion of the mundane world. Christopher Lehrich elaborates by describing the practice of "breaking character," or bringing up "OOC" (Out-of-character) information during "IC" (In-character) scenes.[80] Experienced role-players remain highly conscientious of the IC/OOC division in order to maintain the liminality of the experience. The phase of return is often accompanied by a shift from IC to OOC:

> The social aggregation at the close of play thus amounts to an undoing of this separation: players step back from the in-character world (to whatever extent they postulated themselves as in it) in order to receive rewards or accolades, rehash enjoyable events, and generally begin shifting from a relatively discontinuous and separated game-time to an ordinary social event, itself marked eventually by the dispersal of the participants to their everyday lives.[81]

One of the most distinctive elements of Turner's theory is that ritual provides the potential for community building, or *communitas*. For a ritual behavior to fully affect an individual, the process should be witnessed by a group and this observance constitutes a form of participation. Even if the focus remains on an individual undergoing a rite of passage, the witnesses play their own roles, some in an active manner. In a tribal community, the shaman — or spiritual leader — of the group often oversees the ritual. Other members of the tribe may play supporting roles in the unfolding drama, lending to further immersion. Thus, the participation of the community — whether active or passive — facilitates a sense of social cohesion based on shared experience. A wedding, though technically a union between two people, bears more meaning when witnessed by a group and officiated by a leader. Each participant lends their emotional and spiritual investment into the ritual, enhancing its efficacy and reinforcing bonds within the community.

The process of separation from the mundane and crossing over the threshold entails stripping the participants of their normative positions in the status hierarchies of the secular world and charging them with new, temporary responsibilities within the liminal space. Emergence from the ritual imbues the initiates with a new place in the social order, but also a return to the previous structure. Turner states:

> What is interesting about liminal phenomena for our present purposes is the blend they offer of lowliness and sacredness, of homogeneity and comradeship. We are presented, in such rites, with a "moment in and out of time," and in and out of secular social structure, which reveals, however fleetingly, some recognition (in symbol if not always in language) of a generalized social bond that has ceased to be and has simultaneously *yet to be* fragmented in a multiplicity of structural ties.... This is not ... a matter of giving a general stamp of legitimacy to a society's structural positions. It is rather a matter of giving recognition to an essential and generic human bond, without which there could be no society.[82]

Role-playing — and performance in general — also entails a reconfiguration of social roles. The player is stripped of previous rank in the external world and given equal status to fellow players, though some players enact more central roles in the ritual than others, similar to the lead actor in a play.[83] Individuals are appointed to guide the ritual, a role similar to those enacted by elders in tribal communities. In his article "Designing and Conducting Rituals, Ceremonies, and Celebrations," Adam Blatner describes modern ritual, in which this role is enacted by the Master of Ceremonies (MC):

> The MC role, in which a person helps others design and then conducts the ritual ... would not simply be the one who narrates the event, but more, one who truly aspires to master "the art of ceremony." The role includes a capacity for being sensitive to the needs not only of the key celebrants, but also to the group and its dynamics. A key skill an MC should develop is an ability to discover and create "meaning" as part of the dramatic process.[84]

In traditional drama, the equivalent of the MC would be the director and, in some cases, the playwright. In role-playing, the MC role is enacted by the Gamemaster (GM), also called Storyteller (ST). This individual acts as the "god" of the game, guiding the story and making final determinations on the course of events, similar to a referee in a sports game.

The Storyteller has many responsibilities. First, he/she must possess a clear understanding of the meta-story of the game world, including the back-stories of the characters and history of the game universe. The Storyteller is also responsible for the formation of major plots and the keeping of game secrets. He/she must understand the rules extensively in order to provide an all-important sense of internal consistency for the players, a particularly crucial aspect to playing in a fantasy or science fiction themed world. Ultimately, the Storyteller must possess enough personal charisma and strength of character to guide the ritual of the game, maintain the perception of being a fair facilitator, and keep the players engaged in the story world.[85]

Ultimately, the Storyteller, then, performs a similar role to a religious leader in a sacred context, guiding individuals through the process of liminality. For the ritual to be successful, the players must willingly place the fate of their characters — and, ultimately, their own experience itself— in the hands of the Storyteller, regardless of his/her status respective to theirs in the outside world. Furthermore, players must adhere to the in-character status hierarchies that invariably emerge; even in a group of adventurers of the same age and rank, positions such as Leader, Information Gatherer, "Tank,"[86] and Negotiator eventually establish themselves. A fifty-year old man may find himself taking orders IC from a girl who, in the "real world," is only eighteen. He must submit to his role in order to maintain the consistency of the game world.

Regardless of the culturally specific distinctions, modern role-players inhabit a liminal state and create a sense of *communitas* through the ritual process of "gaming" in its many forms. The result of this process is what Lehrich describes as "genuine social alteration":

> A play group is often formed on an *ad hoc* basis, where some players do not know each other well outside of the game context, and indeed may not have met. Through successful ritual collaboration in a shared space understood as distinct from other social spaces, a new social group forms, enabling friendship and other forms of collaboration that refer to the constructed game-space rather than to other social structures. That is, precisely because gameplay is at once divided from other social spaces and nominally focused upon a limited set of predetermined issues, and because such rituals do act conjunctively by taking given divisions and annulling "winner and loser" categorizations, gameplay tends naturally to formulate an alternative social framework. Particularly for those who find mainstream, dominant social frameworks problematic or dangerous, gameplay can constitute a controlled social space in which to succeed and seek liberation.[87]

As Lehrich suggests, some individuals seek role-playing environments because they have difficulties integrating into mainstream society. Representations abound of socially-awkward "geeks" who "obsess" over fantasy and science fiction worlds in order to avoid interaction with "the real world." The term "escapism" is often applied to these individuals, incurring a pejorative connotation to the both role-playing and gaming. Indeed, many role-players and alternate world enthusiasts spend a good deal of time emphatically distancing their behavior from that of those who "go too far" in their fandom.

For these individuals, hyperinvolvement in role-playing communities may be considered "unhealthy." Stallone warns of such pitfalls in his article on Medieval Reenactments:

> Some people who are not very successful in their everyday lives who need to find self-worth by receiving recognition from others, may start devoting more and more of their time, energy, and resources to their new hobby instead [of] their daily lives. There have been people who will spend much of their hard-earned wages on fabric to create a Tudor costume for the upcoming Twelfth Night Feast, but do not have enough money to pay their telephone bill. As they become more involved in these groups, they may rise to positions and titles of power. Recognition "from above" and the wielding of "power" are addictive to some people and could cause problems in their lives both within the group, at home, and at work.[88]

The problems Stallone describes seem rooted in issues of power-hungriness and an inability to properly prioritize, issues which arise in any social group or hobby. When assessing the amount of financial resources to pour into a ritual, we determine how important that ritual is to us and the group. Extensive spending on a wedding, for example, may seem entirely appropriate; however, when mainstream society views the ritual activity as non-essential or non-productive, extravagant expenditures on costuming and props are more difficult for participants to justify. Perhaps the individual mentioned in Stallone's example viewed participation in the Feast as symbolically more important than mundane concerns.

When hyperinvolvement causes conflict both in the group and outside of it, distancing may indeed become necessary. Lehrich addresses this issue with regard to role-players:

> It could be argued that the shared space of ritual, although it permits and even demands reflection upon social inequalities, ultimately acts not only to affirm these inequalities as natural and given, but also deludes those in inferior positions into thinking that they achieve a measure of equality that is in fact nonexistent. From this perspective, we can see that RPGs may act simultaneously to affirm and assist players psychologically, and at the same time discourage them from acting upon or challenging the inequities of modern social dynamics. Anecdotally, at least, we seem to see this in stereotypes of RPG players as "geeks" or "nerds" who, by participating in gaming, in conventions, and generally in a subculture, are thereby diverted or distracted from real social action or mobilization. To formulate a rather over-

stated Marxist reading, the recognition of RPGs as ritual is confirmed by its ability to serve as an opiate for the oppressed. [89]

My question with regard to this common assumption that participation in alternate worlds inhibits one's ability to interact in the real world remains: How can we be sure that an individual would be better off *without* the social experience of the role-playing environment? If some players experience difficulties in day-to-day interactions, I would suggest that involvement in any social group would be, on some level, beneficial to developing important interpersonal skills and promoting extraversion.

Role-playing scenarios force participants to engage in social interaction and even meander through complex political situations in order to accomplish goals. Role-playing has the potential to enhance social skills by placing individuals in unique hypothetical scenarios and simultaneously providing a safe, liminal space, as stated extensively in the drama therapy and education sections of this chapter. I will explore this connection between community building and role-playing games in the following chapter, which features extensive, ethnographic data on the subject.

3

Interactional Dynamics
in Role-Playing Games

In Chapter 2, I posited the view that the practice of role-playing functions like a modern-day ritual. The activity takes place generally in groups and involves the enactment of various archetypes in order to play out dramas. Role-players perform with each other, calling upon the deep reaches of their imagination and creativity, establishing a safe space within which stories weave themselves. The participants play several roles in these unfolding stories; they act, direct, observe, and co-create an alternate form of reality.

The process of role-playing allows individuals to inhabit an alternate mental space by entering into the "fantastic." This shift in perspective provides players with the opportunity to understand the motivations of others more clearly, expanding their comprehension of mundane reality and existing social dynamics. These skills are considered desirable to role-players, many of whom express having experienced deep feelings of alienation and ostracization from mainstream society. Though engagement in RPGs often incurs further social stigma, the practice of role-playing itself offers a much-needed sense of ritual and community.

Fantasy, Shared Realities, and the Eucatastrophe

Though role-playing games take place in a multitude of settings, the most popular original game, published in 1974, is *Dungeons & Dragons*, which takes place in a fantasy world. As mentioned in Chapter 1, *D&D* draws heavily on the work of J.R.R. Tolkien in *The Hobbit* and *Lord of the Rings.* Tolkien believed that the narrative arcs of "fairy-stories" were transcendent of space and time. Fantastic narratives, for Tolkien, serve three major functions. They allow people to Escape the mundane in order to Recover a sight that was previously obscured. As a result of these processes, the participant in fantasy experiences a sense of Consolation, which Tolkien refers to as *eucatastrophe.* According to Brian Stableford, by eucatastrophe, Tolkien "means a climactic affirmation of both joy and light: pleasure alloyed with moral confidence."[1] He further makes a distinction between the fantasy genre and both speculative fiction and horror, claiming that the narratives in the second two classifications lead to a feeling of "despair" versus "moral rearmament."[2]

Role-playing games arise from a variety of generic traditions; while *D&D* hails from the fantasy tradition, the other most popular collection of RPGs, White Wolf's World of Darkness, emerge from what the game developers refer to as *gothicpunk.* More than the genre itself, the events of the story, the style of Storytelling, and the attitudes of the players create the tone of the experience. For example, regardless of genre, the moment of a character's death may produce an uplifting or despairing effect. A party member's death or devolvement might upset players or might, alternately, provide a sense of release and humor. Some players remain detached observers through such a process and can laugh at the predicaments of their characters, while others may fly into rages or a experience a deep sense of melancholy at their character's demise.

Also, in games like *Vampire,* the characters may be predatory in nature, but have the choice of whether or not they will kill to subsist. Unlike the villain in a horror story, who seems to go on a killing rampage with little-to-no personal reflection on his/her actions, an inherent test of morality and sense of consequence is built into the *Vampire* game system. Thus, on the whole, even RPGs with a darker theme challenge both characters and their players to confront the potential hero within themselves, offering several choices of actions based either on self-interest or altruism. In-game actions are performed with some mixture of both motivations, and the game provides players with the opportunity to observe their own decision-making process and its affect on others within the group.

Stableford's describes the function of fantasy as providing an outlet to step outside of the box of reality and create a new, insightful perspective. He summarizes the benefits of such a practice in the following passage:

> The ability to take up a fantastic viewpoint can ... aid us in putting things in better perspective; what we "recover" in fantasy is actually a clearer sight than we normally employ in viewing the world, because it is a less narrow

sight — a sight which does not take for granted the limitations of mundanity.... To argue thus is to assert that we cannot see reality clearly enough if we are trapped within it, and that only when we can perform the imaginative trick of moving outside the actual can we properly appreciate its bounds.[3]

This definition holds true for the practice of role-playing, regardless of genre. Any shift in the conception of reality is, in a sense, a fantasy: an active practice allowing people to see the mundane in better light. Thus, role-playing scholarship often refers to all RPGs as "fantasy." J. Patrick Williams, Sean Q. Hendricks, and W. Keith Winkler suggest that "fantasy as a fluid, unstable category that is somewhat difficult to map — it is made up of multiple genres or games and gaming subcultures that overlap in some ways, yet differ in others." As a social activity, they broadly classify fantasy gaming as being "grounded in shared worldviews, life-styles, tastes and affinities, as well as collectively-imagined selves/identities."[4]

Just as when reading a book or watching a film, role-players must inhabit a different head space and identify with someone "other" than themselves. RPGs push this identification a step further, allowing that "other person" to evolve as the player's own creation, rather than a conceptualization by an author foisted upon the passive reader of a book. As chapter seven will suggest, these creations often reflect repressed aspects of the player's personality, which are allowed room to breathe and manifest as entities unto themselves. However, the shared nature of these identities also allows for a sense of bonding through storytelling and co-creation. The character starts as a seed of a concept in one player's mind, but evolves through interactions with others in-character, and with player-to-player discussion out-of-character. Thus, identity is actively and consciously created, not just by the individual role-player, but also by the group as a whole.

Theories of Mind

Fantasy role-playing involves fracturing reality and refracting it from a different perspective. This process can provide both a heightened sense of self-awareness for the role-player and a greater overall feeling of unity within the group. Not only can people share repressed, sometimes frightening parts of themselves in a safe space, but they can better understand the perspectives of others. Role-players temporarily identify with a character whose personality traits and choices often differ from their own.

Some characters manifest as similar to the primary Self, differing only in the choices the game world forces them to make. Other characters diverge completely from the primary Self, even representing polar opposites of identification. I offer nine types of characters within this spectrum of self-identification in Chapter 7.

Regardless of the level of divergence between the relative identities of player and character, the process forces players to adopt a *theory of mind*, to think "as if" they were someone else in a unique set of circumstances. According to Jean Piaget, before the age of eight, children perceive the world through a *narcissistic* lens. Narcissism refers to a state in which "the self remains undifferentiated, and thus unconscious of itself ... all affectivity is centered on the child's own body and action, since only with the dissociation of self from the other or non-self does decentration, whether affective or cognitive, become possible."[5] Children eventually shift from this narcissistic perspective, developing the ability to read social responses and anticipate the needs of others. A theory of mind is the conceptual mental framework of one person as developed and adopted in the mind of another. For example, children learn to understand the mentality of their caregivers at later stages of cognitive development. They adapt to the psychology of each of their guardians, modifying their behavior and gearing their decision-making to avoid punishment and seek praise. Psychologist Mike Eslea explains,

> A "theory of mind" ... is something that all people must develop in order to understand the minds of other people. We call it a theory because we can never actually connect with another's mind. There is no objective way to verify the contents of their consciousness or to assess their motivations and desires. Instead, when we interact with other people we can only guess at these things, using our [theory of mind] to work out what they know, think or feel.[6]

Thus, the psychological content of these theories of mind remains hypothetical.

Role-playing allows participants to take theories of mind one step farther. Instead of merely imaging what another might think, the player is forced into situations where he or she must make decisions "as if" they were that person. This practice of enactment is "thinking outside the box" in its most literal connotation; the performers must think outside the box of their own consciousness. Role-playing offers gamers the opportunity to become more open-minded in the broadest sense and experience, both as participant and observer, the thoughts and feelings of the hypothetical self of the character.

Role-Playing Games and the Cultivation of Empathy

Enacting a persona in role-playing scenarios not only provides a mental framework for understanding the consciousness of others, but also an emotional one. In "Vicarious Experience: Staying There Connected with and Through Our Own and Other Characters," Tim Marsh explains how the cultivation of empathy is an essential aspect of "being and self awareness."[7] According to Marsh, role-playing games teach three different forms of empathy: compassionate, cognitive, and emotional. He explains,

> Compassionate empathy can be demonstrated by player-characters responding kindly to other characters. Cognitive empathy can manifest itself through players knowing how other characters are feeling by observation of spectatorship, or through interacting with other characters. Emotional empathy is similar to cognitive empathy, but in addition to knowing how other characters are feeling, the players feel these emotions as their own.[8]

In this regard, RPGs function in the same manner as other forms of improvisational drama, such as drama therapy and educational role-playing. As I detailed in chapter two, therapists and teachers use role-playing to encourage a greater understanding of the minds and experiences of others. The groups Healing the Wounds of History and Geese Theatre, for example, encourage participants to experience multiple roles in a crisis scenario: victims, perpetrators, and spectators. Though the stated goal of RPGs is to provide an entertaining leisure activity, the role-taking process offers the added benefits of enhancing empathy, group conscience, and self-awareness.

Though I kept my questions rather general with regard to people's role-playing experiences, two of the recurring themes echoing through the responses from my interviewees revolved around this unexpected cultivation of empathy. First, gamers report that the practice of role-playing has introduced them to types of people with whom they would not normally interrelate, exposing them to a variety of different paradigms. Second, the enactment of different states of consciousness inherent to immersive role-play often makes players more aware of prejudice and oppression in the "real world" and their own relationship within those systems of power. Ultimately, the open, co-creative space provided by RPGs allows gamers to interface with alternate modes of thinking both in-character and out-of-character. These games offer players the capability to see reality through new perspectives and experience it empathetically through different eyes.

As Gary Alan Fine asserts in his foundational ethnography *Shared Fantasy: Role-Playing Games as Social Worlds*, "Describing the 'typical' gamer by a single example is impossible, probably more misleading than instructive."[9] I asked each of my interviewees the question, "How would you describe most gamers?" While the majority categorizes fellow role-players as "geeks" and "nerds," many of my respondents also emphasize that gamers hail from a multitude of social identifications. They tend to defy falling into neat typologies. Darren describes gamers as "a plethora of fringe people who you would not expect to be involved in this."[10] Kirstyn intimates, "Game attracts such a diverse spectrum of people, many of which I probably would not hang out with under other circumstances. This does not mean these people are bad people. Some are young, some old, some Republican, etc."[11] Kevin, who has role-played for over twenty-nine years and works in a gaming store in the mall, suggests:

> It's hard to say 'most gamers,' because to be perfectly honest, I see such a broad gambit here. I see guys coming in here wearing ties on their lunch hour to buy product ... I see younger folks that come in [wearing] all black and have excessive makeup and are going for that goth look and feel.... They cross a broad spectrum of society."[12]

Certain characteristics, though, seem to recur despite this wide range of participants. Walter agrees that gamers "don't break down nicely or neatly ala gender groups or racial groups or household earning incomes." However, he suggests, "I don't know that there is a majority. You can talk about discrete pluralities. I would say that, in general ... they do tend to be more creative, and they do tend to be more open to new possibilities. That's not always true, it's not an absolute, but that has been a consistent trend."[13] He defines the two most common attributes of gamers as "creative" and "open to new possibilities," two important qualities necessary for development of a theory of mind and immersion into it.

Gaming establishes bonds between people that would otherwise remain nonexistent or underdeveloped. Omega describes how he met his best friend of eight years through gaming and how different their personalities initially were from one another: "He was a type of person who I would never socialize with." He explains:

> Outside of gaming, I wouldn't have even acknowledged his existence. I probably would have made fun of his existence if he tried to enter into my little bubble of a world and he would have done the exact same thing ... he's my best friend now, and I would have never met him if ... we both weren't gamers, and if we both weren't able to extend more courtesy and more option and leeway to those that are gamers outside of those that aren't.[14]

Gaming offers the opportunity for a diverse group of people to interact in new and exciting ways. Because most games emphasize cooperation, both players and characters have to learn to work through personal differences in order to achieve common goals. Gaming scenarios place players in crisis situations where characters must rely on each other for success. These moments of shared adversity can build bonds between people, offering them the chance to look beyond surface forms of identification such as age, race, sex, and occupation.

Role-playing can also work to heal the wounds of damaged relationships. An intuitive Storyteller can shape storylines based on the individual psyches of the characters and their players. By enacting dramas in the safe space of the game, players can experience and examine relationships with others in new, dynamic ways. Omega explains how his strained relationship with his brother improved through such enactments. Though he and his brother's relationship was fraught with violence throughout their youth, he attributes the healing of this bond to role-playing :

> We were able to interact with each other *not as ourselves.* Not with that background of hate. Because he was able to be an Elven Ranger and I was able to be a Halfling Thief. And we were able to be completely strangers and still socialize and see that this person is able to accomplish some of the same things you are through your skills of acting and interaction."[15]

In this example, the self of the "real world," complete with prejudices and painful memories, was temporarily suspended so that alternate archetypes — the Elven Ranger and the Halfling Thief— could become enacted. These identities activated a new aspect of self in each performer and, thus, created a new pattern of interaction between them. The possibility for the building of a bridge between the brothers may have remained impossible without the game. In the sense of the eucatastrophe, the boys were offered the opportunity to Escape in a structured, fantastic, shared world, Recovering a sense of appreciation for each other while previous hurts were Consoled.

Fine suggests, "It is sometimes suggested that these games are similar to psychodrama — that form of psychotherapy developed by Moreno in which participants act out reactions to psychiatrically-significant events."[16] Similarly, Walter asserts that a running joke exists in gaming communities that role-playing is a form of inexpensive therapy. He explains that, as a Storyteller, many of his Non-player characters (NPCs) were created "deliberately or even subconsciously as a psychiatric device."[17] Both player-to-player and player-to-Storyteller interactions can offer insight into individual and group psychology.

However, not all gamers understand how to safely and maturely utilize this tool. Conflict can arise as a result, such as unhealthy power dynamics between players, arguments regarding rules, and a lack of comprehension of the separation of in-game versus out-of-game interactions. Gamers would undoubtedly find the practice of role-playing a more rewarding experience if they understood the potential power of the mechanisms at work. Players need to develop a healthy respect for these mechanisms and for the liminal space of the in-game interaction.

Even through some of the more unpleasant experiences in role-playing environments, these games can help produce a sense of empathy through interaction and exploration of each other's psyches. Desiree insists, "To be able to accurately look around you and have compassion for somebody you know nothing about, sometimes you have to do the role-playing.... 'Why are they acting this way? Can I see how they feel through their eyes?' And maybe learn something. Learn something about humanity, learn something about other people. Try to stretch your mind around that."[18] The "stretching of the mind" that Desiree describes can also work to induce a shift in paradigm, or at least a higher comprehension of the paradigms of others.

Paradigm Shifting

Some participants emphasize that, due to the conflicts built into the game world, they were forced to adopt belief systems alternate to the ones they hold in real life, particularly with respect to race and gender identification. Josh S. describes the challenge involved in portraying the racist attitudes of his non-player characters (NPCs) in *D&D*. He intimated that he is the only person within his family who married within his racial identification, which is Caucasian. He describes role-playing as putting him in "mindsets" that force him to examine bigotry. "I've played a tavernkeeper for a human settlement that doesn't like gnomes or elves. So I have to think.... 'Why would someone blindly hate somebody for no reason?' And it's hard to kind of think of those things."[19] Other players described the process of observing their characters shift from a mindset of racial prejudice to one of inclusion. Kevin explains how the game has forced his dwarf character to accept other members of the party, despite the fact that dwarven culture discriminates against their races as elves and dragons. "Currently, my dwarf is not keen on this concept that there is a dragon in our midst. Thus far he hasn't changed, but I am foreseeing that he will change his attitudes towards this individual dragon as the relationship between the individual characters grows as different events in the time line change and advance."[20] Kevin "foresees" that his character will change attitudes toward the dragon, who is part of a race usually considered monstrous rather than heroic. However, in order to provide a sense of realism to the proceedings, the player does not wish to force the persona to behave against-type.

One of the major "problems" players face is finding a way to unify disparately-motivated characters under a common goal. Since many gamers attempt to represent their characters as distinct entities from their primary selves, they wait for group cohesion to occur organically within the game. The game inherently includes conflicts such as racial tensions in order to present the players with challenges, intensifying the potential for drama. But players, and often their characters, quickly learn that success in scenarios involves cooperation of others. Even in games such as *Vampire* LARPs, in which the players jockey amongst themselves for political position, they often need to make allegiances with other players in order to achieve their ends. This sense of cooperation takes place both in-character, as the personas work together toward a common goal, but also out-of-character, as the players must "play nicely with others" in order to establish the safe space of the shared universe.

Another common type of characterization in which players must develop a theory of mind is alternate gender enactment. The motivations behind the desire to play such a character are multifaceted, but in my research, players often cite a wish to attempt to understand the mindset of the opposite gender. Alex plays females in various sexual scenarios in online games. I asked him why he almost exclusively portrays female sexuality instead of male. He responded, "At first I thought it was a sign that I was sexually confused or frustrated. After deeper analysis of myself, I feel that it's more that I want to see what it's like from a female's perspective. What women go through, and since I can't actually go through it, I can at least simulate."[21]

John has played two long-term female characters in tabletop campaigns. Though he often describes them as dressed seductively, he has yet to engage in any sexual scenarios as these personas. When asked why he chose to play female personas, he responded, "Because it was the most unlike myself. I mean, I'm a pretty masculine guy, I guess, and playing a female character was more of a challenge. I don't know if I did it right, but I tried." I asked him to articulate his process while in-character as a female and he stated that he altered his reactions to events in-game by thinking, "Well this is how *I* would react, so how *wouldn't I* react?"[22] This creative process of behaving in direct opposition with one's primary personality is a common strategy players employ for establishing of an alternate theory of mind.

Walter often plays strong female characters. He considers himself bi-gender identified and androgynous, describing his feminine-masculine split as "seventy-thirty."[23] Role-playing allows him an outlet to express this feminine side, though many of his female characters also possess traditionally masculine attributes, such as combat skills. One exception to this type is Elsbeth, a physically weak character that he enacted in a *Vampire* LARP setting. Since he already considers his mindset to be primarily feminine, his difficulties in portraying her resided more in his ability to convincingly "pass" as female from a physical standpoint. He describes, "My best friend there ... really helped me with the makeup and everything. It took about maybe two hours of preparation and it was cumbersome and uncomfortable, of course. And I feel for women, not having dealt with a corset and a wig and the heels [before]."[24] This experience expanded Walter's theory of mind by developing an understanding for the amount of effort women undergo to portray traditional femininity. Playing a female persona of any physical description is far easier in the relaxed atmosphere of the tabletop setting, whereas LARPs encourage elaborate costuming and movement to enhance immersion into the shared world. Online role-play provides even more opportunities for alternate gender performance, as players are not encumbered by the limitations of their physical appearance.

Some role-players enjoy gender-swapping as a release from the social demands placed upon them in terms of courtship. For men, playing a female character can provide a release from the social pressure to inhabit the role of masculine aggressor. For women, playing male characters can offer an opportunity to behave more dominantly with fewer social repercussions. However, such generalizations are not always true across the board. "Elton" insists that the experience of portraying females online differed little from his "real life" interactions. He explains, "I'm bisexual. I do identify with female characters in interesting ways but it doesn't strike me as anything horribly different from male characters." However, he adds the caveat, "I've been in the homosexual community for a while as well, so men hitting on me doesn't strike me as odd."[25] However, the majority of male role-players playing female characters are less likely to have received extensive aggressive attention from members of the same sex, as such behavior is not generally condoned in society.

One cliché among role-players is that portraying a female character offers inherent advantages by inspiring males to more consistently offer help in the form of items, money, and services. Such offerings are intensified if the male players can verify that the individual presenting the female persona is actually female in "real life." Haley slyly mentions that with male Storytellers, she noticed a clear bias in her favor. "As a girl who's role-playing, I find it interesting how the bigger monsters just don't seem to be thrown at me as much." The male players refrain from IC or OOC courtship toward her due to the fact that her husband also plays in the group, but overall, she believes that female players are "given a lot more leeway than the guys [get] to mess up."[26] As a female player myself, I agree with this statement. In my experience, male players consistently forgive my lack of knowledge of the rules and offer extensive amounts of aid, both IC and OOC.

Interestingly, the behavior patterns of resource provision or protectiveness often manifest even if male players "know" another male is playing a female. When heavily immersed in the game, the player can move beyond the out-of-character knowledge of the others player's sex and react as their character would toward a female. Matthew describes an eventual shift in his ability to engage in an IC romantic relationship between his *Vampire* character, William, and one of Walter's female characters, Ishtari. He explains, "It certainly was awkward. I, at first, did have difficulty imagining [that] a woman [was] speaking with me and not the obvious opposite. At first, the distance I felt, I believe, was more me than it was William." However, Matthew states that he eventually moved past these "immature and confusing thoughts." He describes his characters as "protectors of women," and the IC interaction with Ishtari provided a crucial shift in William's story line. Matthew explains, "In modern times, he had grown cold and distant, and had begun to lost his vibrance and light for his unlife until Ishtari began to make him see differently."[27] Matthew's ultimate ability to perceive Ishtari as female and respond to her accordingly provided important character motivation for William.

In *D&D*, gender-swapping scenarios occur occasionally within characters through spells or items. Players think they have acquired some fantastic piece of armor, for example, but instead, their characters are forced to spend the rest of their existence in the body of the opposite gender. Such items are meant to provide humor to the game, but also present role-play challenges. Omega, who describes his sexual orientation as "nondiscriminative," describes how two of his major characters were forced to change sex in *D&D*: "One started off as a male and then was given the body of a female, and then the other was the body of a male that was inhabited by a female." In the latter case, the gender confusion caused the character, Silverleaf, to become suddenly enraged at a "fop" non-player character (NPC). The NPC was intended simply as a tool for the

Storyteller to provide local color to the town. In a move unanticipated by both Omega and the other players, Silverleaf pulled the fop outside, beat him, and left him for dead. This incident allowed Omega to explore and understand a previously foreign mindset, as he details in the following passage:

> I felt the same rage that homophobes feel in today's society. I felt the same thoughts and the same process and the same atrocities, [similar to how] one religion despises another religion.... And with playing that charac-ter, I understand it now. I still don't agree with it, but at least now I under-stand that, most of the time, these people didn't choose to have these feelings ... I used to blame all bigots for being bigots when, sometimes, that's all that they know.[28]

Omega's experiences as Silverleaf offered a theory of mind for mul-tiple aspects of consciousness: alternate gender identification, sexual ori-entation confusion, and homophobia. This theory of mind also provided a sense of empathy for people with alternate viewpoints, an epiphany that likely would never have taken place outside of the context of shifting per-sonas in the safe environment of the role-playing game.

These shifts in perspective possibly allow gamers to view others more open-mindedly. Having portrayed characters with a variety of different personality traits, backgrounds, demographics, and motivations, gamers tend to exhibit more acceptance of alternate paradigms. Chris explains that his favorite RPG is White Wolf's *Mage: The Ascension* because the game's philosophies and mechanics force players to think outside the box.[29] He explains, "[*Mage* teaches] that there is no such thing as a single para-digm, that we're all really people with our individual ideas whether we like it or not and we're trying to find truth within our own perspective."[30] This explanation, while specific to *Mage*, could easily be applied to the prac-tice of role-playing itself, particularly when players come in conflict with unique types of characters and scenarios. Such paradigm expansion has the potential to influence how players interact with others outside of gam-ing. By studying the effects of issues such as sexism, racism, and religious extremism in-character, they may become more inclusive towards others in their daily life, enhancing overall social cohesion.

Isolation and Societal Stigma

This open-mindedness and willingness to interact with different types of people may result from early feelings of alienation. Almost all of my respondents report experiencing a sense of isolation from their peer group as young children and teenagers. The following list includes various words individuals use to describe themselves and/or their general emotional state as children: outcast, misfit, nerd, geek, loner, anitsocial, shy, "picked on," isolated, sheltered, introverted, anxious, agoraphobic, weepy, elitist, anti-conformist, sensitive, trapped, sullen, terrified, reserved. While many adolescents may identify with the descriptors, my interviewees expressed an overall sense of distance from the mainstream group.

Several respondents describe having no friends growing up, or only one or two. Desiree intimates, "I didn't have a lot of socializing until I was out of the house, which was [at] about twenty ... I didn't belong anywhere. Pretty much was an outcast. Completely on my own, by myself. In a corner. No social skills. No really good friends."[31] Guillermo describes his childhood as "very sheltered and very awkward," speculating that his parents "never understood the need for social interaction."[32] Omega states that before the age of ten, "the only time I ever saw anybody that wasn't family was either when we went to the store or when I went to school." He describes, "From ten to fifteen, I had an issue with people's ignorance and I *chose* not to associate with anybody that I thought was an ignorant person, which means I only talked to teachers because they were the only ones who understood the words that I was using."[33]

Some explained the source of this sense of isolation was often physical circumstances. Josh T. relays, "Up until fifth grade, I lived out in the middle of nowhere. So, pretty much it was me, my brother, and the neighbor three miles away."[34] Matthew suffered from childhood leukemia, which alienated him at times from his peers. He explains, "My social life was varied from very active to almost nonexistent. Being hospitalized at age five and then again at age eleven, I repeatedly experienced changes in friends and people who would speak with me because of my having cancer."[35] Other respondents mention either constantly moving around with their parents or being shuffled between caregivers. Without a stable sense of home, some children have difficulty establishing long-term bonds with friends. "Elton" thinks that his initial difficulty reading people socially combined with his unstable home life, contributing to his desire escape into games:

> We moved, on average, about every nine months. Never was in a place, never was in a school, never had any lasting friends. Everything was changing constantly, which, interestingly enough, is a perfect environment for game because everything *is* changing constantly. I definitely think that my environment growing up had a direct impact on the games and the fact that I was drawn to [them, providing] the environment for me to deal with the crap that went with growing up in such situations that I did.[36]

Immersion in alternate worlds provides a sense of escape from loneliness and disappointment in the real world.

Not all my interviewees immersed themselves in role-playing games early in life, though many indicate having a previous background in theater. While in some ways different in structure and content, role-playing and theater both employ the active enactment of an alternate self. As Henry describes, "Theatre and role-playing are an escape from reality. If you don't like whom you are, or are tired of what you have been, be something else for a few hours."[37] Chris dabbled in theater and high school and majored in the field in college. He states, "There's a subculture within subculture within subculture that defines what a theater person is." He further delineates common qualities of people attracted the craft: "Flexibility, being very eccentric, having a very unique perspective on people, being able to be observant. A lot of actors, especially, are extremely observant. Being about to walk away from anyone's expectations and following your own."[38] Many of these descriptions also apply to role-players.

When I asked my participants how they would classify themselves as teenagers in retrospect, several mentioned being part of a group of "outcasts" or "misfits." Josh T. explains, "In clique fashion, we always termed ourselves the outcasts, but it was in a fashion to where we weren't picked on or anything. We weren't constantly insulted ... we were just left alone."[39] Similarly, Erin describes, "I got picked on a lot. I think every kid gets picked on to some extent. When I was in high school, the kids that nobody else wanted to hang out or talk to ... were my close friends. We were the outcasts of ... 'normal' society overall, but with each other we were just fine."[40] Guillermo correlates the "rejects" with the theater subculture in the following statement: "My friends in high school ... were the rejects, the people that were the theater majors, the people that were the alternative crowd. We were drinking coffee and smoking at the Denny's and that was the bohemian life in Midland, TX."[41] So, though many of my respondents describe a strong feeling of social alienation, several report having bonded with other "misfits" in small social groups.

A few interviewees describe themselves as having an extroverted personality in high school and being involved in a variety of different social groups. I myself fall into this category, as do Chris, John, and Omega. Interestingly, even the extroverted gamers still did not fit neatly into one particular social category. My mother often referred to me as "a chameleon" as a teenager. Omega describes, "I went from hanging out with nobody to hanging out with every type of person who was out there from the jocks, to the dweebs, to the people in chess club, to the people in drama club, to the people who have already dropped out of school, to the people that did illegal substances, to the people that didn't drink soda or have sugar." He further acted as an "activist" for "anybody who was an underdog," attending "a lot of different organizational meetings that were set up to prevent depression and to prevent conformity."[42] Though Omega became extremely socially active, much of his behavior and ideological values promoted rejection of the status quo.

Chris also moonlighted in a myriad of different groups. He describes, "[In] ninth grade, I got to high school, and I met a lot of theater kids there, and a lot of the music kids ... I was technically a jock because I was a swimmer, but I was also involved with the Creative Writing program so I was 'the Writer.' I got into the art crowd."[43] For these individuals, this ability to shift roles in the "real world" may reflect an inherent ability to perform in a pretend setting, and perhaps also indicates a desire to do so. Also, such varied experiences reflect the aforementioned open-mindedness and ability to respect the viewpoints of others.

Josh S. classifies the early social behavior of gamers as falling into two categories: the Supernerds and the After High School Cool People. He describes the Supernerds as "the stereotypical, live in the basement, talk with that nasally voice kind of person and ... they seem to like smaller groups of people and [their] social skills [are] not quite as good as other people I've met." The After High School Cool People are "incredibly sociable people that have a different concept of what 'cool' is, really. You know, the people who like the goth and dark stuff but are still really nice and personable people."[44] Some of my participants described themselves more popular now than they once were, akin to this After High School Cool People category. "Elton" brags, "I like to think I'm gloriously successful. I've got a strikingly beautiful wife, mostly successful businesses, financially successful. I think I'm doing great. I'm definitely still not mainstream, but as an adult, that matters very much less than the politics of high school."[45] Guillermo also mentions this shift in importance, stating, "I don't think that I actually realized it until later, in college, that [my] lifestyle is okay. I don't need this prom queen, Barbie and Ken ... popular lifestyle to be successful in life."[46] Virtually all of my interviewees strongly distanced their personal sense of identity with the Supernerd stereotype.

Interestingly, when I asked my respondents if they participated in any fan behavior, they avoid admitting to any, though I know from looking at their bookshelves and DVD collections that they definitely favor particular genres and series. Scholarship on role-playing commonly correlates involvement with RPGs as related to "other" forms of fandom, particularly involvement with science fiction and fantasy texts. Fine describes the role-playing subculture as a "subsociety [that] overlaps with those of war gamers, science fiction enthusiasts, and medieval history buffs."[47] Daniel MacKay reports, "In my experiences with the recreational community of role-players, I have found that almost all of them share the same score of product art from which they create a community, a subculture, with its own jargon, rituals, and practices." MacKay observes that out-of-character conversation at games tends to revolve around films, comic books, music, novels, video games and television. The majority of these cultural products arise from the science fiction and fantasy genres.[48]

If role-players also commonly participate in other forms of fandom, why would they wish to hide such interests? Unfortunately, popular culture fandom often often incurs negative stigma from society at large, as does the practice as role-playing itself. When I asked if role-playing as a practice had any negative consequences, almost every participant stated that they had seen gaming cause problems for *other* players, but not for them. In communication studies, the phenomena is dubbed the *third-person effect hypothesis*, which "states that people see media messages as having greater impact on others than on themselves."[49] Many role-players attempt to distance themselves from this concept of the Supernerd, creating a category of Otherness in which to place fellow gamers who they feel lack social skills or excessively participate in gaming and fan behavior. This defensive behavior allows role-players to internalize less of the social stigma placed upon role-players by outsiders.

For example, participants often stated that one valuable aspect of role-playing is obtaining access to friendships they never would have made before, but that players should never use gaming as their sole form of socialization. As Chris suggests, "Some people may have no other way of making friends so they use that as their only social outlet and, when that happens, bad emotional things can [result]."[50] Players may take conflicts related to the game too personally and friendships may end, which can also result in the dissolution of the game itself. Guillermo describes a recent example in which he and Chris had to ask a player not to come back to their tabletop game:

> I guess my personal theory, and I never was able to confirm it, was that she came to a lot of these games because she didn't have a lot of social interaction. She was very socially isolated, she didn't have very good social skills.... She would get angry in the middle of game because of mechanics.... She became violent; there was dice-throwing. There were these outbursts that were very childish, immature.[51]

Though the behavior of the player in Guillermo's example is a bit extreme compared to most games in which I have participated, I have witnessed hostility between players. Some individuals become extremely upset when their concept of the rules does not correspond with that of the Storyteller's, especially if their character's failure or death in a scenario results from the disagreement. Walter cites a particular rules dispute in which a player argued with his authority as Storyteller with regard to the physics of the game world. Ultimately, he learned that the Storyteller needs to have a sense of clinical detachment because "allowing yourself to get into that space of brawling and conflict [is] just utterly disruptive."[52] Chris admits, "There are other cases where I may have lost my temper and said some things horrible to people I should never have said. I would like the opportunity to say I'm sorry but I will never get to [do so]."[53]

Part of the challenge in games, then, is learning how to "play well with others," both in-character and out-of-character. Chris explains that though the games are meant to be cooperative, people's inborn competitive mechanisms sometimes activate and debates ensue that can damage relationships. He jokes that while questioning authority is healthy, "It's just very irritating sometimes when the guy that's questioning you doesn't know how to use deodorant and has no friends."[54] This comment reflects another common stereotype about Supernerd gamers: not only do they lack social skills, but they also lack proper bathing habits. Unprompted, Henry felt the need to remark, "Unfortunately the old stereotype of poor hygiene among gamers has too much real evidence to back it up."[55] Comments such as these further highlight the distinction many gamers feel they should make between themselves and the Supernerds.

The participants overwhelmingly also felt the need to emphasize that they engage in social activities outside of gaming in order to distance themselves from this stereotype. Often, gaming groups consist of players who do not know each other outside of the practice of role-playing and who probably would never socialize outside of the context of game. John, the only one of my participants who classified himself as one of the "cool people" in high school, describes how he dislikes being pigeonholed as a "gaming friend," finding the term offensive. He complains that just because people share a common interest in role-playing, their friendship should not be defined by those parameters. He explains, "You have only so much time in life to leave the house and go hang out with people.... If gaming was removed from the situation, I guess we'd be movie buddies or book buddies or any [other] kind of buddies."[56]

Other interviewees strongly stressed the need for moderation in role-players, lest the individual lose touch with the "real world." Kevin states, "I think gaming is a positive practice for people in general so long as those people remember that it is not real life. I've also known a person or two who got so wrapped up in gaming that they lost themselves, and that's not positive."[57] The so-called boundary between fantasy and reality can often be difficult to define, as I will explore in my chapter on identity alteration. However, my participants stress that engagement in many different social and cultural activities is necessary for mental health. Chris maintains,

> To be around ... or talk about role-playing games twenty-four seven to me is extremely unhealthy. I need to pick up and read a book. I need to watch TV. I need to play video games. I need to see a movie. I need to go to a beautiful restaurant with my boyfriend. I need to go to art museums. I need to do all these other things [to] stimulate me ... Role-playing games is an outlet, but it's not my only one. And I think that it's really important for people to try to have different outlets.[58]

Personally, I strongly agree with Chris' statement. However, I think that if an individual lacks sufficient social skills to interact effectively with mainstream society, and role-playing is the only activity where they can feel welcome, than gaming groups offer phenomenal opportunities for growth. Because gamers often admit to having felt socially isolated at some point in their lives, they become much more accepting of the individual quirks of other gamers. Having faced social scrutiny and judgment before, they often remain less judgmental and more open-minded. Combined with the ability to shift roles and adopt new perspectives, gaming can provide a feeling of inclusion for those who often have felt excluded in social life.

Gaming as Ritual

The in-game experiences of glory and hardship are amplified when explored in a group setting. For example, players often describe with fondness the exhilarating moments when a long-term story line reaches a climax. The characters, who have endured several smaller challenges together, now must far more difficult odds. Secret plots are often revealed at these times; the central, elusive villain may finally surface, for example. The characters must present a united front in the conflict, for defeat is imminent without an effective strategy.

These shared experiences often create an intense bond between players. Some participants in my study described such climactic moments with nostalgia. When I asked John to detail one of his positive memories of role-playing, he described a long-running *D&D* campaign that culminated in a final confrontation with an "amazingly powerful dragon, steeped in a pool of positive energy that would continually heal us." He recalls the event with enthusiasm: "I remember seeing the worry, and the fretting, and the fear. And then they got into the battle and the more they fought, the more that they talked to each other and they were really excited ... and at the end of it, they all went outside, were talking to each other, laughing, holding hands, giving each other high fives. Great experience, after they killed that dragon."[59] This example presents a straight-forward, Tolkien-esque quest. A group of adventuring heroes must face a powerful adversary, just as Bilbo and the dwarves must do in *The Hobbit*. The anxiety before the battle lends to the exhilaration after the party members defeat the villain. This shared experience creates a bond out-of-character, a special sense of closeness between players that is unparalleled in most other non-sporting social activities. While experiences such as rock concerts provoke such feelings of unity and excitement, the process of sharing and creating a story with another group of people over a long period of time adds a fascinating dimension to the role-playing dynamic: that of a co-created shared mythology.

These moments sometimes end in tragedy rather than elation, particularly if an important party member dies in the confrontation. The intensity of these moments varies depending on the talent of the Storyteller, the attitudes of the players, and the established bonds between characters. Walter describes the climactic moment of a *Champions* campaign that he ran in high school. One of his NPCs, Donna, had an intimate relationship with one of the player-characters. Because she had become too powerful, she had to sacrifice herself to save the universe, and her in-game lover was forced to kill her. Walter recalls,

> Everyone was crying there. Even thinking about that now ... it was so powerful. Every story about sacrifice, about the nobility of the human character and the ability to persevere despite all odds ... it all really came together then.... It was huge and it reminded us all why we're doing this. Why we're willing to have these fights, and why we're willing to pour hours into this ridiculously complex rules system with freakin' algebra necessary to do it. It was because of moments like that.[60]

Later in his interview, he indicates that the players in this session responded with "stunned silence and weeping."[61] Though the player-character in this example performed a heroic deed by destroying the threat, he did so at the expense of his own love and happiness.

This type of storyline falls under the category of classical Aristotelian tragedy. For Aristotle, tragedy must "excite pity and fear" in the audience.

He indicates that "pity is aroused by unmerited misfortune, fear by the misfortune of [humans] like ourselves."[62] This emotional response, called *catharsis*, allows audience members to expel emotion from within themselves by witnessing the horrifying elements of the story. Tragedy is also often marked by the central character killing someone close to him or her. Aristotle states, "When the tragic incident occurs between those who are near or dear to one another — if, for example, a brother kills, or intends to kill, a brother, a son his father, a mother her son, a son his mother, or any other deed of the kind is done — these are the situations to be looked for by the poet."[63] In addition, Aristotle believes that a certain story length is necessary for tragedy to full take hold of the audience. He explains that "the greater the length, the more beautiful will the piece be by reason of its size, provided that the whole be perspicuous."[64] All of these qualities describe the climax to the above story from Walter's *Champions* campaign. Though the seeds arose from a pre-formulated module published by the game designers entitled *The Coriolis Effect*, the emotional investment of the players into the characters, the romantic angle between one of the player characters and the NPC, and the length of the campaign intensified the experience of the tragedy.[65]

Ultimately, role-playing games hold the potential to produce an even greater sense of catharsis than the plays and epic poems of Aristotle's time. While ancient festivals such as the City Dionysia featured lengthy plays and performances that were spread out over the course of three days, role-playing story lines can take years to reach a climax.[66] Walter claims that the *Coriolis Effect* plot line climaxed after one and a half years of weekly and sometimes biweekly play. Gaming sessions generally last anywhere between three to eight hours; thus, such a powerful moment was achieved after hundreds of hours of gaming. The extent to which players experience such intensity depends on the personalities involved in the game, the length of time invested, and the level of character immersion.

Regardless of these specifics, the practice of role-playing functions as a modern-day ritual. The function of ritual, according to Victor Turner, is to reestablish bonds within a community.[67] As described in Chapter 2, ritual involves a separation from daily life, an immersion into a liminal reality, and a reintegration back into the social group after the ritual experiences transpire.[68] A couple of my participants actively use the concept of ritual to describe role-playing in their language. Kirstyn states, "[Role-playing] became like a ritual — the food to be shared, drinks to be had, the laughs and tears."[69] Walter laments the growing lack of consistent, formalized rituals in modern society. Though all role-playing games require some shift between the outside realm and the liminal, Walter attempts to intensify these distinctions in his currently-run LARP. He formalizes the shift between in-game and out-of-game activities through the following process:

> Everybody knows that when I'm asking them to light candles, the game is closer ... when I walk back into the bedroom, which is where all the costuming is going on ... I'll tell them, "Next time I come out, I'm in character." And when I walk out, there's actually an in-game ritual, but it's also an out-of-game ritual where [my character] walks up, he kneels before the sword to give obeisance to the missing Prince. Then, he looks at everyone, and he says, "*Ave, Quirites.*" Hail citizens. And then they'll repeat back, "*Ave, Caesar.*" Hail Caesar, or in this case ... leader. And, both in-character and out-of-character, that kind of gets everybody [thinking], "Okay, *bam*, the game's on."[70]

Walter intensifies the normal shift between the pre-liminal and liminal stage of the role-playing ritual, which helps players move deeper into the mindset of their characters.

After the game, the players often linger a while longer to discuss the events of the episode. In LARPs, a more formalized gathering is held for announcements, discussion, and nominations for best role-playing and costuming. These traditions help create a sense of closure for the episode, but also enhance the sense of community by allowing everyone to share their favorite moments and offer criticism. In tabletop settings, this time is usually dedicated to issuing out experience points and determining where to spend them, allowing the player to witness how the events of the game directly affect the growth of the character from a meta-perspective. These practices form the post-liminal state, in which participants slowly reintegrate themselves back into the social roles of the "real world."

Rituals generally contain some remnant of a mythological story or inherent archetype. In role-playing, the game system usually provides the language for the enactment of these archetypes, though these symbols themselves often derive from age-old images. The overall plot lines tend to fall into traditional mythological structures, such as classical tragedy or the hero's journey. Walter explains that role-playing enacts "the myths, the archetypes, the themes, the story arcs that speak to primal human experiences. The loss of the mother, avenging the father, finding your place in the universe, finding your true origins, coming of age. I mean, these are things that have existed since ... human beings were sentient."[71] These themes resonate in the deep reaches of the minds of the players and the enactment of them promotes an exceptional level of engagement.

The creators of White Wolf's World of Darkness understand this inherent power of role-playing. They weave terms like "archetype" and "ritual" directly into game concepts and mechanics. For example, players choose various archetypes in *Vampire: The Masquerade* in order to delineate their character's personality. The main rulebook contains an entire section explaining the concept of archetypes and even includes a quote from Carl Jung as an epigram. White Wolf tells its players, "Archetypes encompass not only personalities, but places and things as well. They are a way for the Storyteller to get the players to understand the characters and setting, and to relate them to their own lives. Archetypes help us make sense out of things and help the Storyteller bring the story home."[72]

White Wolf's *Werewolf: The Apocalypse* utilizes traditional notions of tribalism, totemism, and ritual as a framework for their conceptualization of werewolf society. Though brutal and physically powerful, the werewolves in the World of Darkness act less like one-dimensional monsters and more like Native American tribal units. Werewolves possess an inherent connection with the life force and the land, which they call Gaia. Thus, they are the natural enemies of vampires, who live outside of the life force and prey upon it for subsistence.

Werewolf characters must choose archetypes as well, though these assignations are labeled *Auspices* instead. "An auspice," according to White Wolf, "reflects the werewolf's general personality traits and interests, as well as his duties to the pack. All auspices are important, for no werewolf can perform every role for his or her people. When packs include a variety of different auspices, the unit grows stronger as a whole from the diversity of its individual members."[73] Each Auspice reflects phases of the moon, as well as ancient mythological symbols. The five Auspices are: Ragabash, the New Moon, the Trickster; Theurge, the Crescent Moon, the Seer; Philodox, the Half Moon, the Mediator; Galliard, the Gibbous Moon, the Moon Dancer (or Bard); Ahroun, the Full Moon, the Warrior.[74]

This concept of the Auspice establishes a sense of the character's role in the community — or *tribe*— from the outset.[75] Unlike vampire society, in which characters consistently backstab one another for dominance, the "goal" of *Werewolf* is to establish a sense of tribal unity. Werewolves are further distinguished from one another by *breed* and they organize into subgroups known as *packs.*[76] Packs identify themselves through dedication to a particular totem. The book describes totemism in the traditional sense, but also includes modern conceptualizations:

> Many of these totems are great animal spirits, such as Raven or Bear. Others, such as Grandfather Thunder, are more personified. Lesser known,

more esoteric totems, like Almighty Dolla' and the Great Trash Heap, are cryptic and bizarre. These great spirits each have their own special strengths, so the choice of a totem often relates to a pack's goals or strengths. The choice is made during an intense and mystical rite. The pack then receives a *totem spirit*, a spiritual servitor of the totem that can act as their guardian, guide them through the spirit world and even lend them mystical power.[77]

At the close of the *Vampire* rulebook, the writers list Carl Jung, Joseph Campbell, and Mircea Eliade as some of the many sources of inspiration for the World of Darkness.[78] The game designers clearly possess a theoretical familiarity with the power of archetype, myth, totemism, and ritual.

Though RPGs such as *Dungeons & Dragons* also use myth and archetype, the use of these terms in the structure of the White Wolf games provides a metaphoric language for players, offering them a deeper understanding of the practice of role-playing itself. In *Vampire*, for example, *masquerade* refers to the need for vampires to mask their true nature from humans, but also to the act of role performance itself. In *Werewolf*, the players enact tribal practices as a form of nostalgia toward the world's fading, native cultures and their rituals. By doing so, the role-playing practice itself recapitulates traditional, tribal ideals into modern ritual and storytelling forms. In this way, the game designers call the players' attention to the potential for role-playing to act as a unifying communal practice. Such unifying practices are few and far between in our fragmented, Western society.

Interestingly, many of the gamers in my study responded that they did not feel like they were part of a "community" of gamers. Some stated that LARP provides more of a sense of community than tabletop, due the larger numbers of players. Others assumed that I was referring to gaming stores or international conventions when I used the word "community." Omega states, "It took about a year and a half of gaming to realize it wasn't just me and the few that I knew. It was actually a worldwide community that would get together and share in the same likes and dislikes [and who have] the same experience when they're acting as these characters and bringing life to it and seeing a whole new world through their role-playing."[79]

Omega assumes that a community must be large in numbers rather than "few," a response echoed by many of my interviewees. However, Dictionary.com defines community as "a social, religious, occupational, or other group sharing common characteristics or interests and perceived or perceiving itself as distinct in some respect from the larger society within which it exists." Another definition on the site indicates that a community can be "of any size."[80] The sense of social alienation and stigma experienced by many gamers, both in general and as a result of role-playing, obfuscates from the players the deeper sense of belonging that role-playing can provide.

Some of my respondents likened the practice of role-playing to other group ritual activities involving games. "Elton" explains, "Some people take up bowling. Some people take up pool. Some people go and do their own thing within their own social group. This is just what we seized upon." However, he admits that most people fail to see the similarities between role-playing and other forms of gaming. He laments, "Role-playing is not socially accepted in the same realm as a guy's night out having poker or the women going out playing bridge."[81] Kevin makes a point of distinguishing role-playing as a "hobby," rather than just a game. He explains, "It takes a lot of time. And it's a big commitment. It's not just a game, it's really a hobby, and I tell everybody that when I sell them product. If you're looking for a game to open a box, sit down, and play for two hours on a rainy afternoon, don't try role-playing. That's not what you're looking for."[82]

Aside from the time commitment, role-playing differs in other ways as well. While many games offer the benefits of mental exercise and the establishment of group cohesion, role-playing adds aspects of co-creation and narrative structure that other activities lack. These characteristics can deepen the relationships between roleplayers. Chris describes one instance in which the in-game process of co-creation also established an out-of-character bond:

> Especially with your more intense scenes, you can get an intimate connection with somebody. There is this woman I met in my last LARP experience whom I've never met before, ever. And within five minutes, we both had to behave as if we were cousins, [spiritually-speaking]. And we did it, we pulled it off, and we roleplayed to each other like that for a couple of hours. And after that ... how could I not feel close to somebody like that? I mean, [she was] able to *go there* with me, so quick, so fast. I don't even know her last name. I don't even know what her favorite color is, what her birthday is, and thus, I don't know her sign ... I don't know anything about her.... You don't know somebody so quickly outside of role-playing, I think.[83]

The majority of my own role-playing experiences echo the instance Chris describes. Though all games inherently possess personality differences that can erupt in conflict, most role-playing involves tapping into one's personal wellspring of creativity and weaving a story with others. In a powerful way, role-players dip into the content of their unconscious mind, sharing their secret thoughts, desires, and potentialities with each other. Desiree explains:

> When you enter a person's fantasy world, when you enter a person's fantasy character, when you become friends with a person's fantasy character, you become friends with a part of them that they've hidden from most of society. So therefore, not only have I been friends with most of the gamers I've played with before we started playing, I realized that I really wanted to be their friend even in a game world. Even with their fantasy character, which is truly a part of them, very deep in their heart that nobody else knows.[84]

Role-playing offers the possibility for out-of-game relationships to be enhanced though deep engagement with each other's fantasies, both on an individual and communal level.

This chapter has detailed how role-playing allows individuals who feel alienated from the majority of society to experience alternate perspectives, to better understand and empathize with others, and to establish a much-needed sense of community. The next two chapters explain how role-playing scenarios can offer the opportunity for individuals to learn an important variety of skills through problem-solving and scenario-building both in "serious" contexts and as a leisure activity.

4

Role-Playing as Scenario Building and Problem Solving

As we have discussed, role-playing is widely used in a variety of contexts. Role-playing works as a modern-day form of ritual, enforcing social cohesion through shared dramatic experiences. Role-playing also provides a useful tool for training and education purposes. Because of the extensive scope of possibilities inherent to the enactment of roles and situations, a wide range of organizations find its application useful, including corporations, medical establishments, churches, psychologists, prisons, military bases, and educational institutions. While the previous chapters focused on the social dynamics offered by role-playing, the chapter will deal specifically with the extensive array of skills that people can potentially acquire through the enactment of scenarios.

The mainstream media consistently debases RPGs and their participants, labeling role-players "geeks," "dorks," and "nerds." Public perception of individuals who engage in this the subcultural activity ranges from ridicule to moral panic. J. Patrick Williams, Sean Q. Hendricks, and W. Keith Winkler describe the cultural backlash incurred as a result of the popularization of the first RPG, *Dungeons & Dragons*:

> *D&D* was defined as a threat to societal values and interests soon after it emerged on the American mainstream cultural radar in the late 1970s. The threat was manifested primarily in fears of occult worship and negative psychological conditions including suicide, all of which the mass media presented in a stylized and stereotypical fashion. In these and many other popular culture sources, staff writers, apparently unfamiliar with fantasy games, reported the concerns of adults — parents, politicians,

police, and religious leaders — over fantasy games as a source of child corruption.[1]

Paradoxically, when role-playing takes place in so-called "serious games," popular and academic publications often celebrate its benefits. The overall tone of public response toward these games remains positive, emphasizing how role-playing can offer a revolutionary method of training. This chapter explains how, in a variety of contexts, reputable institutions have found the practice of role-playing valuable rather than dangerous. In fact, proponents of so-called "serious games" emphasize the relative safety offered by gaming scenarios. According to David Michael and Sande Chen, authors of *Serious Games: Games that Educate, Train, and Inform,* "Many skills can be taught only by *doing,* and many lessons can be learned only through failure. Serious games allow training to occur in a non-lethal environment."[2]

A difference exists between the way the mainstream views role-playing in institutional environments and role-playing for leisure (RPGs). The mainstream finds role-playing valuable when geared toward a specific "purpose" and when structured and overseen by authority figures such as managers, therapists, educators, and drill sergeants. However, engagement in role-playing for entertainment is dismissed as lacking in any sort of worth and potentially damaging to the psyches of gamers. I would like to problemetize this concept of "serious games" as a distinct unit from RPGs. This chapter will detail the many benefits of role-playing for training purposes, while Chapter 5 will specifically examine how participation in RPGs also encourages the development of important skills in a leisure setting.

The Role-Playing Advantage

The practice of role-playing entails three major functions: scenario building, problem-solving, and skill training. *Scenario building* describes the projection of potential future timelines and the subsequent conjecture regarding the difficulties, benefits, and consequences involved in taking particular sets of actions. The concept was popularized in the field of business by pioneers like Peter Schwartz. In his book *The Art of the Long View,* Schwartz describes techniques originally developed within the Royal/Dutch Shell company and later drawn from first-hand experience with the world's leading institutions and companies, including the White House, BellSouth, PG&E, the EPA, and the International Stock Exchange.[3] According to Uri Avin and Jane Debner, experts distinguish scenario building, which involves asking the question, "What do you think might happen?" from *visioning*, which queries, "What would you like to see happen?"[4] Projecting scenarios involves establishing the givens and uncertainties of a particular course of action. Business modelers then create solutions based on five driving forces: society, technology, environment, politics, and economics (STEPE).[5] Though the concept of scenario building emerged from the field of business, other institutions such as the military have long used scenarios as a means to project potential futures.

Problem-solving is another related function of role-playing. Scenarios place players in difficult situations that often require a high-level of critical analysis for resolution. Players must evaluate the options open to them, such as available resources and potential social reactions to stimuli. Role-playing allows people to find solutions to dilemmas in a safe, low-risk environment, often the with the goal of *skill training* in mind. This chapter details the multitude of different skills researchers claim that role-playing scenarios can train.

Many researchers insist that *active learning* is superior in the development of skill training to *passive* learning. Active learning allows students the opportunity to attain a high level of engagement and interactivity with the material, whereas passive learning favors a unidirectional deliverance of information. Passive learning remains dominant in education, as most traditional teaching environments favor the top-down approach. However, new pedagogical studies often encourage experimentation with active learning techniques.[6] Educators are beginning to recognize the value of "participatory, experiential modes of thinking" as complementary to the standard "distanced, reflective modes," such as detached observation and analysis.[7] According to Beres Joyner and Louise Young, role-play has been touted as the most widely practiced instructional method for the development of interpersonal skills. Role-playing has also become a valuable teaching method for knowledge, skills, and attitude development, often aiding in the transition from classroom to professional setting. Role-playing contributes life and immediacy to academic descriptive material, inspires students to recall more information than they would from lectures, and encourages fun while learning.[8]

Games appeal to contemporary young people who, in our fast-paced lifestyle of high media saturation, expect speed and interactivity. Howard Witt of the *Chicago Tribune* stated recently, "Some researchers even suggest supplanting much of the traditional back-to-basics K-12 curriculum with a new generation of game-based materials to capture the increasingly short attention spans of today's youth."[9] Role-playing offers the benefit of expedient learning when compared with traditional education or the acquisition of "real-world" experience. According to training specialists, scenario leaders "can often demonstrate more ideas, skills, and techniques in a ten minute role-play than in thirty of forty minutes with 'real' people."[10] Furthermore, role-play offers the opportunity for immediate feedback directly after the session, a quality of high didactic value to participants.[11]

In addition, role-playing increases the enjoyment of the learning process while decreasing the risk incurred through real-world experience. Scenarios offer the opportunity to try out different roles or courses of action in a safe atmosphere with little cost to the players. Some authorities even recognize the ritual qualities of role-playing. As pastoral care specialist Pamela Couture eloquently describes, role-playing provides a ritual space in which "stimulation, excitement, and emotion can be appropriately experienced without shame or guilt.... A ritual process in an introductory pastoral care class creates a frame around playfulness that protects creativity and freedom in the learning process and relaxes the frame in seriousness when insight and learning is reinforced."[12] When participants perceive the activity as "just a game," they relax their feelings of investment in success and experience less social stigma for failure.

Role-playing theorists examine the interdependent relationship between task difficulty and reward in both the enjoyment and the potential benefits of games.[13] In professional business scenarios, for example, participants are rewarded by supervisors and peers for "intelligent, rational, and well planned, executive-type decisions."[14] Even players who enjoy various types of games for entertainment — including board and card games — locate their pleasure as rooted in the mental challenges necessary for success and the competitive gratification inherent to outwitting an opponent.[15] Harboring a "love of thought" and a desire for social interaction, players describe their enjoyment in the following way: "You have to actually think and make decisions, but you have fun and socialize, too." Game enthusiasts believe that this rare combination of mental exercise and entertainment cannot be duplicated in traditional classroom settings: "If those situations are taken out of an academic environment and put into an entertaining environment, people discover that they enjoy using their brain a lot more than they thought they did."[16] Thus, the pleasure for gamers is two-fold; they experience their own objectively-observed aptitude, but also the subjectively-perceived rewards of glory and distinction.[17]

Players also gain from their losses. Failure in scenarios can provide important learning opportunities; therefore, the game difficulty must provide a significant challenge for full engagement. As organizational leadership specialist Linda Naimi suggests, "Simulations enable students to apply theory and concepts to realistic situations and to learn from their mistakes as well as from the good decisions they make."[18] Secondary educator Bill MacKenty, who advocates the use of computer games in the classroom as an aid to instruction, insists that "devoid of challenge or risk of failure," games lose their enjoyment value.[19] Children devote large amounts of time and energy into understanding and playing a game, but only given a good challenge and a compelling role. Furthermore, failure can provide immediate feedback and become a valuable tool when combined with thoughtful and deliberate instruction.[20] MacKenty cites an example from his own experience with teaching and the game *Civilization*. The popular and complex *Civilization* computer simulation series challenges players to create a successful culture, forcing them to battle with rival societies for survival and dominance:

> One day when the students and I were playing *Civilization* in class, several boys immediately pounced on the closest city they could find, initiating a war at the very beginning of the game. After a few turns, they lost. So I took the opportunity to talk to them about the misuse of force. The conversation soon segued into a discussion of current events, and the students gained some important insights about war and its consequences.[21]

Such examples challenge the notions of concerned parents and media critics who fear that violence in video games and other areas of popular culture will encourage acceptance of such activities and engagement in them in the real world.

Even without the didactic element of supervised instruction, experienced *Civilization* players discover the folly of overemphasis on the military. The game encourages the balance of other elements of society, such as cultural wonders, governmental guidance, scientific advancements, entertainment, religion, and city improvements. While militarily-based cultures may dominate, they must somehow manage an unhappy populace and might eventually still lose the game if another society attains a "cultural" or "space race" victory. Critics may discourage games such as *Civilization* in educational environments on the basis of inappropriate content, but these simulations are often far more complex and nuanced than they might ostensibly appear. Furthermore, simulations often offer real-world, adult dilemmas, many of which may be faced in the future, either in a domain-specific or more generalized context.

In order to properly map out the extensive benefits games offer for skill training and problem solving, I will detail these gains in terms of two related axes: the psychological dimensions of the skills themselves and the institutional locations facilitating their acquisition. My discussion will include a variety of different educational approaches, ranging from immersive role-play to tactical simulations, as both factors function together in RPGs.

Dimensions of Skill Acquisition

Researchers tout role-playing scenarios as highly useful in encouraging growth across many dimensions of human psychology. These dimensions include — but are not limited to — the following: personal, interpersonal, cultural, cognitive, and professional. Though the studies cited in this section are extensive in scope, they wish to achieve three major goals. Some studies attempt to identify the inherent absence of traits or skills in participants through the use of games. Others detail specific procedures designed to cultivate desired traits or skills in training subjects. Others seek to evaluate the effectiveness of scenarios intended to assess or train. Despite this range of goals, the research remains overwhelmingly positive in favor of role-playing and gaming scenarios, emphasizing their usefulness in instruction.

Personal Skills

I define "personal skills" as aspects of self that remain, for the most part, contained within the individual. Personal skills cultivate the positive attributes of human personality and may also improve one's relationship with one's self. However, the improvement of such characteristics often also enhances one's interactions with others and with the external world at large. Thus, personal skills can often interrelate with interpersonal skills in practice.

Role-playing scenarios provide the opportunity to develop self-confidence, as players practice and learn to succeed at a task.[22] Players also learn spontaneity, for scenarios often force them to "think on their feet"[23] and respond quickly to stimuli.[24] These responses often require creativity on the part of participants,[25] who must improvise solutions to complex problems or adopt alternate identity roles in order to succeed in the simulation. In this sense, role-playing provides a space for players to activate their artistic sensibilities as well as their intellectual ones and can offer a model for creativity that players can apply to the "real world."[26]

Role-playing provides the opportunity for participants to evaluate and understand the consequences of their actions,[27] both tactically and emotionally. Some scenarios train moral sensibilities,[28] inviting participants to examine their ethical value systems in tough decision-making situations.[29] These activities test the player's comprehension of the acceptableness of particular practices and demonstrate the consequences that unethical conduct or poor judgment can incur on one's career and reputation.[30] Journalism educators use scenarios to replicate ethically challenging situations, allowing future reporters to learn snap decision-making under the pressure of fast-breaking events.[31] Military training simulations encourage individuals to develop values such as loyalty, duty, respect, honor, and selfless service.[32] Successful soldiers learn these skills by cultivating the ability to pay attention, follow orders, and work hard. Alternately, if the soldiers decide instead to "party" and minimize their work, they fail.[33] Other governmental bodies also employ scenarios to train ethical conduct. In the game *Quandaries*, for example, the Department of Justice tests their employees understanding of federal ethics rules.[34]

The immediacy of games inspires motivation, stimulates active involvement on the part of participants, and encourages the development of "adult" behaviors for participants of all ages.[35] Stressful or traumatic situations provoke the development of advanced coping skills.[36] Because their actions produce direct, often dire in-game consequences, players learn to assume responsibility as decision makers.[37] Successful role-players learn to prioritize their goals and actions and delay gratification. They must regulate their behaviors and act in deliberate, intentional ways.[38]

Participation in role-playing is also a self-conscious, reflexive process, providing the opportunity for individuals to sharpen their self-awareness and observation abilities.[39] The activation of a "role" inserts the player into a unique, liminal space in which he or she inhabits a split consciousness or dual identity. Unlike trance-work or hypnotism, the primary identity of the role-player is self-aware and yet observational, viewing the actions and motivations enacted by the role-played identity. As described in Chapter 3, this contrast between main identity and persona can aid in the development of self-awareness and enhance the understanding of the subjectivities of others, an important step toward improved interpersonal relations.

Interpersonal Skills

Researchers have widely acknowledged the potential for role-playing to encourage the development of empathy. Acculturation exercises aimed at broadening perspectives on current global cultural issues help participants experience empathy for others who are changing cultures and establish a meaningful understanding of the issues that immigrants face.[40]

Writing instructors develop empathy through role characterizations and produce catharsis in sensitivity and therapy groups.[41] Business instructors concerned with ethics in research procedures design role-playing exercises with the express purpose of encouraging honesty, integrity, and fairness in human experimentation.[42] Medical students engage in extensive role-play training in order to help them develop humanistic skills for interaction with future patients.[43] Furthermore, educational environments employ moral judgment scenarios featuring opposing players with differing levels of moral maturity, which result in prosocial styles of thinking.[44] One such online role-playing environment, *Quest Atlantis*, fosters social responsibility and compassion in nine- to twelve-year olds by assigning players tasks like identifying endangered species.[45]

As described in Chapter 3, the most important mechanism through which role-playing fosters empathy is identity alteration, or adopting a "role" different from one's primary identity. Identity alteration allows individuals the opportunity to place themselves in the shoes of another human being, whether real or imagined. Studies demonstrate that role-playing scenarios in clinical environments encourage participants to develop a "theory of mind" outside of their own and embody it, briefly escaping their own subjective narcissism. This process allows players to understand the motivations of others,[46] adopt their perspectives,[47] and consider their needs.[48]

Role-playing scenarios are excellent tools for developing verbal and nonverbal communication skills among participants.[49] On a preliminary level, these exercises can serve an icebreaking, relaxing function, assisting in immediate group cohesion.[50] Continuous communication[51] is often necessary for success. Role-playing scenarios create "a dynamic and interplaying environment," fostering important individual potential as well as team expression.[52] According to a study on teamwork and online gaming, sharing tasks and subsequent rewards creates an "interdependency [that] builds trust and intimacy among players and also motivates them to maintain good relationships with each other."[53] Ultimately, group role-playing inspires cooperative learning and individual responsibility for the fate of the team.[54]

Team role-playing also builds leadership skills, since every group needs at least one leader. Whether a player volunteers or is assigned the role, the team benefits from nominating a leader, who may expected to make final decisions or serve as the "face" of the group in social negotiations with outside groups or opponents. Group dynamics force leaders to try to maintain collective stability and identity alteration allows leaders to better understand alternate perspectives. College instructor Rebecca Whitehead has taught Introduction to Applied Leadership in an online role-playing environment, where "students form teams, develop goals, discuss problems, and track progress, but they meet only in the virtual world." The exercise caused one student to observe that a good leader, "whether in the real or virtual world, must recognize the personalities and abilities of different group members."[55]

Finally, scenarios provide opportunities for participants to confront dysfunctional behavior within themselves and others, as well as develop strategies for more effective social interaction. Cognitive disabilities resulting from traumatic brain injury, Down syndrome, or autism can hinder a person's ability to find and keep a job due to limitations in social skills.[56] Role-playing offers low-risk social experimentation in a safe environment, while computer simulations test individuals in social cues such as identifying facial expressions and practicing appropriate reactions to the comments of customers and coworkers.[57]

Social skills training also aids people with behavior problems. Educational theorists Howard Muscott and Timothy Gifford posit that such training should be ubiquitous. They claim that modern schools "must meet the challenge of a changing social landscape by restructuring the formal curriculum to include direct instruction in prosocial skills for all students, not just those who currently exhibit, or are at risk of developing, behavioral disorders."[58] Some role-playing games specifically promote prosocial skills in young people, such as *Reach Out Central*. This virtual environment encourages players to travel around a virtual neighborhood building friendships and helping characters through typical life struggles such as dealing with divorce, low self-esteem, and social anxiety.[59]

Alternately, law enforcement training scenarios are not used to teach emotionally troubled people how to more appropriately coexist with others, but rather to train police officers how to deal with people in a conflict or crisis situation.[60] Similarly, scenarios train prison wardens how to deescalate situations rather than to respond with confrontation. These skills could mean the difference between life or death in "real world" crises.[61]

Cultural Skills

Related to the enhancement of interpersonal communication, role-playing can also introduce participants to alternate cultural perspectives. As the world moves toward a more global consciousness, the development of an active understanding of other cultural practices, traditions, and paradigms becomes crucial. Among other influences, wars, natural disasters, and technological changes create a sense of permeability between traditional geographic and socioeconomic boundaries.[62] However, despite exposure from various mass media channels, many people experience difficulty comprehending alternate social perspectives without personal interaction. Thus, some specialists employ role-playing techniques in order to encourage a sense of cultural relativity in their participants.

William James Stover refers to simulations as "the laboratories of political science." He emphasizes the ability for scenarios to produce empathy, insisting that, "Empirical and analytical skills are important, but without empathy, students will never fully appreciate the subtle complexities of global affairs."[63] His simulation reproduces a version of the current Middle East conflict, instructing students on the power of diplomacy by exposing them to experiences for future reference. Scenarios also promote the potential for acculturation, a process which "occurs when different cultures experience continuous contact with one another, leading to subsequent changes in one or both of these cultures."[64] Placing individuals in complex cultural situations can help explore cultural issues and alternative ways to influence potential outcomes. For example, instructors help nursing students learn how to interact with culturally diverse patients using role-playing strategies.[65]

Role-playing scenarios are also used to teach participants about diversity, opening channels of understanding about people with different identities, including ethnicity, race, history, nationality, gender, and sexual orientation. Enactments also enhance participant comprehension on issues of religion and violence.[66] Involvement in such activities could enhance future relationships between human beings who, in the past, felt they shared nothing in common or felt locked in an adversarial interaction due to cultural differences. These simulations especially hold potential power for young, impressionable students and for military professionals whose interactions with people in other countries may produce profound consequences.

Cognitive Skills

Game play is a fundamental, important aspect of child development. Humans cognitively develop through mental and physical repetition and exploration. Psychiatrist John Ratey emphasizes the importance of building and reinforcing synaptic pathways in the brain:

The more that higher skills such as bike-riding and cognition are practiced, the more automatic they become. When first established, these routines require mental strain and stretching — the formation of new and different synapses and connections to neural assemblies. But once the routine is mastered, the mental processing becomes easier. Neurons initially recruited for the learning process are freed to go to other assignments. This is the fundamental nature of learning in the brain.[67]

Activities that some may view as extraneous to "real world concerns"— such as game play or other creative pursuits — actually enhance overall cognitive abilities. The brain works like a muscle; the more humans exercise the mind through extensive and varied forms of activity, the easier cognitive processing becomes in the future. Ratey continues,

> We always have the ability to remodel our brains. To change the wiring in one skill, you must engage in some activity that is unfamiliar, novel to you but related to that skill, because simply repeating that same activity only maintains already established connections. To bolster his creative circuitry, Albert Einstein played the violin. Winston Churchill painted landscapes. You can try puzzles to strengthen connections involved with spatial skills, writing to boost the language area, or debating to help your reasoning networks. Interacting with other intelligent and interesting people is one of the best ways to keep expanding your networks — in the brain and in society.[68]

Role-play, and RPGs in particular, provide participants with such "novel" situations, as well as offering the potential for debate, writing, and "interaction with other intelligent and interesting people."

Role-playing scenarios also afford participants the opportunity to hone a variety of cognitive abilities. Game play allows participants to develop comprehension and mastery of complex concepts in the realms of history, science, economics, and philosophy, to name a few.[69] Immersion in play increases the capacity for attention and concentration.[70] Play of video games in particular improves the internal capacity for visual memory and mental mapping.[71]

Role-playing scenarios aid in the development of systemic thinking, encouraging participants to look beyond situational specifics and uncover overall patterns. Plot-based situations inspire players to "infer things about a character and situation from sketchy details."[72] Educators use role-playing to foster intuitive, pattern-based cognition in students. In one exercise, middle schoolers in Madison, Wisconsin, engaged in a four-week program designed to simulate work in urban planning.[73] The project encouraged students to become "ecological thinkers" and view the city as an interconnected system. The exercise demonstrated for students that cities are shaped by the decisions of individuals and allowed them to participate in that process. Players were then required to offer proposals to city-wide problems, such as parking availability. These projects further aided students in the development of writing, analytical, and presentational skills.[74]

Mitchel Resnick and Uri Wilensky advocate the use of role-playing scenarios to broaden the scientific understanding of "complex systems," such as chaos theory, self-organization, nonlinear dynamics, adaptive conditions, and artificial life.[75] They contend that role-playing exercises inspire students to "explore [the] behaviors of complex systems ... [and] develop better intuition about how complex phenomena can arrive from simple interactions and predictable patterns from random events."[76] Because role-playing requires a level of participation and creativity not usually present in top-down classroom approaches, scenarios help individuals move beyond deterministic, centralized modes of thinking, a crucial step for comprehension of non-linear, probabilistic, counter-intuitive concepts such as chaos theory.[77] In-depth participation facilitates both the understanding of how rules underlie behavior[78] and the establishment of new relationships with the knowledge of underlying scientific phenomena.[79] Resnick and Wilensky describe the process in the following manner:

> Role-playing provides a natural path for helping learners develop an understanding of the causal mechanisms at work in complex systems. By acting out the role of an individual within the system (e.g. an ant within a colony or a molecule within a gas), participants can gain an appreciation for the perspective of the individual while also gaining insight into how interactions among individuals give rise to larger patterns of behavior.[80]

Role-playing exercises illuminate otherwise abstract concepts by adding a level of consciousness and identification not normally present in the traditional learning process.

Business educators use role-playing to foster systemic thinking in the context of corporate organizations. Robert M. Fulmer, J. Bernard Keys, and Stephen A. Stumpe study the influence of simulated business environments on employee comprehension. These researchers use games called *Microworlds* and *Simuworlds*, scenarios in which "players can observe implementation of planning across all functions of the simulated company, and ... see the interrelationships of cause and effect within a compressed time frame."[81] As in the other examples, business modeling encourages participants to discern previously overlooked patterns and interactions in their organization.[82] Participants "discover difficulties in team strategy that can be explained by systems theory. They react to 'pushes and pulls' in the dynamic system being simulated. They learn how to align systems to arrive at success over time, and they learn to better understand the interconnectedness of events."[83]

Other games that encourage systemic thinking include board games such as Risk and chess and "strategy" video games, such as *The Sims* and *Civilization*, in which players view the entire system of the game world while making individual decisions and therefore understand the effect that even the smallest movement can make on the whole.

The role-playing process often involves both storytelling and pretend play, particularly in the enactment of RPGs. Elena Bodrova and Deborah Leong have explored the specific dimensions of storytelling and pretend play in the cognitive development of young children.[84] Influenced by the pioneering work of such theorists as Jean Piaget and Alan Leslie, Bodrova and Leong describe pretend play as a vital psychological developmental feature that emerges around the age of eighteen months, only to grow rapidly in frequency and complexity. They insist, "A child is atypical indeed who does not spend many preschool hours engaged in pretense, sometimes, alone, but most often with others. Like language acquisition, pretend play may be a universal, rapidly acquired human competence."[85] The peculiarity of pretend play, however, lies in the fact that children represent the world not as it exists in actuality, but as a meaningful and deliberate construction of how it might exist otherwise, as a result of their personal influence.

Bodrova and Leong cite play as linked to a variety of important cognitive functions, such as memory, oral language, self-regulation, increased literacy skills, and the ability to recognize and represent things symbolically.[86] More specifically, storytelling and pretend play facilitate the ability for the mind to create narrative structures, a skill important to the process of recalling and relaying information related to experiential events.[87] Bodrova and Leong believe that storytelling and pretend play lend to basic developmental tools for children, who "tend to construct play scenarios and talk about what they learn or have experienced." Stories provide them with the opportunity to "use metaphors to help distance themselves from the characters and the context being portrayed, which affords a feeling of safety and allows them to enact upsetting events more easily."[88] These tools are by no means limited to the experience of children; the use of narrative and pretend scenarios abounds in the psychic life of adulthood as well, particularly in such "leisure" activities as theater, written fiction, film, and television.

Chase play in children and animals involves the reenactment of predator-prey relationships for "entertainment" purposes. Entertainment, in

Stephanie Owens' and Francis' Steen's formulation, is both engaging and pedagogical. Thus, "playing" at the predator-prey interaction, while enjoyable, creates the cognitive framework for evolutionary adaptation. Children and animals learn the skills to pursue and evade by enacting chase play, crucial patterns for more serious survival situations.[89] Though chase play may appear to be a rather rudimentary form of role-play, Owens and Steen state that such enactments provide the root for more complex forms of culture, which they refer to as "evolved pedagogy, which suggests that evolution has designed a cognitive adaptation for utilizing the environment creatively to construct appropriate learning situations, guided by boredom and that particular reward of pretend play, thrill." They continue,

> Sociocultural forms of pretend play, such as mass media entertainment, may tap into this ancient system, targeting a motivational system that is calibrated for an environment long since gone. Secondly, it suggests that the learning processes that are involved are largely unconscious and may be cognitively impenetrable. Even when we engage in activities simply because we find them entertaining, we are likely to be engaged in an evolved form of unconscious learning. These entailments of the model have broad consequences for our understanding of culture, for instance in the areas of children and television, mass entertainment, and political propaganda, not only in the present, but also in a historical perspective.[90]

This model for understanding our cognitive impulse toward play offers an exciting conceptualization of the evolutionary need for culture and for the enactment of roles within an entertainment framework. Cultural products such as RPGs present a form of advanced pretend play, evolutionarily adapted to react to environmental pressures over time.

Professional Skills

On a practical level, employers and educators regularly utilize role-playing scenarios to enhance employee performance in job-related skills. Games provide the opportunity for players to experience hypothetical realities and step into the shoes of historical figures or professional roles, such as doctors, medics, firefighters, and mayors, facing the complex challenges involved with each job.[91] Developers are currently creating prototypes for new educational games that immerse players in such professional roles as urban planners, medical ethicists, journalists, and graphic designers. One video game program, called *Zoo Tycoon*, allows elementary school children to "build virtual zoos by selecting animals, creating appropriate habitats, managing food budgets and even setting the prices of popcorn at the concession stands."[92] Another Live Action game, entitled *Oh Deer!*, imparts lessons about how scarcity and abundance of interrelated natural resources can impact plant and animal life cycles.[93]

Private and governmental institutions widely employ role-playing applications as a means of assessment and training. Medical students engage in role-playing throughout their residencies in order to gain practice in diagnosis, history-taking, and disease management.[94] Role-playing scenarios also give physicians the chance to assess the "bedside manner" of future doctors and correct any unethical behaviors or awkward communication skills. Military scenarios such as paintball games and historical reenactments provide participants with a sense of the experience of fighting in a "real" war.[95] U.S. Army recruiters develop military-life video games in order to ascertain a potential soldier's compatibility with military life, complete with target shooting, barking drill instructors, and other training exercises that offer character-building points.[96]

Authorities also use scenarios as a means to assess the potential risk associated with crisis situations. In Columbia, Missouri, three schools played out a "mock gunman" scenario in which police, students, and teachers faced armed intruders. The exercises included handguns and mock bomb explosions in order to enhance the immersion of the participants with the overall goal of coordinating emergency plans between law enforcement and local schools.[97] In another exercise, a panel of banking industry insiders presented an ID-theft scenario complete with a fake bank at a Charlotte, North Carolina, conference.[98] This scenario demonstrated to attending lawyers and bankers the step-by-step process involved in identifying perpetrators, offering invaluable instruction in this modern information age. Other financially-oriented scenarios teach young people how to manage their money, including games such as *Credit Counts*, ran by the Central Bank of Kansas City.[99]

Some businesses hire improvisational actors to inspire creativity and enhance performance skills among their employees.[100] Performers use theater techniques to teach professionals to think faster on their feet, appear more persuasive, and present technical material without boring audiences.[101] As Tom Yorton of Chicago's Second City describes: "The skills required to be a great improviser are also skills you wished you had learned in business school.... [You learn] how to listen, how to read a room, how to react to tough problems in the moment, how to create trust and a tight ensemble."[102] As will be discussed in Chapter 5, players can also acquire such skills in RPGs, despite their informal setting.

Societal Locations of Role-Playing Scenarios

The following examples demonstrate the use of role-playing and scenario-based games in various important societal locations.

Military

The U.S. military has utilized games in training soldiers for many centuries. The game of chess, which dates back to the seventh century A.D., "is considered one of the best representations of warfare in the pre-gunpowder age."[103] Traditionally taught to officers-in-training to improve their battlefield performance, chess finds roots in even earlier war games, leading authors Chen and Michael to suggest that "there can be little doubt that warfare and games go hand in hand."[104] Modern war games originating in the seventeenth century add to chess more complex terrain, more contemporary military units, and more sophisticated scenarios.[105]

The military has shown specific interest in computers and their training potential. According to Chen and Michael, "Computers provide both an impartial referee and an untiring 'rules gopher' who ensures that the players follow the situation-appropriate rules of movement, weapon effects, physical laws, and so on."[106] The current generation's youthful experience with video games provides them with a host of natural advantages over previous recruits, including: improved hand-to-eye coordination, more efficient processing of fast-changing visual information, improved ability to multitask, improved target differentiation, improved target prioritization, ability to work within a team using minimal communication, desensitization of shooting at a human target, and willingness to take aggressive action.[107] The authors insist:

> To say that the military, particularly the United States military, is "interested" in video games for training is to make an incredible understatement. The "President's Budget Request for Fiscal Year 2003, National Defense Section" specified $10 billion for training. For the Pentagon, simulation equipment and war games take up $4 billion a year. To further demonstrate the military's commitment to training games, the United States encouraged other NATO members to use games for training at a conference in October 2004 called Exploiting Commercial Games for Military Use.[108]

The most famous application of computers for military training remains simulators, including fixed-wing aircraft, helicopter, tank, and humvee simulators. The military also uses computer games as a form of recruitment. *America's Army*, released in 2002, attempts to provide verisimilitude of the battle experience.[109] The realism and enjoyment factor of the game has given the Army more of a positive impression than any other recruiting endeavors, helping them to acquire volunteers at fifteen percent of the cost of normal recruitment methods.[110]

The military also employs non-combat-oriented games, such as *Tactical Iraqi*, which enhances communication between soldiers and Middle Easterners by utilizing speech recognition technology to correct language errors.[111] *VECTOR* teaches the local language, but also utilizes cognitive and emotional modeling to enhance cultural training, instructing soldiers "to use situation-appropriate gestures to avoid offending simulated members of the native population." The military trains combat medics on simulators as well, preparing them for a host of situations from life-support to physical examinations. "The uncertainty of their safety combined with loud noises and precarious situations can be unsettling to those who need to quickly and accurately save lives," explains Chen and Michael. "A simulation provides the next-best scenario other than wartime experience for training medics."[112]

Though the military's enthusiasm for the development of video games and communication technologies such as the Internet has certainly accelerated advancements in technology, not everyone supports their intentions. Timothy Gifford and Howard Muscott critique the military's funding of virtual reality, stating:

> The military and entertainment establishments continue to pour large amounts of resources into the development of VR which, at their best are neutral and at their worst continue to promote violent themes and ultimately violent behavior in our youth. Initial entertainment applications of VR technology including arcade games such as the Virtuality game *Dactyl Nightmare*, which utilizes programming based upon seek and destroy plots that serve violent outcomes and foster aggressive goal attainment.[113]

The authors stress that virtual reality technology should be used to foster prosocial behaviors rather than violent ones, since immersion into computerized scenarios can influence potential behaviors in the "real world."

Despite criticisms such as these, so-called war games abound both in the military and in civilian use. To a certain degree, nearly all role-playing games integrate some form of "combat." *Warhammer,* for example, employs hundreds of small figurines on miniaturized terrain in tactical war maneuvers. Though *Warhammer* remains technically a civilian game, the skills necessary for success are identical to those required of military officers. *Warhammer* tournament player Matt Byrd originally learned how to play the game "in the Navy, when the sailors aboard his ship would stage skirmishes with a gaming set to pass the time."[114] While these skirmishes worked to "pass the time," they also helped train and reinforce important military planning skills.

Other civilian war games include Live Action Role-playing (LARP) troupes such as Amtgard and the Society for Creative Anachronism (SCA), which feature combat simulations with varying degrees of accuracy with regard to weaponry and armor. Gamers also physically compete at Paintball and Lasertag, favoring projectile, gun-like weapons over the more antiquated swords and other weaponry utilized in organizations such as the SCA. One recent adaptation, Airsoft, offers elements of war reenactment, paintball and live-action role-play by providing military simulations employing guns loaded with plastic pellets.[115] These games offer players the opportunity to experience war-like conditions without incurring the risks involved in actual combat.

Government

The use of role-playing scenarios in governmental training drills extends far beyond the military. The government values the educational potential of games at many levels, including national, state, county, and municipality.[116] According to William James Stover, political scientists use simulations "in areas as diverse as comparative politics, electoral campaigning, local, state, and national American politics, legislative behavior, domestic and international law, budget making, international relations, public policy making, and national security."[117]

"First Responder" simulations allow the national government to practice strategies for handling emergency scenarios and national disasters. First Responder employees include the police, fire fighters, and emergency medicine technicians, each of whom need extensive training.[118] Games help the government prepare for "black swan" situations — events that lie "beyond the realm of normal expectations." The Department of Homeland Security, the FBI, and other federal agencies attempt to predict and respond to these unpredictable catastrophes. In the computer game *Angel Five*, FBI agents learn crisis management by coordinating resources between federal, state, and local departments. The Department of Justice funded a similar game, *Incident Commander*, which standardizes response methods for dealing with national disasters and terrorist attacks. *Dangerous Contact* provides USDA administrators modeling for handling infectious disease outbreaks.[119]

Homeland Security has created live-action scenarios with dummy victims for large-scare disaster preparedness across the United States, though Chen and Michael state that these exercises "tie up personnel and equipment and open up the possibility of litigation, and even panic, in the citizenry."[120] Video game scenarios, on the other hand, can run repeatedly and vary in locations and severity, feats difficult to duplicate in the "real world." *3D Wild Land Fire Simulation*, for example, provides first responders with a computerized wild fire, complete "with physically realistic fire propagation."[121] The FEMA website even features a site entitled "FEMA for KIDS," teaching children disaster preparation and damage reduction.[122]

Scenarios serve other purposes at the governmental level as well. Some believe that simulations hold the power to influence public policy decisions. The Markle Foundation, a non-profit organization, developed *SimHealth* in the '90s. This game helped politicians, the White House, academics, insurers, consultants, and the general public better understand the issues involved with health care policy.[123] Simulations are also accepted as useful tools for modeling scientific behavior. NASA's *Distributed Earth Model and Orbiter Simulation* provides ground crews with 3D depictions of the events transpiring on space missions. The Federal Aviation Administration trains air traffic controllers by utilizing advanced scenarios to replicate air traffic patterns at airports. Similarly, the Maritime Administration trains marine pilots on "a full-scale simulator designed to mimic a ship's bridge, with a computer generated projection of actual ports and waterways around the world."[124]

Finally, at the state and provincial levels, games train people in a variety of areas, such as budgeting and allocating funds, hunter education certification, boat safety and operation education, and driver training.[125]

Education

Some educators value both live-action and computer-based scenarios to aid with student learning. Though use of computer games in the classroom remains a relatively new phenomenon, Chen and Michael insist that "education based on the methods of question, answer, and discussion dates back to ancient Greece and the dawn of civilization."[126] Educators eventually adopted books, television, and movies as "new media" to supplement already existing patterns of teaching. Computer education, particularly the use of games, represents the most recent effort to integrate technology with educative principals.

In a study conducted by researchers from the NTL Institute for Behavioral Sciences in Alexandria, Virginia, retention rates "increase to seventy-five to eighty percent when catering to the learning style of games, compared to the five percent ... rate of lecture-based instruction."[127] Even if such numbers reflect an exaggeration on the part of the researchers, the fact that games show a significant impact on education is difficult to deny. In the 1969 book *Serious Games*, Clark Abt describes a junior high school simulation called *Grand Strategy*, which replicated events from World War I:

> The game unfolded much like WWI, with an entanglement of alliances between students that led to global war. Just before lunch, the students were told they would get a chance to play the game again in the afternoon. Some students went to the school library during lunch to study the history of the Great War. The afternoon game, played with the experience of the morning and the results of the "active learning" (the self-motivated research of WWI in the school library) resulted in a peaceful compromise [in the game].[128]

Few junior high students would find themselves motivated to study during their lunch break without the excitement and competition associated with the gaming experience. Abt further suggests that games can motivate students who have difficulties learning from conventional methods. Within the context of gaming, withdrawn and shy students sometimes become active and communicative.[129] Chen and Michael state: "Serious games provide a way for students to not just memorize facts, but also to gain experience and create their own internalized 'model' for how what they can learn is applied to their life."[130]

Video games used for teaching fall within a spectrum. One end of the spectrum contains games known as *edutainment*, specifically designed for use in the classroom or during study time. The other end of the spectrum features Commercial Off-the-Shelf (COTS) games, which developers design for the purpose of entertainment, but which may also offer educational elements and may train skills, even unwittingly. A game such as *Mario Teaches Typing*, for example, falls somewhere in the middle of the spectrum by featuring the popular video game character Super Mario in an instructive role. Furthermore, teachers have found several COTS games useful in classroom settings, including the following: *Wall Street Trader, Start-up, Airport Tycoon, Zoo Tycoon, Dance Dance Revolution,*[131] *The Oregon Trail, SimCity, Age of Empires, Age of Mythology, American Civil War: Gettysburg, Rome: Total War,* and the *Civilization* series.[132]

Many educators favor online role-playing environments as a supplement or replacement for traditional classrooms. Some instructors emphasize the use of MUD Oriented Objects (MOOs) such as LinguaMOO and Massively Multiplayer Online Role-playing Games (MMORPGs) such as *World of Warcraft* and *Second Life* as innovative educational tools. Students now can take entire courses and earn degrees online without ever interacting with a class or instructor in-person; role-playing environments offer added flexibility. According to Ray Braswell and Marcus Childress,

> Chat rooms may improve the immediacy of interaction between students, and students are becoming more comfortable with the concept of "talking" by typing to others online. Some students prefer, and thrive in, an online environment (as opposed to a face-to-face class) as it allows them time to more completely formulate their thoughts as they respond to the class discussion. Virtual online worlds provide an additional level of personality that is missing from the typical chat room environment.[133]

Virtual and live-action gaming environments offer alternatives to traditional teaching methods and exciting new realms of possibility for conveying concepts.

Corporations

Large companies require employee training specific to the needs of their organization. Many of the skills taught in college classrooms have no direct application in the corporate world; likewise, employees cannot learn the particulars of every job description in the generalized environment of a college campus. Companies employ live-action and virtual scenarios to offer employees a safe environment to build vital job-related skills.

While much corporate training previously took place via training films and videos, many companies now look to e-learning for a cost-effective alternative. Though CD-ROMs and webpages are effective training tools, the process of e-learning remains largely passive. "To really learn," Chen and Michael assert, "instead of simply memorizing answers, trainees need to be involved in what's being taught, to actively weigh consequences and mull over decisions."[134]

In 2004, John Beck and Stephen Wade reported that out of twenty-five hundred workers, eighty-one percent of those thirty-four and younger self-reported as moderate or frequent gamers.[135] The workforce is composed increasingly of people from the video game generation; these individuals come to expect and respond well to an increased level of interaction in skill-training environments. Immersion in the world of the information forces employees to engage with the material rather than ignore or forget it.[136]

Healthcare

Simulations allow doctors and nurses-in-training to perfect their diagnosis and surgery skills. Surgeons with video game experience perform thirty-seven percent better and twenty-seven percent faster at laparoscopies and suturing than surgeons who had never gamed.[137] Pamela Andreatta directs the Clinical Simulation Center at the University of Michigan Medical School at Ann Arbor. The program offers two types of simulations. The software-based scenarios can recreate any series of medical conditions or physical events. The program also offers a simulation room similar to a Star Trek Holodeck called The Cave, in which physicians can practice procedures repeatedly so that the psychomotor aspects become automatic, "an obvious boon for patient safety."[138]

In addition to training healthcare professionals how to perform difficult procedures and how best to interact with patients, games benefit individuals with mental, physical, and emotional difficulties. Mark Weiderhold's presentation at the 2004 Serious Games Summit emphasized the potential for the use of games in modern medicine. Video games can distract patients during painful medical procedures, simulations can improve rehabilitation, virtual reality environments can improve motor skills, and games can assist with therapeutic interventions.[139]

For patients with physical ailments, immersive environments can aid significantly with the healing process. As Chen and Michaels describe:

> How much pain a person experiences often depends on how much conscious attention the person gives to the pain signals. Video games and virtual reality (VR), with their ability to immerse the individual in a computer-generated environment, have been shown to be effective in focusing a patient's attention away from their medical treatment and the pain they are experiencing. Immersed in the world of the game, they are not as consciously aware of what is going on around them, and they miss a proportion of the pain signals.[140]

Gaming scenarios also train patients in the realm of self-management. In *Watch, Discover, Think, and Act,* children with asthma learn proper self-care through the aid of a computer game, resulting in fewer hospitalizations, increased functional status, greater knowledge of asthma management, better symptom scores, and better child self-management behavior.[141] Similarly, computer programs such as *Packie & Marlon* and *Glucoboy* assist children with diabetes self-management.

Games also assist patients with mental difficulties. Chen and Michael state:

> Studies have shown that people respond to games in many of the same ways that they respond to real-life events. They react with fear in frightening situations, excitement during high-speed races, and so on. Thus in a sense, games are real experiences, and learning how to face a situation in a game can provide the foundation for learning how to face the situation in real life.[142]

First-person shooter games can assist in conquering psychological pho-bias.[143] The video game *Full Spectrum Warrior* diagnoses and treats Iraq veterans with Post-Traumatic Stress Disorder (PTSD).[144] Psychologists use *Second Life* as a tool to help patients suffering from cerebral palsy, Asberger's syndrome, and autism, allowing for normal social interaction in a "judg-ment-free environment."[145]

Furthermore, games aid healthy players, providing instruction on topics such as nutrition, sexually transmitted diseases, and physi-cal fitness.[146] *Squire Quest*, a medieval themed game where a squire becomes a knight by designing healthy meals for the royal family and bat-tling "vegetable-destroying enemies," inspired Houston-area fourth graders to increase their fruit and vegetable intake by one a day. Some games also promote physical fitness. Video games such as *Dance Dance Revolution* offer aerobic exercise, leading them to be dubbed "fit-ness games," "exergaming," and "exertainment."[147] Live-Action Role-playing groups such as Amtgard and SCA allow players to physically reenact battles and are considered by some to be both a sport and a game.

Summary

Games provide a multitude of possibilities for skill-acquisition, sce-nario-building, and problem-solving. The insistence by critics that role-playing and video games only encourage escapism and mental deterioration is patently false in light of the mountain of evidence supporting the pos-itive effects of such activities. On some level, games always must retain an element of "fun," involve little risk, and feature a certain detachment from the "real world." These elements of play may upset people who feel that adults should "put away childish things" and focus on work rather than entertainment, an attitude inherited from the Puritan work ethic. Accord-ing to Stephanie Owens and Francis Steen, for a behavior to be viewed as "entertaining," it must satisfy three central requirements: the players must perceive it as "fun," they must be involved in the process both emotion-ally and imaginatively, and the activity must possess a tacit pedagogical effect.[148] Therefore, virtually no leisure activities fail to teach their partic-ipants on some level.

Though mainstream sources misunderstand and subsequently dis-miss role-playing games as escapist, time-wasting, and even potentially dangerous, the evidence from academic and professional sources clearly delineate innumerous positive benefits. Even RPGs developed solely with the intention of leisure in mind — such as *World of Warcraft* and *Dungeons & Dragons* — exercise and enhance social and mental processes on multiple dimensions. The following chapter will provide an ethnography delineating the variety of skills taught through participation in RPGs.

5

Tactical and Social
Problem Solving

Like professional role-playing and other types of games, RPGs offer participants the opportunity to gain experience in a variety of distinct situations. As their characters undergo challenges and grow in strength, the players also develop important skills. Role-playing scenarios force players to wrestle with several types of "problems," including mental puzzles, combat tactics, and social maneuvering. While working through these scenarios, gamers develop models for understanding and adapting to "real life" situations. Not only do RPGs allow participants to escape the mundane world for a time, they also train gamers how to view reality as similar to a game system, with physical and social rules that they can decode.

The following ethnography provides examples of typical "problems" players face in role-playing games. As one of my respondents, "Elton," suggests, "If you don't have problems, you don't have a game."[1] Conflict is an inherent component of plot and story development; the players in these scenarios must find ways to overcome the obstacles presented to their characters. In this chapter, I suggest that the same cognitive process involved in early pretend play often leads to a later interest in more systematized styles of role-playing. The system establishes an internally consistent framework of rules within which all actions within the game must fall. Gamers learn how to solve problems based upon these elaborate guidelines, enhancing their overall ability to think systemically and overcome adversity.

Though a wide variety of person-to-person role-playing games exist on the market, the two most popular and enduring game systems remain the various versions of *Dungeons & Dragons* and White Wolf's World of Darkness. Within White Wolf's oeuvre, *Vampire: The Masquerade* is the game most commonly referenced by my participants. Traditionally, *Dungeons & Dragons* tends to emphasize physical and combat-oriented puzzles, whereas *Vampire* focuses on story-driven, social problems. However, both systems inherently include each of these problem-solving aspects, adding to a unique richness of experience. While this study focuses almost entirely on person-to-person role-playing, the same principles that I describe can easily be applied to virtual RPGs. Indeed, many of my own formative role-playing experiences have transpired online rather than in-person.

This chapter explains how and why adults feel the need to add a game system when engaging in the early activity of child play. It then explores how role-playing scenarios encourage a high level of complex thinking skills and how most role-players exhibit an inherent capacity for processing information and applying it creatively; the various problems players solve in-character, including puzzles, combat tactics, and social maneuvering; and finally, the how role-playing encourages individuals to perceive reality like a game and think "outside of the box," applying the skills they acquire in the game to "real life" situations.

The Necessity of the Game System

When asked about their initial RPG experiences, many gamers in my study describe initial attempts to role-play without a coherent sense of structure. This type of "game" is commonly referred to as "pretend play," and involves the creation of a shared reality that can shift and bend according to the immediate desires of the players. Young people, who are often inundated with a myriad of rules imposed by adults, experience this mutability of structure as pleasurable.

However, as gamers grow older and their minds develop a greater sense of cognitive sophistication, they begin to see the necessity for some form of rule set within which to establish pretend play. The *game system* establishes the rules of reality within which pretense seems more plausible, adding to the experience of immersion and reducing cognitive dissonance. This framework also provides the mechanisms by which player measure success or failure, helping to mediate disputes and lending to a greater sense of satisfaction when players achieve their characters' goals.

The mastering and manipulation of a manageable system of rules to reality is especially pleasurable in modern-day society. Fine explains, "A gamer, today's Everyman, is battered by forces outside his control; he is at the mercy of restrictions, superiors, and bureaucrats. Gaming is said to provide not only an escape from worldly pressures, but a feeling of control or efficacy over an environment — even if it is a fantastic environment."[2] According to Fine, this feeling of mastery is especially experienced by the Storyteller, who acts as the "God" of the world, making ultimate rule calls and weaving the story for the players. Fine states, "[The Storyteller] chooses how the game will be constructed, both in terms of the setting and the scenario. In theory, he is the dreamer; he is in control."[3] However, the players also learn the rule system and negotiate with the Storyteller over rulings; their actions necessarily influence the world of the game, establishing some measure of mutually-shared control.

A few of my interviewees describe that their initial gaming experiences lacked a coherent sense of mechanics and structure. As mentioned in chapter four, the practice of role-playing develops from the pretend play of young children. Several of my subjects indicate an early involvement with pretense. Chris describes engaging in extensive amounts of pretend play with his cousin as a child: "If you were to ask him, he would have stories upon stories upon stories. We have written entire novels over a weekend ... of us spending time together, playing pretend. That was a favorite thing to do."[4]

Gamers often define role-playing as a distinct practice from simple pretend play as it specifically involves a game system. Alex actively distinguishes role-playing from pretend play in his interview, stating, "There have been quite a few role-playing games that I've been through, that is, excluding the games of 'Cops and Robbers' and 'Super-hero' that we played as children. I believe my first experience was with *Dungeons & Dragons* back in high school."[5] I suspect that the early creation of characters and pretend worlds leads to an interest in the more formalized practice of role-playing later in life.

Because many role-playing systems require an intensive amount of research and rule-learning before play, gamers may initially try a looser format. For a game to achieve longevity, however, the participants must establish and enforce a set of rules, or the practice quickly devolves into chaos and dissolution. Haley mentions, "I've been role-playing for four years seriously. And, then, back when I was, like, fourteen, we tried to role-play and just ended up having parties that didn't have anything to do with role-playing."[6] Chris describes his first attempt at "running a game," i.e. performing the role of Storyteller for the players, as a "beautiful disaster." He explains, "We tried to create some system, but it just never came out. So [my friend] says to me, 'Play in my tabletop role-playing game — it's *Vampire*— and see what it's like. Translate that to your LARP and see if you can pull it off that way.'"[7] Though Chris claims that first game was one of the best he has ever run due to the free-form pretend play, he eventually had to learn the rules in order to maintain a consistent game world with a large player-base. The lack of a coherent rule system allowed for enjoyment and creativity in pretend play, but not for potential longevity within the group.

Thus, the game system functions as a social contract between players that allows for pretend play within an established framework. This framework generally involves rules for the construction of the skill set of the character and for the resolution of conflict. John indicates conflict as necessary "to propel the story." He explains, "It wouldn't be fair to subjectively decide who wins a conflict. There has to be a predetermined method to resolving conflict. I think that's the core of any role-playing game: how do you resolve conflict?"[8] This predetermined method, referred to in role-playing theory as *fortune*, is generally statistical in nature.[9] Fortune often involves the rolling of dice or the enacting of rock-paper-scissors in order to create a sense of probability in conflict resolution. Fortune generates greater excitement for the game and adds an element of the unknown into the proceedings. A player may construct a character with a high chance of success at a particular endeavor, but ultimately, the dice decide the outcome. The game system sets the parameters of the world and the Storyteller weaves the plot. Then, the players respond based on their individual motivations. The fortune system provides the ultimate results. As John suggests, "The dice aren't partial ... it's just the way of the universe. Every time you roll that die a different number is going to come up. Sometimes it's going to be low, sometimes it's going to be high, but the dice themselves can tell a story."[10] Most role-players attempt to shape their characters in order to achieve the maximum statistical advantage within the restrictions of the framework, a process known as *min-maxing*. As Walter puts it, "You need to see the wires behind the curtain and know how to manipulate those wires."[11] Gamers will often pour countless hours into memorizing the rules of a particular game system. Some players find this process pleasurable and prefer the tactical aspect of gaming, while others soon become frustrated if the *campaign* lacks a coherent story. The term campaign harkens back to the early relationship between role-playing games and military simulations. A campaign is a particular story arc or quest that the players must complete, a process which may take several game sessions. For some role-players, the campaign merely functions as loose story facilitating combat or the enactment of particular skills granted by the game system. By denoting the enactment of scenarios as "campaigns," the very language of the original RPGs encouraged players to view combat as the primary focus of gaming. Matthew explains, "Tabletop RPGs as they were introduced to me initially felt like a dungeon crawl/action film with no major plot — also known as Roll-Playing — the emphasis being on rolling dice to see if your character succeeded or failed."[12]

White Wolf Studios, the game developers responsible for *Vampire: The Masquerade* and other games in the World of Darkness, attempted to rectify this overemphasis on combat by restructuring the language of their manuals. "Campaigns" were renamed "Chronicles";[13] the "Dungeonmaster" became the "Storyteller."[14] Despite this shift in terminology, many players in White Wolf games still tend to min-max their characters in order to achieve maximum social and combat effectiveness. For these individuals, mastering the game system is a vital and important part of the role-playing process. In order to succeed at RPGs, players must display at least some understanding of the system. A player may detail an extensive background and heavily immerse him or herself into the character, but the character may die easily if the player "builds" him or her weakly within the framework of the system.

Role-Playing and Higher-Level Thinking

RPGs challenge players to think at a higher level. Examination of the game from such a methodical, mathematical standpoint is an acquired skill. Josh S. explains how learning the complex rules of *Dungeons & Dragons* prepared him for higher-level thinking in college, teaching him "how to study." He explains,

> The kind of chemistry books that I have to study and read are incredibly similar to *D&D* rules in 3.5, honestly ... I'd read the combat section, and then I'd read another chapter dealing with magic. And they'd tell you how they work ... but you have to read both those sections and put them together. And that's the way it worked in Chemistry ... they have minute rules and they have exceptions and they have contingencies and you just have to memorize all of those things and know them. Eventually it just becomes second nature. [15]

Through intense engagement with complex game systems, role-playing games can also increase player's mathematical abilities. In her study on the potential skills players acquire through RPGs, Heather Mello states:

Respondents reported improved statistical or probability skills, which "applied in more day to day stuff," or "in other situations involving variables and chance, I can figure the odds better by thinking of it in terms of dice systems." More interesting, one respondent stated, "understanding of dice mechanics allowed me to get a job as a statistician," a human capital skill that literally paid off.[16]

Similarly, one of my respondents, Walter, describes the trials involved in mastering the system for *Champions,* a RPG based on the superheroic genre. He admits, "[*Champions*] was difficult for a bunch of high school kids — none of us were strong in math — do deal with. But I got very good at number crunching because of that, actually, oddly enough. And that's served me well."[17]

The process of learning a new game system can sometimes confuse and disgruntle new players due to the intensive amount of study required. Desiree complains that gaming "became frustrating because it was all that the other players could think of, and I felt that I was kind of dragging behind because I had other things I needed to get [done]. For me, role-playing was something that was fun; it was something intriguing. It was something I enjoyed doing and it began to feel too much like a job. Like homework."[18] I myself often feel overwhelmed at the sheer amount of work required to compete with other gamers in a strategic capacity.

Not only do RPGs allow players to develop higher level cognitive skills, but people who engage in these games may possess inherent abilities that lend to their interest and success. For instance, gamers tend to demonstrate an inherent voraciousness with regard to the consumption of fiction and non-fiction texts. Many of my respondents indicate displaying an exceptional interest in reading, research, and story writing at an early age. When asked to describe his childhood, for example, Darren responded, "I spent most of my time reading whatever I could get my hands on."[19] Similarly, "Elton" immersed himself in books. He offers the following anecdote: "I was the nerd. I was the geek. I was the know-it-all. I was the guy who stood up and class and told the teacher, 'No, no, no. *Encyclopædia Britannica* says this,' and they'd ask me how [I knew] and I'd say, 'Because I read it.' And I was in third grade."[20] I myself experienced intense interest in textual and contextual analysis at a young age, which eventually led to my involvement in role-playing games. These skills particularly aided me in the development of story meta-plot and in back story research for my characters.

I asked my respondents to describe themselves and other gamers and they almost invariably pointed to an inherent intellectual capability.

Hyper-intelligence tends to distinguish individuals from their peers during adolescence, contributing to a sense of alienation from the larger social group. As described in Chapter 3, many gamers indicate having experienced a sense of isolation in their youth. When I asked my interviewees to indicate their social identity in secondary school, they often labeled themselves and their friends the "outcasts," "misfits," "geeks," or "nerds." Erin described herself in high school as "an artsy-fartsy nerd. I have a lot of hobbies and crafts and things that I do, and I always made sure that I had all of my classes taken care of and I had high grades."[21] Christopher confesses, "Yes, I am a big, huge nerd. I can have a two-hour conversation with my cousin ... about a *Star Wars* novel, that's pretty nerdy."[22]

Kevin relates the term "nerd" to those individuals who display an interest in trivia and are capable of absorbing high levels of information. He admits, "Most gamers definitely have what the world would consider a geek or nerd aspect to them [in] that they focus on [the] minutiae and details of things that the rest of the world could care less about."[23] Gary Alan Fine also emphasizes this quality, stating, "What most distinguishes gamers from others is their specialized knowledge of topics relevant to the game, and this is both a cause of their involvement and a result of their participation."[24] While such interests can alienate gamers from mainstream social groups, hyper-intelligence, self-directed research, and the capacity for remembering large amounts of information affords gamers several advantages. Such skills are often necessary to understand the complex mechanics involved in many RPGs and to flesh out the story lines within game worlds.

Such individuals desire a challenge from their entertainment pursuits, and RPGs create manageable crises that players must face. Gaming scenarios tend to offer three types of "problems" for players to solve: puzzles, tactics, and social negotiation. Fine describes the role-playing scenario as "a set of forces in the setting that provide the motivation for the characters."[25] He explains, "These scenarios can range from very simple ones, such as the existence of a dungeons filled with monsters and treasures, to more complex issues, such as a mysterious blight that has affected local vineyards."[26] The following sections will explain several examples in which RPGs force players to solve certain problems in order for the players to succeed and proceed with the story line.

Puzzle Solving and Combat Tactics

RPGs often feature extensive puzzle solving and tactical combat scenarios. Since RPGs originated as advanced forms of war gaming, combat

was the initial emphasis of the game. The first version of *Dungeons &
Dragons* revolved around exploring cavernous dungeons, defeating monsters, and acquiring treasure. Later games, such as M. A. Barker's *Empire
of the Petal Throne*, expanded upon this concept considerably, offering
extensive political, economic, and social details. More recent games, such
as White Wolf's many titles, avoid the dungeon model completely and
instead offer a detailed, multifaceted world of supernatural beings in which
players can freely roam. However, the various versions of *D&D* are still
touted as the most widely-played RPGs.

Thus, players who favor *Dungeons & Dragons* emphasize enjoying
puzzles, tactics, and fortune-resolved combat, indicating that these aspects
are the "point of the game." As Josh T. describes, "Puzzles and strategic
[problems], those have *D&D* written all over them. I mean, that's the
bread and butter of *Dungeons & Dragons*. It's combat and dungeon-crawl-
ing, puzzles and such."[27] John explains that puzzles arrive in many forms,
stating: "There've been door puzzles: pull this latch, activate that key.
Those kind of physical puzzles. There have been mind puzzles too, [like]
trying to figure out intertextual [aspects, such as]: Who is the real villain,
the one that you're supposed to pursue, the one with whom conflict will
bring resolution?"[28]

Regardless of how these puzzles manifest, solving them provides an
essential component to RPG scenarios. Games such as *Dungeons & Dragons,* tend to present these puzzles overtly and completion becomes necessary for the continuation of the story. Players must disarm traps, unlock
doors, and figure out how best to attack monsters while considering specific
strengths and vulnerabilities. This process is known as a *questing* or *dungeon crawling* and is the thematic focus of most game modules, as well as
most level-based computer games and online MMORPGs. As a reward
for their hard work and exposure to danger, players may acquire "loot"
from the dungeon or monster and receive leveling points to enhance their
character's statistics. If specifically assigned to a quest by an NPC, the
characters must often return some trophy to prove the success of their
mission.

In a dungeon crawl, the characters must utilize their specific talents
to proceed through a series of chambers. These chambers generally feature monsters, traps, or treasure. Danger pervades these adventures in the
obvious form of aggressive creatures, but also in more innocuous places,
such as the rooms themselves. In the following passage, Kevin describes
playing a particular *D&D* situation in which the main puzzle for the group
to solve was exiting the room itself:

> We wound up in a chamber that, shortly after we entered ... sealed off on
> us. We could find no means of exit other than a four-foot tall pedestal in the
> center of the room that had six knobs on it that appeared to turn, or shift,
> or move. There were three player-characters, so each of us took two knobs
> and simultaneously turned all of them. As it turned out, there was a negative
> effect upon each of the characters, but there was a positive effect, and we
> were all able to exit that particular chamber.[29]

In this example, the group had to solve a puzzle in order to proceed. Puzzles often have many solutions, and in this case, the group's decision
incurred both positive and negative consequences. John details the myriad of puzzles offered to him over his several years of gaming experience,
highlighting one particularly frustrating example:

> I guess the greatest problem I've ever had to solve was.... The Secret of
> Nine. And it was the most difficult kind of riddle because we had no place
> to start ... and it wasn't even an abstract construct. It was just a word: nine.
> That was it and we had to figure out what that meant. We had to probe
> with bizarre, off-the-wall questions. And I remember we all just sat around
> for three or four hours. [The players] were so disgruntled ... but we did it ...
> One of the players finally rattled off the nine different alignments in *Dun-
> geons & Dragons* and that was the solution to the riddle, which is pretty
> weird.[30]

By *alignment*, John refers to the system by which *Dungeons & Dragons*
designates morality. Each character chooses an alignment, or moral ori-
entation. The nine archetypal alignments in the game are as follows: the
Lawful Good "Crusader," the Neutral Good "Benefactor," the Chaotic
Good "Rebel," the Lawful Neutral "Judge," the True Neutral "Undecided,"
the Chaotic Neutral "Free Spirit," the Lawful Evil "Dominator," the Neutral Evil "Malefactor," and the Chaotic Evil "Destroyer."[31] Characters must
behave according to their respective alignments or face consequences from
the Storyteller. In the Secret of Nine, part of the difficulty John's party
had in solving the riddle was the relative inconsequentiality of the "secret"
with regard to the plot. Though alignments are central to game mechanics, part of the language of the framework they generally function as role-
playing aids rather than in-game aspects within the context of the story.

Such inconsequential riddles may cause frustration, particularly when
these conundrums take a significant amount of game time to solve. Some
gamers actively dislike the typical *D&D* game style because of the propensity for such arbitrary situations. Without a sufficient balance between
challenge, reward, and a compelling storyline, players often become
irritated. Guillermo describes a particularly frustrating situation in which
he was stuck in an elaborate dungeon, fighting oversized ants with no

obvious story motivation. Recalling the story, he states that he kept thinking, "'I just want out of here and I want my reward.' And that was the problem. It was constantly doing [tasks with] no reward. There was no [one saying], 'Well, congratulations. Here. The princess kisses you and thanks you.'"[32]

The central concept of struggle and subsequent reward promotes character growth, but also subsequently offers potential for the growth of the player. In behaviorist terms, the characters experience a set of positive and negative reinforcements from the game world. They must navigate through the universe, learning and adapting as a result of each unique scenario. They receive their "reward" as a testament to their success. In some cases, blatant rewards manifest, like the acquisition of treasure or a position of power. Alternately, one's reward might seem small, like a word of approval from a superior or even the continued existence of their character.

Walter details one scenario from his LARP in which a new player faced an ambush and survived, a reward in itself. He explains, "[The player] was delighted when another tactician, another acknowledged tactical mind in the game ... said that her character had survived this assassination attempt. She had done incredibly well in the fighting and had made the correct tactical decision at every combat round and at every juncture."[33] The in-game incident and subsequent reward helped build the player's out-of-game confidence level. Exuding confidence can mean the difference between success and failure in many situations, both in-game and out-of-game. According to my interviews, success in role-playing scenarios does tend to translate into success in other areas of life, as I detail in the final section of this paper.

One interesting aspect of role-playing tactics is the ability for players to alter time for various purposes. While engaged in "combat," players will often spend several hours ironing out what feats their characters will perform, reexamining rules, and establishing the results of the battle through the fortune system. This extensive process segments time into sequential *rounds*, in which each player is allowed to perform actions by taking designated turns. Guillermo explains how this technical aspect functioned in one of John's *D&D* campaigns: "When we first began playing, it was very combat driven and very mechanical ... there were countdowns, it was 'Well, let's start on 25 ... 24....' And he would, literally, count it. It was all mathematical to him. So he would actually [say], 'This person does ... seven damage plus eight divided by two,' mechanically saying it out loud."[34]

Part of the benefit of enacting scenarios is being offered the opportunity to slow actions down and examine them at each step. In the

Vampire RPG, a combat round only accounts for three seconds of time in the game.[35] However, with a multitude of players, the fortune resolution of one round might take several minutes. Thus, although vampires move extremely fast, the game slows the process of combat down in order for players to fully examine each decision. When a crucial mistake is made, the players can learn from these mishaps and alter their decision-making in future scenarios. Similarly, when characters succeed, they can rehash their ingenious solutions with other players, regaling them with stories out-of-character. Players consider this regaling pleasurable, allowing them the opportunity to relive their successes, but it also serves the purpose of reinforcing the lessons learned in the situation.

This slowing down of time into manageable segments may be an essential aspect of human consciousness. In dissociative theory, people who endure traumatic events often feel a shift in their perception of time. In times of crisis, every second may mean the difference between life and death, so reality is perceived as slowing down. By dissociating, the mind is offered the opportunity to examine each moment more fully than it normally could. The individual perceives him or herself as oddly distant from the events transpiring. This process of slowing and distancing, known as *depersonalization,* creates enough emotional space to afford the individual the chance to make rational decisions. Dissociation specialist Marlene Steinberg states,

> Feeling that the clock has stopped in the outside world gives the person the latitude to focus on quickening thoughts of self-preservation. The numbing of emotions stills anxiety and wards off panic, allowing the person to perform automatically, as if some higher power has taken control. In all, these perceptual alterations combine to enable someone in grave danger to defy death or, failing that, to accept it gracefully.[36]

Depersonalization remains an important psychological mechanism, developed to handle situations in which the individual's decision-making process directly correlates with survival.

Role-playing scenarios offer a similar process for gamers, but they experience these moments as pleasurable rather than traumatic. In a relaxed, safe atmosphere, gamers can enact life-or-death situations with a sense of emotional distance and slowing of time. The experiences "happen" to their characters rather than their primary selves; similarly, people in dissociative states will sometimes create alternate personalities that will experience traumatic situations in their stead.[37]

In the case of dissociation, these "alters" will often protect the primary personality from the memories of the trauma through various degrees of amnesia.[38] Role-players, on the other hand, experience the events in-game along with their characters and often actively direct the actions of these personas in order to maximize their effectiveness. This process is similar to Steinberg's description of people acting "as if some higher power has taken control" when in a dissociative state. In the case of role-players, this higher power simply reflects the primary self, who views the situation more objectively than the character. The player understands the meta-plot and the game mechanics and makes decisions accordingly. However, the player must also provide IC justification for why their character would make such decisions, lest the other players accuse them of *meta-gaming*— making in-character decisions based on out-of-character information. Ultimately, most tactical moves involve some combination of the motivations of the character and the objective, "higher" self.

Time can also speed up in role-playing games. The meta-plot of a game universe may span thousands of years, locating the actions of the characters within a long continuum of time. In addition, the players must also elide certain details of their characters' story, condensing their history into workable fragments. In the invention of my vampire character Viviane, the Storyteller and I highlighted a few key scenes out of her first one hundred years of "unlife." These events were considered part of her *back story*, or background, as they preceded the events of the actual game. For my five-hundred year old character, Eustacia, I wrote a twenty-three page background, which spanned the years 1510–1580. Even within this extensive back story, I had to condense many of her interactions into representative moments. Then, in order to bridge the gap between 1580 and present day, entire centuries of her back story were covered by a few sentences. This speeding up of time and establishment of a meta-plot allows players to examine the characters in the larger context of the story and understand how certain actions affect the world systemically.

In some cases, time will speed up in between episodes of the story, in which characters will experience *downtime*. Some Storytellers require players to submit "homework" to relay their downtime actions. In Walter's *Vampire* LARP, the actual time between games is usually one month; in-game, however, six months passes during downtime. Downtime allows players to experience the sense of a character's development over time. If a character survives a game session, they receive *experience points*, which are used to enhance the statistics on their character sheet. Downtime allows players to feasibly explain these sudden leaps in their characters' abilities within the realm of the story. To increase the Melee skill for my character, for example, I may use a downtime action to train with a Master Swordsperson for a certain span of time. Characters who are allied with each other will often trade skills during this time, training in order to fill the gaps in their respective skill sets. This bending of time allows the mechanical aspects of the game system to be explained through storytelling, adding to the experience of immersion.

Aside from tactics and puzzles, game scenarios also offer social problems for the players to solve. Players must face the inherent struggle between competition and cooperation within specific contexts. The Storyteller presents the players with complex situations in which they must figure out who to trust, how to work together, how to manipulate others to gain advantage, and how to eliminate competitors. Depending on the scenario, one or all of these strategies may produce successful results.

Social Problem Solving

Characters rarely succeed in a vacuum. *Solo gaming* sometimes take place, in which only one player interacts with the Storyteller. However, the majority of games feature multiple players. While the characters in the game may or may not form a cohesive unit with similar goals and personalities, they must work together regardless in order to solve many of the game-related problems. In *Dungeons & Dragons,* characters are called a *party* of adventurers when grouped together to achieve a specific purpose. In *Vampire,* the party is instead dubbed a *coterie.*[39] In *Werewolf: The Apocalypse,* characters are grouped in a *pack.*[40] Regardless of the terminology, the concept of the "party" is central to understanding the dynamics of role-playing groups.

Like the Fellowship in Tolkien's *Lord of the Rings,* each character offers his or her own unique talents to the group. A Warrior may excel at close-range combat, but may need a Wizard or an Archer to attack from afar. The combined strengths of the group may defeat the villain, but a Healer remains necessary to mend the wounds incurred by the battle or to revive fallen party members. When I asked John what skills he learned from role-playing, he responded: "How to work with others, the team-building exercise.... Not every character class or character concept has a full array of every possible human skill. In order to play a well balanced game, every individual player must come to the table and add something to the team effort. If they can do that, then they generally succeed."[41] Part of the challenge of gaming, then, is for players to utilize the strengths of their character to maximum advantage, while allowing other party members to compensate for their weaknesses.

Role-playing scenarios often feature ethical dilemmas in which one member of the party must decide whether or not to embark on a course of action that could incur negative repercussions on others. Some situations involve the imperilment of other party members, where the character must choose between saving one character and aiding the larger group/community. Desiree describes adopting a utilitarian approach to such problems, indicating the challenge as the following: "Sometimes you have to protect one to protect all. Sometimes the one you're trying to protect will be ... the one that will make or break you. If you lose him, the whole team could be in complete catastrophe."[42]

Josh S. describes one situation in which he had to solve three problems at once in one scenario: a party member was drowning, a number of aggressive assailants were attacking, and a third group of misfits were poisoning the water supply. His character was forced to address each of these problems in the proper sequential order. He describes how he succeeded in the following passage:

> This character had to assess what needed to happen first to get his friends out alive and still accomplish everything.... He dove in right after he threw oil at the bridge and made his friend set [it] on fire. He got his friend out from the water, and then, as the bridge burned down, the other party tried to go across this little rope thing that was up above.... [My character] immediately assessed the situation and then oriented himself for what he needed to get done first, and then solved the problems in the order that he had to solve them in.[43]

Much of the decision-making process in these ethical situations involves weighing one's personal feelings for other members of the group with the necessary tasks at hand. If the players do not properly prioritize their actions, they often fail.

Ultimately, the challenges of an adventuring party are both social and tactical. Some groups cooperate easily with each other. These characters may possess similar goals or personalities or experience an early emotional chemistry with one another. In other situations, the characters clash with regard to their motivations and paradigms. The Storyteller may present the group with a problem to solve, but the entire game session is instead spent attempting to resolve conflicts between characters and establish cohesion.

To retain the sense of an "authentic" immersive experience, many role-players will not force their characters to act out of accordance with their concepts or natures. However, Guillermo suggests that an excessive amount of in-character bickering can derail the game. He states, "Sometimes, I've had very good experiences. I've had experiences with people [where] we meet, we don't really have a reason for getting together, we find a common purpose. And then you meet other characters that are going to be antagonistic.... And it [does not seem] conducive to have these characters built that way because, well, it's an adventuring game."[44] Some players create characters with interesting concepts, but who ultimately conflict with the overall goals of the game. While internal conflict within the party can instigate character and player growth, excessively antisocial characters become "unplayable" within the context of a successful adventuring party.

Sometimes, the players solve in-party conflicts through nefarious means. Erin offers an example where her adventuring party attacked a female wererat, an Evilly-aligned, anthropomorphic creature that is part human and part rodent. The party decided to keep the wererat as a slave rather than killing it, much to the disdain of her character. A warlock had recently joined the party, who her character also disliked. She eventually "solved" the problems of having these two disreputable individuals in the party in the following manner: she killed the wererat, then framed the murder on the warlock, who was put on trial and eventually executed.[45]

Some players enact characters that are designated as Evil rather than Good in *D&D* terms. Evil characters make decisions based on pleasure and self-interest rather than compassion or altruistic motivations. Omega describes an example in which his Evilly-aligned *D&D* character, Silverleaf, betrayed his entire party in order to save himself:

> [Silverleaf] has double-crossed an adventuring party, making it so it was fatal for two of the party members. He conned his way into becoming the one who was trusted with all the goods and all the treasure that they had gotten through the entire time ... he made his getaway with all of their loot and all of their treasure and all of their healing potions and their entire existence.... And it's quite a dastardly thing to do, but it needed to be done. It was either him or them, so, of course, he chose himself.[46]

While asserting that such actions "needed to be done" within the context of the character motivations, Omega distances his own beliefs from the character's paradigm. He states, "Although I have hopes that [Silverleaf] will become somewhat of a Good character in the future, he is far from it at this point." Players often report watching with a certain detached horror as their characters engage in actions they themselves find detestable. The extent to which the enactment of such behaviors relates to repressed energies within the player is further explored in chapter seven.

Regardless of the player's individual motivation, the problem of group cohesion can often bring ruin upon the characters if not solved. Though choices such as Silverleaf's above betrayal might bring immediate rewards to the character, he or she will generally face consequences from the game world. The Storyteller may decide to punish the character directly or the surviving party members may refuse to cooperate with the character in the future.

Though the majority of RPGs favor cooperation over competition, some gaming environments favor a competitive style of play, in which the players must compete with each other in order to achieve dominance. *Vampire* LARPs present players with this challenge. While players may cooperate to gain advantage in the game, ultimately, most players seeks to attain higher rank in the hierarchy of vampiric society or more personal or supernatural power. To achieve these goals successfully, characters often must backstab and manipulate one another. Therefore, much of the game centers around the cultivation of trust, whether deserved or not.

The Vampire Social Experiment

"Elton" claims that, in *Vampire* LARPS, the most interesting problems arise from the players themselves. "The Storyteller's job," he states, "a lot of the time is to just take problems and throw them at the character to challenge them and force them to grow, because a lot of the whole game is about growth."[47] However, in most instances, he believes that the resolution of inter-character conflicts should remain the central theme of the game. The LARP format involves larger groups of players and fewer Storytellers, resembling more of an improvisational theater troupe than a war gaming scenario. Thus, the Storyteller and the plot remain secondary to the in-character social dynamics.

In *Vampire*, inherent to each character is a set of political affiliations and motivations that generally will conflict with the designs and machinations of others. As Elton puts it, "I've created a problem just by creating a character."[48] Gamers refer to the form of role-play that focuses on competition between participants as *Player-versus-Player* (PvP). LARPs and MMORPGs that allow player-killing thrive on such inter-character conflict. Players will sometimes group together with the express purpose of eliminating another player who they consider an opponent, only to shift these short-lived allegiances when advantageous.

In Walter's tabletop *Vampire* Chronicle, for example, my character Viviane had a close mentorship under another vampire, Annabelle, for over a hundred years. This century-long relationship was severed when Annabelle shirked an important tradition in order to gain power and Viviane sided against her politically. Annabelle publicly humiliated Viviane and later orchestrated an attack against her, making both her displeasure and the termination of their mentorship clear. Despite their century-long allegiance, these two women found themselves suddenly at odds with each other when the political situation changed.

Such situations are built into the theme of the *Vampire: The Masquerade* universe. Many participants in my study demonstrated familiarity with White Wolf's universe. They highlight three major "problems" offered by the game developers: the problem of basic survival, the problem of ascension to Princedom, and the problem of Diablerie. These three scenarios sometimes only manifest in *Player-versus-Environment* (PvE) situations, the traditional non-zero-sum, cooperative style of role-play in which the Storyteller presents the characters with adversaries. However, particularly in a LARP setting, they often become PvP conflicts.

Because vampires are predatory in nature and seek power, they often wish to eliminate each other in order to gain resources and influence. Chris details one scenario in which his character planned to defend himself against an attack from a rival group. He explains, "A group of players [were] basically [going to] kick down the door of my office and shoot me. And that's an easy one. You set up explosives in your room, you walk out, you leave a camera in there, when the guys walk in to shoot you, you just turn on the button and go *boom*."[49] In such a situation, the players are each other's main rivals and the Storyteller merely officiates the conflict.

Vampires must also face the danger of destruction at the hands their human prey. They must hide their true nature from humans by blending into society through an elaborate system of masking, called Masquerade.[50] Vampires run the world behind the scenes by controlling key humans, creating their own social hierarchy, similar to a secret society. But they also have to pretend to be mortal in order to "pass" in human society and avoid detection and death. If vampires "break the Masquerade" and reveal themselves to humans, they incur consequences. Other vampires may destroy them as a protective measure or the humans themselves might eliminate them.

Thus, a typical "problem" involves avoiding detection. Vampires must remember to breathe and blink in order to appear human. Chris cites an example involving his first *Vampire* character, Tye, in which he "broke the Masquerade." He explains:

> Every mistake I made as a new player I made with him. Like in *Vampire*, you don't ever tell other people about vampires, so the first fucking thing I did, naturally, was do that, was tell people about vampires. You know, and then the Storyteller comes down hard on you. And after that, it's very

difficult to make a character that still does that, even though in a lot of ways you probably should still do that because the younger character should still be able to make those mistakes.[51]

In this game world, basic survival and the ability to subsist is, in and of itself, a major problem to solve. As a player, Chris learned through his mistakes and, thus, avoided making them with future characters, lending to greater success in later scenarios.

The second social problem in *Vampire* is the ascension to Princedom.[52] Vampire society within each city resembles the Italian city-states of the Renaissance. A vampire rises to the rank of Prince based on influence, prestige, and resources and must maneuver to retain that power over his or her vassals. The Prince has the ultimate right to kill any vampires within his or her realm, but must also cultivate allies in order to defend himself against usurpers. Thus, the Prince must establish a delicate political balance. The Prince keeps the other vampires at bay by offering *Status* within the society, an elaborate system of accolades vampires use to jockey for position. Some Status is awarded as a result of deeds performed on behalf of the city, though vampires also compete for minor political positions within the Prince's regime.

In one LARP in which I participated, the Prince flagrantly insulted the largest power block of the city. My character, Eustacia, was assigned to the position of Seneschal, or second-in-command.[53] Eustacia would have to constantly remind this character to behave with proper etiquette, but he continued to insult the other characters. Because his character was exceptionally powerful compared to everyone else's, the other players spent an exorbitant amount of time plotting creative ways to eliminate him and ascend the ranks. However, because these players marked themselves socially as resistant to the Prince's rule, Eustacia, who believed strongly in tradition, viewed them as renegades. Eventually, I brought in another character of mine, Viviane, to take the role of Prince, who was physically stronger than Eustacia and could better defend the city. I had already introduced her into the game continuum on the online forum. Thus, as a player, she was a "tool" at my disposal, and I used her to solve the Princehood dilemma in that circumstance.

Sometimes, the Ascension to Princedom problem results in a large number of character deaths. In a game revolving around immortal characters, the mortality rate in *Vampire: The Masquerade* is surprisingly high. Because the characters do not die naturally and are predatory in nature, they consistently seek to manipulate and eliminate each other, like pieces on a chessboard. Sometimes, these vast plots backfire and the underdog wins. Walter describes a scenario in which a fight for survival inadvertently resulted in his character's ascension to the rank of Prince:

> Elsbeth was infamous for most of her career and I will say that out of the maybe forty-five or fifty people that started that game, a year later, I was the only original character left.... She was bloodhunted, which means that the regime in power put her on a prescription list ... and the entire community would come after her. She had to figure out who were her allies, who she could trust, where her safe harbors were, what resources she had at her disposal both personally and politically, who she could cut deals with, what she could promise to people, and basically how she could survive, how she could live.... And, eventually, she was the Prince. She had literally outlasted, destroyed, out-maneuvered, undermined everybody. And that was ... an intense strategical thing because the entire time, I was dealing with a character [that was] physically fragile ... and I managed to do all of that without ever being in a physical combat.[54]

He further mentions, "And I always say LARP is a marathon. It's a game of attrition, looking at it from a strategical standpoint. You just have to keep surviving."[55]

This theme of political machinations is reminiscent of Machiavelli's *The Prince*. Darren quips that *Vampire* scenarios are "sort of like Machiavelli with training wheels."[56] Individuals who undergo the *Vampire* world for any extended period of time soon must learn how to socially maneuver in order for their characters to succeed. "Elton" offers a description of how one of his more intricate plots allowed him to better understand social interaction in real life:

> I think probably the most rewarding one was where I had a ... hugely elaborate Machiavellian plot ... and all these varied threads came together in a single plot and then exploded exactly on my cue and with exactly the results that I wanted. And the person that I had orchestrated this plot against went down in flames and it was a brilliant plot. I think moments like that [are rewarding], where you can have a plan like that and actually work the social dynamic. And then you [think], "Hey, I know how this dynamic works now."[57]

Another important problem in the *Vampire* game world is the issue of *Diablerie*. Diablerie is tantamount to spiritual cannibalism and occurs when one vampire first drinks the entirety of another's blood, then continues to consume their opponent's soul in order to acquire their power.[58] Diablerie is illegal in vampiric society and can incur three potential consequences: the soul of the other vampire may take control of the Diablerist's body, the other vampires may discover and kill the Diablerist, or the Beast within the Diablerist may overwhelm the human side, which also results in lack of control over the body. "Elton" explains how he attempted to survive as a Diablerist in a LARP. He states, "The problem became: How do get away with it? Because there are ways to detect that and a vampire would know inherently to eliminate anybody who would cross such a taboo boundary." He further describes a Diablerist as a "serial killer, a hardened criminal" and explains that murder "had the same consequences in-game. He ended up very quickly found out and dead."[59]

Over the course of seven years of play, my tabletop vampire, Viviane, Diablerized twice. Her sins remained obvious, detectably marked on her aura, but she escaped execution. Her main struggle transpired internally, as her conscious Self fought her inner Beast for psychic dominance, similar to the Ego and Superego battling the Id in Freudian terminology. This inner battle becomes just as important to the *Vampire* concept as the Machiavellian plots as the monster within battles for dominance with the human side. Thus, the struggle in *Vampire* is as much an external political battle as it is an internal battle with one's own selfishness and one's desire to take from others without giving back. Unlike the set-in-stone Alignments of *D&D,* the moral behavior of *Vampire* characters is mutable, shifting based on situation. The game world presents gradations of evil, and the characters fall within a spectrum along that continuum. While Viviane committed evil acts, she knew other vampires who behaved in far more evil ways than she did. She justified her behavior as necessary and rational given her set of circumstances.

Vampire scenarios are, therefore, thematically multi-layered and complex. They transcend the problem of attaining and maintaining power. The nature of the desire for power itself eventually manifests as the central problem to solve, as the repercussions of greed are both metaphorically and literally built into the game mechanics. Thus, *Vampire* players learn how to socially manipulate others, but they also learn to locate and navigate their own self-centeredness. In the safe environment of the game, players can observe the unfolding of the ramifications of their "bad behavior." Thus, through these stories, gamers can enact certain taboo behaviors, but also learn the value of moderation.

"Real Life" as Game Scenario

Though the practice of gaming encourages participants to develop a variety of skills, I believe the most important of these abilities is learning how to think "outside the box." Because players must keep game systems and meta-plots in mind when they make decisions, many gamers start to adopt a view of reality that looks beyond the surface and identifies the inherent structures underlying all things. On a mechanical level, Josh S. claims that learning the system to *Dungeons & Dragons* allowed him to later comprehend the complex structures of molecules. On a social level, *Vampire* teaches players to look for the hidden strings behind all public displays of power. Henry states, "Any social situation can be [simulated] in a roleplaying game; business negotiation, flirtation leading to sexual encounters, a duel of wit, or subtle use of insults and threats to unhinge an opponent and perform character assassinations."[60] These situations provide training opportunities and encourage gamers to look beyond surface explanations of reality.

In addition, people who play RPGs tend to feel marginalized by the mainstream culture at large. My interviewees often indicate feeling initially isolated from their peers and seeking role-playing games as a bonding experience. Many of my respondents feel that role-playing offers them the opportunity to find friends with similar interests in a low-stress social environment, but involvement in these shared realities further divides gamers from non-gamers and can exacerbate their feelings of ostracization from society.

Thus, much of the process of gaming involves not only attempting to solve life-or-death scenarios through probabilistic statistics, but also learning how to solve the "problem" of social integration and cohesion. When asked what he learned from role-playing scenarios, Henry responded, "[that] there are few personalities that can successfully survive the world without destroying themselves, and everyone must change and be able to adapt to the requirements of social order."[61] Also, when players are forced into the "spotlight" through games as either Storytellers or characters in leadership positions, they must quickly learn how to hold the attention of others and communicate effectively. One of the respondents in Karen Mello's study claims, "I believe that I've become a better public speaker from my experience of being a convention GM. It is an environment where I am the center of attention of a group of strangers and I must be able to communicate effectively with them."[62]

As a consequence, many role-players not only view the lessons acquired from gaming as directly applicable to actual situations, but also begin to view "real life" as a game. Another one of Mello's interviewees states, "[I] used to be shy and reluctant to approach strangers when traveling. When I tried seeing the situation as a (gaming) encounter, I could often negotiate the situation with more ease and confidence. This has eventually internalized itself so that I can now handle these situations with confidence."[63]

My respondents describe fantastical scenarios involving magical abilities and ever-present danger. They presumably will never face such situations in reality. Yet, almost all of them, without hesitation, were able to draw direct correlations between the problems they had to solve in-game and issues they face every day. When I asked Chris if he anticipated having to deal with the kinds of problems faced in *Vampire* scenarios in real life, he responded:

> God, I hope not. Probably, at some point, I'm sure ... you know, people want my job, and in order for them to have my job, I have to be gone. So they do things to try to dispose of me. They try to get me in trouble. They try to find flaws in what I do [and in] my work. And yeah, kind of the same thing, really. Because if I lose my job, I lose my life.[64]

Other respondents similarly characterize the world of business as akin to role-playing situations. Omega likens the problem of party cohesion in role-playing scenarios to the necessity for employees to find a sense of unity in work environments. He explains, "[Gaming] has also taught me to better read a variety of people's personality quirks, their skills at negotiation, their 'tells' on what they do and don't like. It helps your interactions on how to get around some of the differences that you and a person might have, but you have to unite in a common goal."[65] Desiree adopts an alternate approach, comparing the ethical decision-making process involved in gaming to the unfortunate necessity of firing employees. She remarks, "Sometimes you've got to try to figure out which employee or which person you work with is better to keep and which one's better for the team. And it sucks, because sometimes you see a really great potential, and you see a really great person, but you just have to let them drown. You have to let them go to save the others, because they're the weaker one."[66]

The lessons learned from role-playing are specific to the individual. Omega describes his difficulties in real life work situations: "I worked someplace, they said something I didn't agree with, I said, 'Well, you can take your job and shove it. There's two thousand out there I can go for.'"[67] The lesson he needed to learn from gaming, therefore, was how to form a better, cohesive unit with coworkers. Desiree, on the other hand, describes herself in her interview as a "healer."[68] Gaming taught her to accept that, in some situations, workers for which she felt a personal affection had to be fired, like sacrificing a character for the good of the group in a role-playing scenario. Experimentation with alternate selves allows gamers to perceive their own failings and weaknesses and to develop a stronger sense of introspection.

Ultimately, gaming allows participants to develop an exceptional awareness the consequences of their own actions and how reality possesses its own inherent "systems," in its many physical and social manifestations. For some, understanding and manipulating these systems can translate to success both in-game and out. Respondents also emphasized that, rather than training them in skills they did not already possess, gaming allowed them to hone preexisting talents. Role-playing allows players to better understand predictable patterns of human behavior and build models for responding to such patterns. Chris emphasizes this point in the following passage:

> I've always been a very ... mischievous political person. So, office politics is second nature and so is something like a *Vampire* LARP, 'cause they're both the same ... I think maybe that a *Vampire* LARP had refined that [skill] in a way. It gave me experiences like: "Okay, I met this personality type, I'm understanding how they work." Humans are archetypes, ultimately, and I'll familiarize myself with that personality type. People that I work with sometimes remind me of people that I LARP with and I sometimes manipulate them the same way. And it works, usually.[69]

Thus, gamers use the successful strategies and mentalities of their characters to navigate the social waters of the everyday world.

Several of my interviewees described "real life" situations where they chose to think like their character and react accordingly. In an amusing anecdote, John describes how adopting the hedonistic impulses of one of his characters aided in relations with his spouse. He intimates, "Not too long ago, I was in an argument with my wife ... and instead of getting mad, I thought to myself, 'What would Findo do?' So I went to Sonic and I picked up some smoothies and some treats or some eats ... and I brought those home and I had sex that night. Thank you Findo ... it was a great option."[70] The adoption of various appropriate roles is often necessary for success in specific interactions. In the above example, John shifts from an angry emotional persona to a hedonistic one, affording him "success" in his dilemma.

Life situations often require such shifts in role and RPGs allows players to experience these changes as embodied enactments of persona. As I will detail in the final two chapters of this volume, the practice of role-playing facilitates the playful exploration of such roles and creates a metaphoric language for articulating and understanding them. The game system provides the rules of engagement, but ultimately, the creativity and risk-taking ability of the individual offer the greatest advantages with regard to role immersion.

6

Role-Playing as
Alteration of Identity

Perhaps the most fascinating aspect of the process of role-playing lies in the ability to shift personality characteristics within the parameters of the game environment. Games and scenarios allow participants the opportunity to "try on different hats" of selfhood, experimenting with the adoption of personality characteristics that either amplify or contradict aspects of their primary identities. Role-playing environments provide a safe atmosphere for people to collectively enact new modes of self-expression and experience a sense of ego permeability while still maintaining their primary identity in the "real world."

The formation of identity begins in early childhood through immersion in pretend play and further solidifies in adolescence. By the time the individual reaches adulthood, he or she must negotiate between the different social roles designated by the culture and somehow perceive the Self as a unified whole. In our postmodern world, however, interactions with multiple cultural forms of expression produce an awareness of the inner multiplicity of identity. For adults engaged in role-playing games and other forms of online communication, the distinctness of these selves becomes more apparent. Thus, gaming provides a release from the pressures of social expectation, as well as an opportunity to explore repressed facets of inner consciousness.

The Pleasure of Identity Elasticity

Many gamers begin to immerse themselves in role-playing at a young age. Pre-adolescent "play" activities provide the nascent building blocks for more sophisticated role-playing practices. These activities include, but are not limited to: engaging in pretend play and storytelling activities, challenging the rules of reality through imagination, adopting future social roles in game activities, reinventing identity through the creation of alternate selves and personal story lines, developing alternate "worlds," and conversing with Imaginary Friends. Thus, engagement in role-playing games evolves out of an extension and expansion of childhood creative processes, which become more sophisticated and complicated as the individual's consciousness matures.

Pretend Play

The practice of *pretend play* appears to be vital to the development of many cognitive skills amongst children ages four and above. According to psychologist Sook-Yi Kim, pretend-play emerges as early as eighteen months of age, expanding rapidly in frequency and complexity in later childhood.[1] "A child is atypical indeed," Kim states, "who does not spend many preschool hours engaged in pretense, sometimes alone, but most often with others. Like language acquisition, pretend play may be a universal, rapidly acquired human competence."[2]

Kim also emphasizes the importance of storytelling in the function of human development. Storytelling "reflects moral standards, lifestyles, fantasy, humor, emotions, and different ways of knowing" and allows children to examine their present and future social roles.[3] In effect, modern RPGs merge pretend play with storytelling, allowing children of all ages to enact roles of their own creation within a consistent narrative and the framework of an imagined time and space. Thus, RPGs provide the benefits of both activities in structured and exciting ways.

Pretend play, on some level, involves a temporary alteration of the individual's concept of self. In early development, the child's sense of self maintains a flexibility and plasticity that they must relinquish in future years. Play provides a mental and emotional outlet for this malleability of the self-concept; the child experiences games as pleasurable because they provide an escape from the rigors and pressures of socialization.

Sigmund Freud refers to the *pleasure principle* as the time before adulthood when human beings are primarily motivated by seeking pleasure and avoiding pain.[4] As children mature, they must transition from a mental space of pure pleasure-seeking to an acceptance of the *reality principle* by adopting the conceptual framework of the dominant social paradigm. "In taming the impulses of the Id," Freud states, "the Ego replaces the pleasure principle, which was earlier the sole regulating factor, by the so-called reality principle, which indeed pursues the same ends but takes into account the conditions imposed by the outside world."[5] For instance, a child might believe in Santa Claus or the Tooth Fairy because such concepts bring pleasure and excitement. At a certain age, however, adults believe they must make apparent to the child the "reality" of the imaginary nature of such figures. The worldview of the child must shift in order to find accordance with more mature mindsets. A large part of the parenting process involves imposing prohibitions upon children against partaking in certain pleasurable activities at inappropriate times. The standardized education system further guides children toward a body of common knowledge and epistemology, framing the questions and answers pertinent to adult life. These practices direct the young mind toward the conceptualizations of reality necessary for the nuances of complex social functioning.

Game play is often dismissed as "childish" by adults who, through the process of socialization, have become ensconced in traditional institutional power structures. Part of the adoption of the reality principle involves "putting away childish things." Instead, the individual must gear his or her life toward acquiring the skills necessary for success in the professional, domestic, and social spheres. However, many children's games actually work to prepare them for these exact goals. Playing with dolls teaches children how to nurture and care for children. Games like "Cops and Robbers" and "Cowboys and Indians" allow kids to channel their aggressive tendencies into a sense of heroic mastery, potentially paving the way for future occupations in areas such as the military and law enforcement. "Playing House" is a way for kids to mimic their parents in the domestic sphere, recreating home life on a microcosmic level, while allowing children to "change the rules" as they see fit.

Paracosms

Through game play, children can occupy any psychic space they wish. Perception is — ultimately — reality and the child can manifest the stuff of dreams through imagination and creativity. For a child engaged in play, humans can fly, unicorns and dragons can exist, and animals can speak. Some children engage in a more structured form of pretend play in which they create entire worlds, combining external stimuli with their own inner creativity to form what David Cohen and Stephen A. MacKeith call *paracosms*.

In *The Development of Imagination: The Private Worlds of Childhood,* Cohen and MacKeith detail sixty-four paracosms created by children six and older. The children created these inner worlds for a number of reasons, though each paracosm tends to be long-lasting, heavily structured, and internally consistent.[6] The respondents in the study reported a range of different childhood experiences and backgrounds. While some shared their worlds with encouraging parents or eager siblings, others guarded their paracosms as tightly-held secrets. Some worlds involved extensive characterizations of the inhabitants, while others simply provided a sense of order and structure, such as an island dedicated to an elaborate railway system, complete with schedules.[7] Cohen and MacKeith insist against essentializing anything about the content of these worlds and the motivations behind creating them:

> These worlds are worth discovering for their own odd logic, their charm
> and, sometimes, because one can glimpse through their structure the reasons
> the children needed them. We try to avoid over-simple analysis in this book
> of the sort that suggests that because children had an unhappy childhood,
> they devised a cuddlesome imaginary world where they were loved and in
> total control. But sometimes it seems clear that there were emotional factors
> at work which might push a creative child to make up this kind of work.[8]

Some children appear to possess a particular propensity to invent these kinds of worlds despite radically different upbringings. This fact suggests that the ability to invent paracosms may be an inherent aptitude related to creativity.

While many children "shelve" their paracosms as they reach adulthood, some creators rely on these worlds as predecessors for future artistic projects. Famous authors such as the Brontë sisters created elaborate paracosms as children, as did Peter Ustinov, W. H. Auden, and Jacques Borel.[9] The creation of fantasy worlds may arise in part from early involvement in the development of paracosms. J.R.R. Tolkien, who created his elaborate Middle-earth later in life, displayed a "lively imagination" as a schoolchild, composing a story about dragons at age seven. This story no doubt provided the initial seeds for later stories such as *The Hobbit*. Similarly, M.A.R. Barker had established the rudiments of his world *The Empire of the Petal Throne* by the age of ten.[10] Barker later developed his paracosm into a role-playing game, complete with its own socio-cultural and linguistic structures. Gary Alan Fine suggests that, for both Barker and Tolkien, the establishment and maintenance of these paracosms required a level of personal investment above and beyond a brief flight of fancy. He states,

> Both men describe their fantasy histories, languages, and mythologies as
> being *real*. I do not suggest that either is delusional. They separate their

"belief" in their creations from their belief in the existence of the world in which they reside. Yet they treat their creations *as if* they are real, maintaining their "fabric of belief," and that they themselves are only historians, writing the record of a civilization.... These worlds are living realities for these men, and engrossment is possible to a degree that most of us find impossible in our own daydreams.[11]

The extent to which the creators of paracosms invent time and energy into the realization of their worlds affects their level of immersion, which Fine refers to as *engrossment.*

The practice of role-playing also involves a certain level of engrossment in fantasy worlds, though the participants co-create the content of their paracosms. Though the RPG designers may establish the initial parameters of the world structure through manuals and modules, the Storyteller can alter aspects of the world or can choose to create his or her own reality, utilizing only the barest structure of the game mechanics. Even if a player creates only one character in a larger scheme of the paracosm, that character affects and helps shape the world, sometimes even to a large degree. The player may develop an elaborate character back story, for example, that the Storyteller then works into the meta-plot, or Grand Narrative, of the story line.

Identity Alteration

If the external rules of reality can shift at a whim, so too can the internal ones; the self can become whatever the child wishes. Often, this desire manifests by pretending to be someone other than who one "really is." Though the personality traits of these new identities vary, these selves often possess magical talents or an important destiny. Freud theorized, for example, about a common child's fantasy called the *family romance.* This daydream represents "a conscious fantasy, later repressed, in which a child imagines that their birth parents are not actual but adoptive parents, or that their birth was the outcome of maternal infidelity. Typically, the fantasy parents are of noble lineage, or at least of a higher social class than the real parents."[12] The family romance represents one example of how children often imagine their "secret" identities as possessing inherently important and special qualities.

The theme of the family romance is prevalent in fantasy literature, a genre many children find appealing specifically because the rules of reality are easily bent. In many fantasy stories — and in their mythical/folktale roots — the hero is often raised humbly on a farm or in a forge, only to learn his destiny as the inheritor of a kingdom or of magical powers or both. Frodo, the primary hero in Tolkien's *The Lord of the Rings*, believes himself to be a humble, unimportant hobbit, but later learns that he must save the world by destroying the One Ring of Power, for he alone can resist its lure. In the same narrative, the character Strider first appears as a lowly ranger, but later must rise to his own destiny by claiming his birthright and ruling as High King of Middle-earth. These heroes must shake off the limitations of their previous social roles and inhabit their new ones through important rites of passage throughout the story.

By temporarily identifying with the heroes in fantasy stories and by creating their own narratives, children attempt to understand their own social place in the flow of cultural memory. Instead of remaining relatively powerless, small individuals, they imagine themselves to be the movers and shakers of the world, essential to the continuation of the universe. *The International Dictionary of Psychoanalysis* details the psychological motivation for such fantasies in the following passage:

> The family romance ... differs from children's sexual theories in that it does not address general questions about the origins of life but rather the question, "Who am I?"—where "I" denotes not an agency of the mind (or ego) but the result of an effort to place oneself in a history, and hence the attempt to form the basis of a knowledge.[13]

In this sense, identity play may actually work to enhance self-esteem and provide the child with a sense of agency in a world over which they otherwise feel they have little control. Releasing one's preordained identity and adopting another can allow for a psychic sense of freedom. Psychologists sometimes refer to this process of conscious identity alteration as *impersonation* when enacted by young children.

Imaginary Friends

Some children adopt so-called Imaginary Friends while engaged in the process of pretend play. In the case of an Imaginary Friend, the child's central identity remains consistent, but he or she projects alternate personality traits onto an invisible target or inanimate object. The child often imbues these entities with unique names, appearances, and idiosyncrasies, such as likes/dislikes and strengths/weaknesses.

Often, these attributes directly contradict the child's self-concept; the Imaginary Friend possesses capabilities that the individual perceives the self to personally lack. In "Characteristics and Correlates of Fantasy in School-Age Children: Imaginary Companions, Impersonation, and Social Understanding," Stephanie Carlson et al. provide a detailed analysis of the Imaginary Friends of a group of young children. The researchers suggest that, out of a sample of one hundred children up to the age of seven, sixty-five percent reported interacting with Imaginary Friends at some point in their lives.[14] Some examples of Imaginary Friends described in the study are:

1. *The Good Indian (also known as Don Vont):* Invisible 5-year-old boy with black hair and brown pants. The Good Indian originally appeared when the child spent a lot of time in the woods, at the beach, and reading.
2. *Skateboard Guy:* An Invisible 11-year-old boy who lives the child's pocket, wears "cool" shirts, and has a fancy skateboard. Skateboard Guy can do many tricks on his skateboard and likes to see how fast the child can run.
3. *Robert:* An invisible male panther who has black fur with blue eyes. Robert lives in the jungle and the child met Robert in his dreams.
4. *Sergeant Savage:* A GI Joe doll who is sometimes also an invisible person. Sergeant Savage is one hundred years old with white-brown hair and wears a Band-aid on his forehead, boxer gloves, and a pilot jacket. He lives at bases and sleeps in sleeping bag. The child likes Savage's shotgun, but dislikes his face.[15]

These examples reflect clear distinctions between the personality of the child's primary self and the projected identity of the Imaginary Friend.

The creation of Imaginary Friends — and, in some cases, Imaginary Worlds for the Friends to inhabit — appears to correlate with several cognitive advantages. When compared to other children, kids who create Imaginary Companions are more creative, less shy, more sociable, participate in more family activities, possess good coping skills, and show more positive affect when playing with others.[16] They can more easily create a theory of mind with reference to other people's psyches. On the other hand, in clinical research, psychologists tend to associate the creation of Imaginary Friends with trauma, loneliness, and/or emotional distress. The development of Imaginary Companions and "elaborated play identities" — or impersonated characters — is also common amongst children with Dissociative disorders. However, Carlson et al. warn that "care must be taken to distinguish the normal phenomena from the pathological."[17] Like Cohen and MacKeith in their study of paracosms, these researchers avoid making the claim that these activities arise solely from emotional difficulties. I will explore Dissociative Identity Disorder and its potential relationship with the ability to create alternate personas later in this chapter.

I believe that interactions with alternate forms of consciousness — either real or imagined — further define the characteristics of the self as the child attempts to understand his or her place in the social realm. Semiotically speaking, we understand what something *is* only by placing it in direct opposition with what the object *is not*. In this case, the object in question is the self-concept, which is constantly defined and refined through interaction with real and imagined entities. The processes of embodiment of alternate selves and of imbuing an external object with personified characteristics allow the child to make sense of the fragments of the psyche and explore potential personality traits. This process need not terminate in early childhood. Role-playing games offer adolescents and adults the opportunity to creatively explore their own inner multiplicity and inhabit shared, co-created worlds.

Role Discovery

Role-playing allows for even deeper self-exploration during the period of adolescence. Younger children engaged in pretend play adopt alternate roles with ease, able to shift from mystical roles — such as "wizard" or "elf" — to more mundane roles — such as "father" or "teacher" — without experiencing ego confusion. As the individual matures, however, the psyche strives for a coherent sense of self in order to better integrate into social groups. Role-playing games offer a dual benefit within this process: they relieve the pressure incurred by the imposition of existing social roles by the "real world" and they allow adolescents to practice alternate roles in a risk-free environment. This process can continue throughout adulthood, as the initial identity concepts develop and mature through time and experience within the game.

The human psyche needs to experience itself as unified and coherent in order to avoid unpleasant ruptures in consciousness. Psychoanalyst Erik Erikson details eight stages of psychosocial development that he believes are inherent to the maturation process of all human beings. He emphasizes the importance of the fifth stage of development, in which the adolescent mind struggles to achieve what he terms a "stable sense of ego identity."[18] For an individual to perceive ego identity as stable, he or she must perceive little contradiction between his or her behavior from moment to moment. One must view the ego-self as behaving in predictable patterns and must experience little cognitive dissonance when the inevitable ruptures in consciousness occur.

The development of a stable sense of ego identity remains an ongoing process throughout young adulthood. Erikson describes the development of ego identity in the following passage:

> The young person, in order to experience wholeness, must feel a progressive continuity between that which he has come to be during the long years of childhood and that which he promises to be in the anticipated future; between that which he conceived himself to be and that which he perceives others to see in him and expect of him. Individually speaking, identity includes, but is more than, the sum of all the successive identifications of those early years when the child wanted to be, and often was forced to become, like the people he depended on.[19]

Such personality characteristics manifest as integrated aspects of the exterior world. Erikson explains, "The search for a new and yet reliable identity can perhaps best be seen in the persistent adolescent endeavor to define, overdefine, and redefine themselves and each other in ruthless comparison, while a search for reliable alignments can be recognized in the restless testing of the newest possibilities and the oldest in values."[20] The adolescent absorbs the personality qualities, belief systems, tastes, preferences, and stylistic expressions of individuals whom they admire, adapting and reformulating the particulars to reflect their own desired sense of self.

Identity formation is an arduous process of trial and error. The adolescent may display radically different representations of self throughout the identity stage and is often heavily influenced by the reactions of peers and authorities. According to Erikson, should the individual fail to achieve a satisfying concept of self, issues of identity confusion will plague him or her throughout the rest of the life cycle. Role confusion persists past this point, an overall feeling of alienation or fragmentation, which may result in a lack of direction and self-confidence.[21] Later theorists refer to the confusion of ego establishment during adolescence as "self-discrepancy." Psychologist Peter Wright describes, "Self-discrepancy is conceptualized as an aspect of self-concept, and has been described as the difference between the following: how I actually see myself now, how I would ideally like to be, and how I think I should or ought to be. These facets of self ... may not always be congruous and the greater the dissonance between individuals' perceptions of their possible selves, the more discomfort they are likely to experience."[22]

Wright further cites the work of E.T. Higgins, describing three "domains of the Self": the Actual, the Ideal, and the Ought. The Actual Self refers to the personality characteristics the individual believes him or herself to possess and is also referred to as the "self-concept." The Ideal Self represents the qualities the individual would like to possess, while the Ought Self is the culmination of the attributes that the Actual Self or a significant other wishes the individual would display. The individual uses the Ideal Self and the Ought Self as "self-guides" to regulate behavior.[23]

Wright speculates that role-playing remains particularly useful for bridging the gaps between self-discrepancy by providing "a growing awareness of different possible selves."[24] Thus, engagement in role-playing games may offer substantial rewards for participants during the difficult period of ego development. Indeed, many of my informants indicated that they originally immersed themselves in RPGs during adolescence. Regardless of the individual's level of ego confusion, the active exploration of one's facets of personality can provide a sense of self-awareness the individual may not have initially possessed.

Role Multiplicity in Adulthood

Even if the mature adult achieves a sense of a stable ego identity, the "self" as a singular, coherent entity remains an untenable concept, especially in postmodernity. The self is a fragmented and contradictory mélange of images, concepts, and memories. Though the ego would like to believe that identity remains stable throughout the myriad of experiences and challenges faced in a lifetime, each presentation of self represents an unconscious construction, pieced together through trial and error. Humans adopt many faces to suit social and environmental pressures, shifting between them as circumstances demand with little awareness.

Social psychologist Erving Goffman's groundbreaking book *The Presentation of Self in Everyday Life* articulates the ways in which daily life is much like a theatrical performance. Social convention dictates that individuals must obfuscate their inner motives, passions, and fears in order to adopt their necessary and respective roles as circumstance dictates. Humans learn these scripts through the socialization process of youth and become invested in them, internalizing the rules of each role and playing them out as if they were natural. Though we battle to perceive ourselves as independent entities, unaffected by the sway of public opinion and expectation, our brains are hardwired to seek acceptance, approval, and integration with others.

We present certain signals to others in order to indicate involvement in the group. Goffman calls these signals "fronts," which include clothing style, mannerisms, and speech patterns:

One may take the term "personal front" to refer to the other items of expressive equipment, the items that we most intimately identify with the performer himself and that we naturally expect will follow the performer wherever he goes. As part of a personal front we may include: insignia of office or rank; clothing; sex, age and racial characteristics; size and looks; posture; speech patterns; facial expressions; bodily gestures; and the like. Some of these vehicles for conveying sign ... are relatively fixed and over a span of time do not vary for the individual from one situation to another. On the other hand, some of the sign vehicles are relatively mobile or transitory, such as facial expression, and can vary during a performance from one moment to the next.[25]

On a basic level, each individual must adopt various roles in order to adequately integrate in society. My own daily social roles include student, teacher, daughter, sister, significant other, and friend, among several other minor roles. Part of success in adulthood involves learning how to best negotiate these roles with as little internal and external conflict as possible.

Identity alteration in role-playing games allows individuals the ability to "practice" roles in a low-consequence environment. I will describe a role-playing character of my own as an example to illustrate the possibilities role-playing environments afford in the area of identity development.

The character in my own repertoire that I have played the longest is Viviane Georgette Morceau, a century-old vampire. By blood, Viviane belongs to Clan Toreador, a group of socialites and artists. Because of her association with this Clan, Viviane is expected to follow a particular set of social practices, including displaying high levels of wit, eloquence, articulation, charisma, beauty, etiquette, education, passion, and intellectual prowess. When I first developed Viviane at the age of twenty-one, my own skills in these areas were comparatively limited. I quickly had to learn to over-represent my personal competencies in order to reflect those of my character. This process included adopting more affected and snobbish manners of speech. In order to accurately represent her vast experience and education, I also felt compelled to increase my knowledge in various areas with which she would be familiar, including art, architecture, psychology, and history.

In the ten years in which I have played Viviane, the character herself had to undergo dramatic identity transformations. Her original self-concept of carefree, hedonistic socialite shifted as she faced political and physical warfare. Skills such as Intimidation and Melee grew in importance. At one point, she took control of a group of vampires and was dubbed

"Prince" of the city. As a player, I had to face the complexities of leadership, which involved managing conflicts between characters and maintaining order in the Domain. Viviane was forced with much reluctance to relinquish her desire for frivolous self-satisfaction in order to negotiate the more serious concerns of the individuals under her rule. At another point in her history, Viviane was given custodianship of a mental asylum, and her roles shifted yet again to those of psychologist and director of the institution. She began to dress differently to acknowledge these shifts, abandoning her cocktail dresses for more austere and bland professional clothing. She presented an alternate "front," in Goffman's terms, in order to signify her shift in role.

While the exact roles Viviane had to enact will never manifest in my own personal life, participation in these scenarios encouraged me to develop aspects of my own identity — such as etiquette and leadership. The game world presented challenges that tested these characteristics to an extent I had not previously experienced. The cultivation of these personality aspects allowed me the tools to transition into more mature social roles in "real world," such as college instructor and discussion leader. The Socialite aspects of her personality, on the other hand, allowed me the opportunity to practice smoother leisure interactions — my "cocktail party" charm, if you will.

Role-playing offers participants an alternate platform on which to practice social roles and adopt alternate modes of identification. Such a "stage" is particularly valuable when exploring roles not acceptable or available through conventional channels, such as characteristics that might be considered "evil" or "selfish." Players can alternately embody a version of their Ideal Selves by projecting characteristics they do not believe themselves to actually possess, or by over-accentuating aspects of their Actual personality. Chapter 7 further details the various character types that players typically enact.

Disassociation and Identity

In addition to the various identities that our social roles force us to inhabit, Sherry Turkle suggests that the postmodern condition predicates the proliferation of even more expressions of self. Faced with constant changes in career direction, gender roles, and technologies, the postmodern person must learn fluidity rather than rigidity.[26] This fluidity applies not just to our values, attitudes, and behaviors, but also to our very sense of ego-concept. In order to adapt to the rapidity of social change and the bombardment of conflicting messages, our psyches develop a sense of multiplicity. For Turkle, individuals experience this multiplicity of identity most explicitly when engaging in online communities. "When people adopt an online persona," Turkle explains, "they cross a boundary into highly charged territory. Some feel an uncomfortable sense of fragmentation, some a sense of relief. Some sense the possibilities for self-discovery, even self-transformation."[27]

Whether online or in-person, this boundary-crossing occurs when one participates in role-playing, though online environments can offer possibilities for more extreme shifts in identity. Online, one can represent the self in ways completely removed from physicality: male can become female, young can become old, weak can become strong, etc. Immersion into alternate worlds is an alteration of consciousness; the individual begins to view his or her self differently when projecting different or exaggerated personality traits. Even when portraying an identity exceptionally different from the Actual self-concept, the player must find a point of identification with that "alter" and manifest his/her behaviors accordingly. Repeated immersion further solidifies these personas into more tangible mental forms.

A deeper understanding of the mind's ability to create multiple senses of self can be achieved through examination of the process of *dissociation*. Dissociation as a psychological concept refers to a particular set of coping mechanisms the mind inherently possesses in order to deal with extreme moments of conflict, pain, or trauma. According to Marlene Steinberg, these coping mechanisms include:

1. Amnesia. The inability of one's memory to account for a specific and significant block of time.
2. Depersonalization. A feeling of detachment from one's Self or the examination of the Self as an outsider would. This mechanism may also include the sensation of separation from parts of one's body or detachment from one's emotions, like an automaton or robot.
3. Derealization. An experience of detachment from one's environment or a sense that one's surroundings and those who were previously familiar have become unreal or foreign.
4. Identity confusion. A feeling of uncertainty, puzzlement, or conflict about who one "is." This state is often perceived by the subject as a continuous internal struggle to define one's self in a particular way and may also relate specifically to one's sexual identity.
5. Identity alteration. A shift in role or identity accompanied by observable changes in behavior such as speaking in a different

voice or using different names. This subject may experience this shift as a personality switch or a loss of control over the body to someone else within him/her.[28]

When these coping mechanisms occur in high frequencies and in conjunction with each other, the individual may develop Dissociative Identity Disorder (DID), also called Multiple Personality Disorder (MPD). The mind discovers ways to avoid becoming debilitated by trauma, including the development of alternate identities who fulfill needed roles, "taking control" of the body at key moments. Unfortunately, the inclusion of the word "disorder" in the name of the condition predisposes the world at large to view dissociative individuals as exhibiting a sickness that needs to be rectified. I believe this belief to be inherently derogatory. Many of the so-called symptoms of dissociation can alternately be viewed as advantages, resulting from an active, creative, and intelligent basic consciousness.

The ultimate goal of therapy for dissociative individuals is a process known as Integration. Usually, an Integrator is chosen — also known as the Narrator — and that individual serves as a mediator between each of the alternate selves. The Integrator begins to break down some of the dissociative processes, working to share and combine memories and create a sense of unity. The Integrator allows for each alternate identity to experience awareness in the body at once, familiarizes alters who have been previously estranged, and reconciles the relationship between alters who perceive themselves to be in direct conflict with each other.

Though dissociative theory presents fascinating explanations for the creation of alternate selves, I hesitate to suggest that such behaviors result exclusively from trauma for three reasons. First, fantastical escapism manifests in the minds of many children who have what most people would consider a "normal" or "healthy" upbringing. As I described earlier in this chapter, the development of alter-egos, Imaginary Friends, and paracosms do not always correlate with childhood trauma or alienation. Though children engage in these activities to varying degrees, immersion into alternate modes of reality appears to be a consistent function of the child mind regardless of circumstance.

Second, these behaviors quite possibly manifest as a result of the creative drive inherent in all human beings. Some individuals possess the ability to access deeper wells of creative power than others, but humans by nature are designed to draw inspiration from the depths of the unconscious and represent these concepts in external, symbolic forms. These forms range from architecture to music to art to storytelling. Society often attempts to either quell or redirect highly creative individuals, channeling their abilities into "products" that are deemed "valuable" by the group. Thus, most creative displays by adults are, in effect, harvested from a younger, more chaotic mindset. What, then, is the essential difference between the creation of an Imaginary Friend and the creation of characters in a bestselling novel? Both processes involve the suspension of the primary ego in order to express the mentality of a hypothetical other self or selves. The difference lies only in the ability to translate that talent into a societally-acceptable, economically-feasible medium. In essence, the impulses are exactly the same and the creation of alter-egos in early life lays the groundwork for the construction of more "mature" narrative structures later in life.

Third, though clinical psychology as a discipline has the potential to offer amazing insights into the inner workings of the human mind, more often than not, psychologists use their findings to prove the "pathology" of an individual, rather than to celebrate his or her uniqueness. The practice of labeling immediately produces an "us" versus "them" mentality that roughly corresponds with "normal" versus "sick." Individuals who display a high level of creativity, such as Vincent Van Gogh, are often touted as lunatics based on their unorthodox behavior patterns and roller-coaster like emotions. However, if these artists can acquire patronage or acclaim, they become "rehabilitated" and even celebrated by the culture at large.

Indeed, critics are fascinated by such unorthodox behaviors and often equate genius with insanity; the biographies of few creative people read as "normal" in the mainstream sense. Offering examples such as William James and Sigmund Freud, Erikson suggests that "trained minds of genius ... have a special identity and special identity problems."[29] These individuals feel an intense amount of pressure to utilize their gifts to produce something of value to the world, an impulse that transcends the needs of simple day-to-day survival. Erikson believes, however, that such "special identity problems" afford these individuals the ability to "[formulate] initially what we can then proceed to observe as universally human."[30] Erikson explains, "We can study the identity crisis also in the lives of creative individuals who could resolve it for themselves only by offering to their contemporaries a new model of resolution such as that expressed in works of art or in original deeds, and who furthermore are eager to tell us all about it in diaries, letters, and self-representations."[31]

Though few people possess the potential for "genius" in the sense that Erikson defines it, role-playing involves self-reflection in the form of an identity crisis that manifests through an artistic medium. Like other artists, people who participate in role-playing games or attend fan conventions are also often deemed by the mainstream as "abnormal" and subsequently marginalized. However, role-playing faces further stigma in that the mainstream has yet to acknowledge it as an art form. Daniel MacKay's 2001 study *The Fantasy Role-Playing Game: A New Performance Art* seeks to establish the legitimacy of role-playing within the realm of artistic creation. MacKay states, "Inevitably, the emergent art form of the twenty-first century, like cinema was for the twentieth century, will be some manifestation of an immersive and interactive narrative form of story creation."[32] For MacKay, role-playing games represent manifestations of these emergent art forms, which would make the role-player a new type of artist.

Psychosynthesis

How can scholars begin to conceive of concepts such as identity alteration in less pejorative terms, associating it less with trauma and more with a general sense of creativity? Turkle addresses this issue by emphasizing that, because of our increased multiplicity due to the post-modern condition, the necessity for a strong Integration of selves remains important. Turkle insists:

> Without any principle of coherence, the self spins off in all directions. Multiplicity is not viable if it means shifting among personalities that cannot communicate. Multiplicity is not acceptable if means being confused to the point of immobility ... [one must develop] a healthy protean self. It is capable, like Proteus, of fluid transformations but is grounded in coherence and moral outlook. It is multiple but integrated. You can have a sense of self without being one self.[33]

Turkle suggests that if individuals develop and maintain a strong sense of Integration, the inherent multiplicity of roles and identifications within us can still establish a sense of cohesion.

This conception of one primary ego identifying and regulating several secondary selves was proposed by psychoanalyst Robert Assagioli in the early twentieth century as an effective therapeutic technique. Assagioli, a contemporary of Freud's, conceptualized the splitting of consciousness as a normal process inherent to the psyche and urged therapists and scholars toward a more positive view of the mechanism. His theory, *psychosynthesis*, offers a view of psychotherapy that involves embracing the multitude of aspects of each of our so-called "sub-personalities" and conceptual archetypes. Rather than emphasizing the pathology of dissociative behavior, he insists — like Goffman — that each of us emulates particular roles throughout our lives. Proper exploration of these roles and integration of each of their functions will allow human beings to achieve a sense of the *Transpersonal*, or spiritual unity. Comparing the subdivision of the psyche with other biochemical processes, he claims,

> The same thing occurs in the human psyche, in which processes of dissolution and reconstruction are being carried on incessantly. Sometimes these processes of psychological assimilation (one might say of ingestion and digestion) take place easily and spontaneously, but often psychological indigestion and toxic conditions occur and psychopathological abscesses and tumors are developed in the unconscious of the individual.[34]

Assagioli believes that his approach to therapy, psychosynthesis, can effectively guide this process of Integration after the "natural" process of ego identity dissolution.

Assagioli's conceptualization of the potential benefits of psychological fragmentation offers a framework for understanding ego alteration outside of the context of trauma and pathology. If we are all — on some level — multiple, then dissociative theory can offer explanations for how the process works in the brain and why some people exhibit these mechanisms in a more severe manner than others. However our intellectual conceptions of the identity alteration process need not be relegated to the "us" vs. "them" mentality previously described.

If human beings, by nature, create alternate selves and the post-modern condition predisposes us to further fragment our sense of identity, than role-playing games provide a fascinating outlet for self-expression. The primary self remains awake and active when role-playing, acting as Integrator by facilitating the transition between in-character (IC) and out-of-character (OOC) interactions. Also, the practice of role-playing represents both a creative expression and a communal activity. In this way, the playful negotiation between selves remains controlled and safe for the participants.

If humans feel an inherent impulse toward the creation of alternate selves, from where does the *content* of these identities arise? White Wolf's The World of Darkness actively encourages its role-players to adopt specific "archetypes," explaining these character concepts in terms of Carl Jung's idea of the collective unconscious.

Archetypal Enactment

The personality traits enacted through role-playing characters do not merely reflect minor idiosyncrasies, though more developed identities do possess individual quirks. Instead, the majority of assumed identities take on a more universal aspect. The work of Carl Jung details this universality in symbolic language. According to Jung, at the dawn of consciousness, human beings produced certain psychological schema for understanding their relationship to the world. These concepts are still embedded in our unconscious minds in the form of ancient *archetypes*. In *Man and His Symbols*, Jung defines archetypes in the following way:

> What we properly call instincts are physiological urges, and are perceived by the senses. But at the same time, they also manifest themselves in fantasies and often reveal their presence only by symbolic images ... [these archetypes] are without known origin; and they reproduce themselves in any time or in any part of the world — even where transmission by direct descent or cross-fertilization through migration must be ruled out.[35]

According to Jung, humans cross-culturally share a *collective unconscious*. The recurring symbols and archetypes in dreams are actually powerful psychic remnants of ancient forms of understanding, developed during the advent of human language. Certain symbols became powerfully important as the structures of our brain evolved and these essential images repeat themselves cross-culturally.

When playing roles, both in game-play and in the "real world," humans unconsciously enact symbolic structures. Certain character types recur throughout dramatic narratives and hold particular power in the deep imaginations of audiences. Embodied within these archetypes is a model for behavior within a particular framework. Archetypes offer a complex symbolic identity resonating from the depths of human consciousness.

Role-playing games provide a forum for the emulation of alternate identities and these identities combine age-old archetypes with individually-imbued characteristics. An individual's Actual Self might remain an adolescent student, but within the game world, that same player can portray a powerful warrior, wizard, or healer. The Actual Self may emulate characteristics of integrity and compassion, but the self in the game world instead may explore ethical quandaries by embodying, for example, the archetype of the villain or the rogue. Such explorations offer several benefits for participants. The player can emotionally — and, sometimes, viscerally — experience alternate modes of consciousness and stories that differ from those of their mundane existence. Role-players can practice personality aspects, many of which may be archetypal in nature, and can then objectively view the distinction between their own Actual identity and the performed identity. This enactment process allows the individual to decide to either adopt such traits or to avoid them, depending on his or her response to the events and emotions in-game.

Popular archetypes emerge in mythological narratives and further reproduce in many of our current entertainment genres. Structuralists such as Vladimir Propp, Claude Levi-Strauss, Erich Neumann, and Joseph Campbell have attempted to unearth the fundamental units of human culture through analysis of myths cross-culturally. Propp's work, *The Morphology of the Folktale,* charts the narratives of over four hundred Russian fairy tales, discovering a fundamentally similar chronological and thematic structure in each.

Propp lists thirty-one important plot points that duplicate themselves throughout each of these stories, despite the appearance of surface-level distinctions.[36] Propp then identifies seven major "spheres of action" for the dramatis personae: the *hero*; the *villain*; the *donor*; the *helper*; the *princess*— and, by extension, her father; the *dispatcher*; and the *false hero.* The hero must depart on some sort of search, be branded, pursued, and defeat his adversaries, marrying the princess and ascending the throne. The villain is placed in contrast to the hero, presenting a source of struggle or pursuit. Along the way, the hero receives aid from various persons. The donor prepares and provides the hero with a "magical agent," such as a special weapon or item necessary for success upon the quest. The helper character assists the hero in various ways, including spatial transference, liquidation of misfortune or lack, rescue from pursuit, offering solutions to difficult tasks, and transfiguring the hero in some important way. The princess represents "a sought-for person," and her father generally acts to protect her by assigning difficult tasks to the hero and punishing the villain or false hero. The dispatcher serves an incidental function, making the initial lack known to the hero and sending him off on his quest. The false hero takes credit for the hero's actions or tries to marry the princess.[37] According to Propp, though the surface characteristics of these myths may change, the basic roles remain inherent to the structure of fairy tales.

Though Propp's work centers primarily upon Russian folktales, his basic formulation resonates with many mythological narratives around the world. Joseph Campbell's important book, *The Hero with a Thousand Faces,* delineates a more universal hero's journey, which he dubs the *monomyth.* The monomyth represents the individual rite of passage each person must face as they transition from childhood to adulthood. The hero provides an idealized model for the psyche to experience through the story and potentially enact through societal rites of initiation. According to Campbell:

> The hero ... is the man or woman who has been able to battle his personal and local historical limitations to the generally valid, normal human forms. Such a one's visions, ideas, and inspirations come pristine from the primary springs of human life and thought. Hence they are eloquent, not of the present, disintegrating society and psyche, but of the unquenched source through which society is reborn. The hero has died as a modern man; but as eternal man — perfected, unspecified, universal man — he has been reborn. His second solemn task and deed therefore (... as all the mythologies of man indicate) is to return then to us, transfigured, and teach the lesson he has learned of life renewed.[38]

The hero provides a crucial inspiration for the human spirit, and thus, the monomyth appears across cultures, across historical time, and across generic convention. In modern Western entertainment, for example, the monomyth is most explicitly replicated in the fantasy genre, though archetypally heroic characters appear in science fiction, horror, action-adventure, and romance, to name a few.

In role-playing games, players often recreate heroic quests. The archetypes foregrounded by folktales and mythology are most commonly recognizable in fantasy-based RPGs such as *Dungeons & Dragons* (*D&D*) and *Marvel Super Heroes,* though even in horror-based RPGs such as *Vampire: the Masquerade* and *Call of Cthulhu,* the players perform heroic deeds and secondary characters often serve Propp's basic functions. The Warrior class in *D&D* most superficially duplicates the classic hero — a physically strong and brave character who must fight monsters to save his or her friends and society from peril. However, most RPGs operate more in line with Tolkien's version of the hero quest, where individuals within a Fellowship bring their respective, unique talents to bear upon the crisis at hand. Usually players choose archetypes that differ from those of other players in the group in order to provide strategic benefits, as well as more extensive role-playing opportunities.

The various editions of *Advanced Dungeons & Dragons* most clearly replicate common mythological archetypes, borrowing heavily from fantasy authors such as J. R. R. Tolkien. In *D&D,* the common character exhibits two important characteristics — class and race. The majority of these attributes reflect age-old mythological symbols. M. Joseph Young, one of the authors of the *Multiverser* role-playing system, succinctly describes these character attributes, as well as providing hints as to their genealogical roots.[39] The following section offers a summary of many of the descriptions on his website.

Archetypal Classes in *Dungeons & Dragons*

The **Warrior/Fighter** is the standard infantry soldier, able to use any weapons and tactics, though he or she is usually most comfortable fighting with feet on the ground. Several subclasses are associated with the warrior. The **Cavalier** is the mounted knight, typified by the reality of late middle ages combat and the legends of Camelot. The cavalier is bound by the dictates of chivalry, must be courageous at all times, and is drawn from the upper classes of society. The **Paladin**, usually represented by Lancelot du Lac of the Arthurian tradition, combines the cavalry prowess and bravery of the cavalier with a limited form of the spiritual power and devotion of the Cleric. The **Ranger**, "clearly modeled on Strider/Aragorn and the Rangers of Tolkien's *Lord of the Rings*," possesses skill in tracking and herbalism, gaining a little magic at higher levels. The **Berserker**, drawn from Viking lore, describes undisciplined fighters who work themselves into a fierce frenzy before battle and are sometimes able to transmogrify into wolves and bears.[40] **Barbarians**, modeled after the design of Conan, are powerful brutish fighters from primitive areas who fear and disdain civilization and magic, but will occasionally band together "for a good brawl." Many barbarian abilities are connected to the kind of land in which their tribe lives.

Another major class in *Dungeons & Dragons* is the **Cleric**. The cleric, "although in many ways the clergyman of the party, is actually a knight of holy orders, dedicated to his god and his faith more than to fighting."[41] This class combines healing magic with somewhat limited combat skills. Related to the cleric is the **Druid**. Modeled after past Celtic legends, druids possess weaker defenses and stronger attacks than other clerics. Druidic magic is slightly more offensive and less curative and, like berserkers, druids gain the ability at higher levels to change to various animals. Gary Gygax, the originator of *Dungeons & Dragons*, describes the Druidic moral philosophy as "true neutral," meaning that these characters view "good and evil, law and chaos as balancing forces of nature, which are necessary for the continuation of all things."[42] His further description reflects some knowledge of the historical Druidic tradition mixed with his own conceptual enhancements:

> Druids can be visualized as medieval cousins of what the ancient Celtic sect of Druids would have become had it survived the Roman conquest. They hold trees (particularly oak and ash), the sun, and the moon as deities. Mistletoe is the holy symbol of the druids, and it gives power to their spells. They have an obligation to protect trees and wild plants, crops, and never

destroy woodlands ... no matter [ ] the circumstances. Even though a woods, for example, [was] evilly hostile, druids would not destroy it, although nothing would prevent them from changing the nature of the place if the desire and wherewithal existed. In a similar fashion, they avoid slaying wild animals or even domestic ones except as necessary for self-preservation and sustenance.[43]

Many of these characteristics are also reminiscent of Tom Bombadil and the Ents in Tolkien's *Lord of the Rings*, creatures who protect the wood as sacred groves but who rarely interfere in the causes of the external world, preferring to maintain the balance between good and evil. In *The Lord of the Rings,* The Ent Treebeard succinctly summarizes this "true neutral" philosophy: "Wizards are always troubled about the future. I do not like worrying about the future. I am not altogether on anybody's *side,* because nobody is altogether on my *side,* if you understand me: nobody cares for the woods as I care for them."[44]

The **Wizard** is the third major class in this classic RPG. Wizards are more dedicated to the pursuit of magic than to any other thing, even gods and moral attitudes.[45] In *D&D,* spells are divided into specific "schools" or "spheres," representing the discipline in which the wizard would have academically specialized. *D&D* offers individualized classes for certain specialized schools, including **Illusionists**, whose magic revolves primarily on making reality appear different.[46] Another powerful character type is the **Psionicist**, who uses highly developed mental powers as if they were magic, exerting control over reality.

The Wizard archetype present in *D&D* hearkens back to Gandalf the Grey in *The Hobbit* and *The Lord of the Rings*, though Tolkien's magic is far less defined and delineated than Gary Gygax's. According to David Day, Tolkien's books characterize Gandalf as a "comic, eccentric fairy-tale magician" who "has something of the character of the absent-minded professor and muddled conjurer about him."[47] Day articulates the Wizard's traditional role of "mentor, advisor, and tour guide for the hero (or anti-hero),"[48] otherwise known as the Helper or Donor in the Proppian designations of the terms. Day explains, "Wizards are extremely useful and versatile as vehicles for developing fairy-tale plots as their presence in so many tales testifies. Wizards usually provide a narrative with: a reluctant hero, secret maps, translations of ancient documents, supernatural weapons (how to use), some monsters (how to kill), location of treasure (how to steal), and an escape plan (negotiable)."[49]

In role-playing games, however, the wizard can also inhabit the role of Hero, depending on the configuration of the party: the personality characteristics of the players and their alter-egos, the goals of the characters, etc. Thus, while certain archetypes may have served a specific function in the plot historically, the story changes considerably when actual individuals inhabit it. In addition, some players enjoy playing "against type" or modifying the original archetype by adding character idiosyncrasies.

D&D's fourth overarching class is that of the **Rogue**. Rogues follow their own individual creed and sometimes swindle, beguile, or fool others for personal gain or amusement. One subclass of the Rogue is the **Thief**, or "expert treasure finder," who is trained in arts of stealth. Basic thief abilities include moving sneakily, surprising opponents, pilfering objects, and opening locked doors and boxes. Young cites Bilbo Baggins of Tolkien's *The Hobbit* as "a fair example." Another Rogue class is the **Assassin**, who earns his or her living by killing others. Assassins are the ultimate spies and must represent themselves as Evil regardless of their motivations for selecting jobs. Assassins cooperate in guilds but prefer to work alone. The Rogue subclass of **Bard**, "a minstrel/thespian pushed up a notch," learn the arts of stealth and combat before "pursuing a pseudoreligious career as musical magicians."[50] Bard characters tend to be excellent at singing, dancing, storytelling, and other types of performance, wandering to different lands earning money for their entertainment.

Rogues find their roots in the age-old archetype of the Trickster. According to Louis Hyde in *Trickster Makes This World*, this archetype consistently challenges rigid assumptions and traditions.[51] Instead of settling in a particular location, Trickster characters tend to live nomadically. In Hyde's words, the Trickster "is the spirit of the road at dusk, the one that runs from town to town but belongs to neither. There are strangers on that road, and thieves, and in the underbrush a sly beast whose stomach has not heard about your letter of passage."[52] This archetype also challenges common conceptions of ethical behavior by blurring distinctions in a multiplicity of ways:

> In short, trickster is a boundary-crosser. Every group has its edge, its sense of in and out, and trickster is always there, at the gates of the city and the gates of life, making sure there is commerce. He also attends the internal boundaries by which groups articulate their social life. We constantly distinguish — right and wrong, sacred and profane, cleans and dirty, male and female, young and old, living and dead — and in every case trickster will cross the line and confuse the distinction. Trickster is the creative idiot, therefore, the wise fool, the gray-haired baby, the cross-dresser, the speaker of sacred profanities. Where someone's sense of honorable behavior has left him unable to act, trickster will appear to suggest an amoral action,

something right/wrong that will get life going again. Trickster is the mythic embodiment of ambiguity and ambivalence, doubleness and duplicity, contradiction and paradox.[53]

Trickster characters represent the passage from one space to the next and the blurring of distinctive boundaries. Thus, rogues are often masters at disguise, stealth, and riddles. Young attributes rogue-like characteristics to Tolkien's Bilbo Baggins, who engages in riddles with Gollum, finds secret doors to the dragon's cave, steals treasure from Smaug, etc. The hobbit's modern manifestations of the Trickster attributes form the template for the more contemporary rogue archetype in role-playing games.

Archetypal Races in *Dungeons & Dragons*

D&D only offers a handful of playable races, though the *Monster Manual* offers a larger variety of creatures arising from a multitude of different mythological sources. The most common playable race is **Human**, since, according to Young, the game is designed to prefer this class. In early editions of *Advanced Dungeons & Dragons*, only humans could start as one class and later change to a different one, offering the benefits of both.[54] Though the game designers relaxed stringent restrictions such as these in later editions, providing in-game advantages for playing a human in a fantasy world seems slightly counterintuitive. Perhaps players enjoy the theme of the triumph of humanity even within the possibilities of a strange, magical world.

Still, players can create characters with alternate races. One such race is the **Halfling**, based upon the hobbits in Tolkien's work. Young describes halflings in similar way to their depictions in *The Hobbit* and *The Lord of the Rings*. He states, "These little people stand about three feet tall and have large hairy feet. They are in the main quiet, decent people. In the words of one of their number, 'Adventures make one late for dinner.' However, occasionally one of their number will get a peculiarity, become a bit odd, and for some reason — perhaps a genetic flaw — become an adventurer."[55]

According to Day, Tolkien once wrote to his publisher that he made hobbits small "partly to exhibit the pettiness of man, plain unimaginative, parochial man ... and mostly to show up, in creatures of very small physical power, the amazing and unexpected heroism of ordinary men 'at a pinch.'"[56] Though Tolkien's hobbits possess attributes specific to the rural Englishmen, the archetype appears in the travels of many a hero's journey as the friendly innkeeper or the country bumpkin. The qualities exhibited here as pertaining to Halflings also represent the humble environment and expectations from which the hero originates in standard formulations of the monomyth.

A similar race to the Dwarf is the **Gnome**. Gnomes are more tolerant than Dwarves of other races and of magic, and are skilled with illusions and machines. Gnomes have an intricate society based on their love of all kinds of arts, pranks, and long life. They love indulgence and celebrate on a grand scale. All gnomes must learn some form of art by the time they come of age, be it music, painting, cooking, building, or any other form that is considered creative.[57] Subraces of gnomes include Surface Gnomes, Svirfneblin (underground-dwelling), Tinker Gnomes (technologically-minded), Rock Gnomes, Forest Gnomes, Chaos Gnomes (flamboyant), Whisper Gnomes (sly and stealthy), Ice Gnomes, and Fire Gnomes.

The alchemist Paracelsus may have originated the term of Gnome in the sixteenth century, adding the "earth gnome" to his list of elementals.[58] He describes them as taciturn, little old men who could shift to the size of giants and were greedy, malicious, and miserable creatures. These personality qualities are not found in the Gnomes of *D&D*; instead, these qualities more resemble the Duergar dwarves.[59] The gnome is often featured in Germanic fairy tales, including those by the Brothers Grimm, usually resembling a gnarled old man, who lives deep underground and guards buried treasure. In European folklore, mythical creatures such as goblins and dwarves are often represented as gnomes, and vice versa, so some confusion arises. The hugely popular "garden gnomes," ceramic dolls first designed in the mid–nineteenth century, further altered the conception of the creature. Based on Germanic myths, the garden gnomes reside on their owner's lawns, reflecting the stories of the gnomes' willingness to help in the garden at night.[60] The garden gnome embodies the playful spirit invoked by the archetype in *D&D*, though Gygax's formulation of the gnome remains at least partially an original, modern conception.

The characteristics of **Dwarves** in *D&D* vary depending on their subrace. Dwarves mine for precious gems, gold, and silver and are characterized by their greed, superstition, and mistrust of magic. According to the website "Literary Sources of *D&D*," Dwarves are an amalgamation of many tales:

> The primary sources, especially for D&D dwarven society and lifespans, are *The Hobbit* and *Lord of the Rings; Three Hearts and Three Lions* [by Poul Anderson] is also an important source, but not as much so as Tolkien's works. (Also, the terms "dwarves" and "dwarven" were coined by Tolkien. The original forms are dwarfs and dwarfish, as evidenced by Disney's movie

Snow White and the Seven Dwarfs). The Germanic story *The Ring of the Nibelungen* and the "Rumpelstiltskin" fairy tale retold by the Brothers Grimm are probably close ancestors of D&D dwarves. Germanic lore depicts dwarves as living in caves, guarding mineral wealth, and being very skillful in making things from stone and minerals. French folklore (and from that, *Three Hearts and Three Lions*) depict dwarves as forest-dwellers, similar to *D&D*'s hill dwarves. The dwarven ability to detect the slope of an underground passage is specifically mentioned in *Three Hearts and Three Lions*, which is most likely the immediate source for inclusion of that ability in *D&D*.[61]

The archetypal tradition of the Dwarf is long and rich and players commonly choose this race to role-play. Other types of dwarves also exist in the game. Hill dwarves, the most common sub-race in *D&D*, stand around four feet tall and at least one hundred fifty pounds. Their skin runs from deep tan to light brown, their bright eyes are almost never blue, their cheeks are ruddy, and they can have brown, black, or gray hair.[62] The Duergar dwarves, also called Gray dwarfs, live deep underground, are thinner than other dwarves, and have gray hair and skin.[63] The Duergar tend to be evil and avaricious.

The other most commonly-played race is that of the **Elves**. The elven lifespan is remarkably long and they almost never die of old age. They tend to possess an innate beauty and easy gracefulness and are often viewed as both wondrous and haughty by other races, though their natural detachment is seen by some as xenophobia or introversion. Slightly shorter than the average human, elves are noticeably more graceful and slender than humans and their features are more angular and defined, including long, pointed ears and wide, almond-shaped eyes.[64] Most elven characters in *D&D* are High elves, though other sub-races exist. The Gray elves tend to avoid anyone not of the elven kind. Wood elves (also called Sylvan elves) are even more reclusive, not mixing with the organized societies of other races on any repeated or regular basis. Wood elves possess a strong affinity toward trees and woodland creatures.[65] Drow elves (or Dark elves) tend to be evil, dark of skin, and white of hair. The Drow dwell in underground in the deep reaches of the earth.

The Elves of *D&D* strongly resemble their counterparts in *The Lord of the Rings*. The Sindaran elves in Tolkien are represented by Celeborn and Galadriel of Lothlorien as well as the Wood elves of Mirkwood. Drow-like elves, on the other hand, are not represented explicitly in the series. Old Norse texts refer to "black elves" (or "swart elves") who live in subterranean realm, but these creatures seem "virtually interchangeable" with

Norse references to dwarves, gnomes, giants, and demons.[66] *D&D* makes clear distinctions between archetypes that often get confused with each other in myth and folklore.

This chapter delineates the major archetypes present in *Dungeons & Dragons*, which strongly resemble recognizable figures in mythological narratives. However, many other role-playing systems exist, and within them a multitude of other archetypes. Game systems such as the World of Darkness take into account modern formulations of character types as well as ancient ones and the archetypes tend more toward deeper psychological aspects rather than surface racial or professional qualities. In *Vampire: the Masquerade*, for example, the majority of Vampires hail from specific bloodlines, including the Toreador, the Ventrue, and the Nosferatu. Bloodlines — also referred to as Clans — function similarly to racial characteristics in *D&D*. For example, the Toreador tend toward artistry and high society, the Ventrue toward leadership and finance, and the Nosferatu toward stealth and information gathering.[67]

However, personality aspects are complexified by the system; characters also possess a Nature — or basic personality type — and Demeanor — or outward personality type. Sample archetypes within these categories include Caregiver, Fanatic, Judge, Loner, and Visionary.[68] Such characteristics reflect a depth of identity not found within the high fantasy game system of *Dungeons & Dragons*. Ultimately, though, each individual role-player invests his or her character with varying levels of psychological depth, regardless of the genre or game system from which their character originates.

Summary

The roots of the creation of alternate identities in the human psyche can be traced to early childhood. Children begin to investigate their sense of self in early childhood through pretend play, storytelling, impersonation, and the creation of paracosms and Imaginary Friends. In adolescence, they seek a stable sense of ego identity through interaction with particular groups and the internalization of social codes and mores. As adults, they learn to adopt particular fronts, playing multiple roles depending on context.

In the postmodern world — particularly with the advent of online communities — humans must establish a stronger fluidity of identity in order to adapt to the fast pace of cultural change. They develop a sense of multiplicity within the self, rather than focusing on a rigid set of ego characteristics. These multiple identities are also known as "sub-personalities" and they tend to reflect archetypes. Archetypes are symbolic structures, bubbling up through the collective unconscious and are easily identified by their continual recurrence in mythology cross-culturally. The earliest and most influential role-playing system, *Dungeons & Dragons,* highlights major mythological archetypes, allowing players to enact these age-old symbolic roles while adding their own creative flair to their characters.

The playful enactment and negotiation of identity is a primary attribute of role-playing games. Rather than representing what some perceive as an "abnormal" escapism into fantasy, role-players tap into their own inherent archetypal structures and explore them in the safe space of the game world. Combined with the other two functions of problem-solving and community building, identity alteration is the third important psychological aspect of role-playing. The final chapter of this volume will provide an ethnographic evaluation of identity alteration within role-playing environments, explaining how players develop their personas and establishing a typography to delineate how the characters relate to the each player's primary sense of self.

7

Character Evolution and Types of Identity Alteration

Finally, we will venture to explore the content of the actual roles the players enact. I use the term "venture" because these characters remain somewhat ephemeral conceptually throughout their "existence" in the minds of gamers. Attempting to understand the cause of their inception, the motivations behind their enactment, and the reasons fueling their evolution over time can often seem a frustrating process. Creativity is, by nature, an unconscious process. Pinpointing its stages requires a certain level of self-awareness and reflection. Fortunately, many of my informants offered flashes of insight into these issues.

This chapter will highlight several key factors with regard to the creation and enactment of role-playing characters, including the inception of the character, which begins as an overall Gestalt of concept. The concept then blossoms and evolves through the development of a background, co-creation with other role-players, in-game interactions, and advancements in the story line. Next, we will detail a typology for the various types of characters. These categories are based less on the archetypal essence of the persona and more on the player's feeling of "sameness" between their primary identity and the character concept. Often, the characters work to serve a certain function for role-players, be it psychological exploration, boundary transgression, or simple stress relief. Guided by the manner in which my respondents describe their characters, I offer nine major types of roles: the Doppelganger Self, the Devoid Self, the Augmented Self, the Fragmented Self, the Repressed Self, the Idealized Self, the Oppositional Self, the Experimental Self, and the Taboo Self. However, as characters often refuse to fit neatly into categories, even archetypal ones, some characters will share qualities of multiple categories.

Finally, we will explore the relationship between the characters and their players, including the extent to which these entities "exist" within the minds of their creators before and after the events of the game cease. The level of connectivity between the primary sense of self and the character changes from player to player. Ultimately, however, the process of creating, enacting, and evolving a role-playing character appears to leave a lasting impression in the minds and hearts of players.

The Evolution of the Character Concept

The evolution of a role-playing character is analogous to the planting and growth of a flower. Like a flower, the genesis of a character arises from a single seed. That seed may stem from a particular fascination of the player — something he or she needs to express or wishes to explore. The player plants the seed in the soil, creating a foundation for the concept. The soil, in this case, may include various character building activities, such as back story writing, the allocation of points on a character sheet, or costuming. These activities allow the character concept to grow roots before ever interacting with the game environment or the other players. Once the player solidifies their concept, the newly formed seed begins to sprout as a result of environmental influences, such as the Storyteller, other player characters, the game system, and various in-game scenarios. Thus, the player may possess an initial idea of how the character will evolve, but that concept will necessarily shift based on the unfolding interactions with the external environment. Finally, with enough time and energy, the character can open like a flower, developing into a multifaceted, complex persona.

There are four central stages to the evolution of role-playing characters. The first stage involves the **Genesis**— or origin/inception — of the character concept. Most character concepts arise from some combination of inherent archetypes, game-specific mechanics or abilities, narratives from literature, popular culture references, and personal experiences. The second stage involves the **Development** of the character, in which the player builds upon the initial idea through various creative exercises meant to make the concept more material in his or her mind. The third stage involves **Interaction** between the character and the game world. In this stage, the character shifts from being a mere concept to an actual persona that must make certain decisions based upon situations outside of the player's control. Given enough time and devotion, the character may reach the final stage of development based upon these various interactions, the **Realization** of the character. When a character becomes fully Realized, the player has a distinct sense of the character's past and present motivations, their complexities and idiosyncrasies. A fully Realized character will still develop and evolve over time based on new scenarios and interactions, but the player has established a strong understanding of the persona as a distinct entity, rather than just a concept.

In addition, at each stage of development, characters possess a particular relationship with their players. I prefer to think of the player as the Primary ego identity; in other words, the player's Primary sense of self represents the individual who operates in daily, "real world" activities. Players still experience the Self as a stable, unified sense of identity, even when enacting the persona. However, the more immersed in the game world the players become, the more they perceive the character as a distinct entity from the Primary Self. Thus, this chapter will describe nine different ways that the player experiences their character with relationship to their daily identities. The goal of the typology is to establish the concept that fully Realized characters manifest as distinct Selves, with various degrees of similarities and differences from the Primary ego identity.

The Four Stages of Character Evolution

The first stage of the evolution of character is the act of creation, or the Genesis stage. The impetus behind creating a character can stem from many sources, including the following:

- The Storyteller or a fellow player may ask someone to play a particular persona in order to further a story line or to fill an archetypal gap in the group.
- The player may find inspiration from a work of literature, a popular culture text, an historical time period, or a personal experience.
- The player may wish to create a character in order to role-play with their out-of-character (OOC) friends.
- The player may feel the need to explore an underdeveloped aspect of their own psyche or of the game world in general.

Regardless of the reasoning behind creating a character, the Genesis stage represents the beginning of the creative process. Creativity, by nature, is often stimulated by other imaginative works. Players will draw inspiration both from one another and from the various external texts that have influenced them in their lifetime.

The Development stage allows the player to more fully delineate the details of their character before introducing him or her into the game world. This process usually involves some combination of the following character building activities: searching for avatar pictures, purchasing costuming, writing back stories detailing the character's history, creating timelines, painting or drawing the character, exchanging ideas with other players, and allocating points on the character sheets provided by the game system. Though the Development stage can be co-creative, this part of character evolution usually marks the last point at which the player has creative control over the character. Once the character enters the game, during the Interaction stage, the player can influence the events transpiring in the story, but cannot fully control the world. The Storyteller ultimately decides the fate of the character, though other players certainly help influence the unfolding of the plot. In this way, the Interaction stage distinguishes role-playing from other, more solitary forms of character creation, such as novel writing.

After a fair amount of time and game immersion, certain character concepts may evolve into fully developed entities. The players of these personas often describe the strange experience of a mild form of splitting of their consciousness, in which the primary Self and the character think and behave differently from one another. Though aspects of the character may remain consistent, the persona has evolved as a result of the unique experiences and circumstances provided by the context of the game world. I refer to this final stage as the Realization of the character, though the ultimate evolution of the persona usually ends up varying widely from the original concept. The concept functions as a form of hypothetical guideline, whereas the execution of the character within the constraints of the game scenarios creates the actual contours of the persona.

Furthermore, the character may experience multiple levels of Realization the longer the player explores his or her limits. For example, I have played Viviane for over ten years in three distinct *Vampire: The Masquerade* games. As a persona, her personality has ranged from coldly sociopathic to wildly hedonistic to philosophically profound, depending upon the game-related circumstances and my own OOC-related experience of reality. In the first game, she engaged in various unfortunate and diabolical acts, a story line which ended with Viviane allowing herself to die out of sheer nihilism and despair. However, I continued to play Viviane as a

Realized entity in two other games, with alternate scenarios. Thus, I have continued to explore the depths of her psyche with each new interaction. Viviane has evolved as a character alongside my own personal evolution as a player; one might even say we learn from one another's experiences, both in the "real world" and the game.

The Genesis and Development of the Character Concept

Characters arise from a variety of sources and motivations. Sometimes, the Storyteller will request that a gamer design a specific type of character to fill skill-related gaps in the party, performing the role of a cleric or warrior, for example. Other times, a player may wish to explore a particular concept, time period, or culture. Regardless of the reasoning behind its inception, players agree that the original concept rarely reflects the way the personality of the character develops over time. According to Gary Alan Fine, "Players must construct a Gestalt — a conception of what their character is like — that is necessarily highly stereotyped, and then play according to that conception."[1] Players then "work from scant, sometimes contradictory information to construct a meaningful identity."[2] This Gestalt establishes a preliminary theory of mind, creating a tentative space within the player's mental framework for the character to inhabit.

This Gestalt holds the initial seed of the persona, which further blossoms through several types of character-building activities. The player establishes the basic characteristics of the persona by creating a character sheet, utilizing the rules of the game system. The character sheet gives the player an initial sense of the strengths and weaknesses of their persona and sometimes establishes personality idiosyncrasies that work to enhance roleplaying and deepen interactions. Other character-building activities include: outside research into related fields, background writing, costuming, purchasing specific dice, painting miniatures, drawing pictures of the character, etc. Character creation can also develop through out-of-character conversation with other players through a process of co-creation. These character-building activities broaden the scope of the player's conception of their character before game play even begins.

Though not all role-players invest a large amount of time into character creation and development, several of my respondents described extensive character-building activities. The first step toward a character "coming to life" requires the player to personalize the archetype offered by the game system. As "Elton" states, "The [games] all force you into a particular role.

And you take that stereotypical character and play with it for a while, tweak it, and add in your own flavor and eventually you get your own character."[3] Josh S. describes this "tweaking" process in detail, explaining the inception of Jeremiah, his character in a *Vampire* LARP:

> Starting out ... I made the stats card up, [thinking] "I want to be a dexterity-based fighter." And that's where it starts. No name. No idea where I would be. Then, the name generally just pops in my head after I've been working on the numbers.... It's not something strange or out of the blue. It just shows up. "Well, my *name* is Jeremiah." Then, generally I give my characters accents, because it helps me transition into being the character ... [*in a southern accent*] "Well, Iaaahm Jeremiaaah." Once I get those two things, then the character kind of grows from there. I'll [think], "If I were this guy, what would I do?" Well, [in the] Old West, I'd play cards, because I don't like working outside. Cause Jeremiah doesn't like working outside. It could have gone either way; it could have gone, "Well he loves to work, he's a workaholic" ... but it didn't. That didn't call to me. So the character makes himself.[4]

Josh first established the Gestalt for his character — the name, abilities, and location of origin. During this process, particular personality aspects began to bubble up from Josh's imagination, leading him to speculate that the character "makes himself." Once the players access their inner well of creativity, they often describe the experience of watching the characters develop of their own accord, already established as preliminary entities.

Josh S.'s explanation of the inception of Jeremiah is remarkably similar to the way in which I create characters. Almost all my personas have high social and mental aspects, while I tend to undervalue physical attributes; I generally dislike combat, both in- and out-of-character. Thus, despite my original character concept, my characters almost always have high appearance, charisma, and intelligence scores. I then decide what culture and time period from which the character hails. Within this culture, I detail what sort of occupation the character will perform, which usually manifests as some form of intellectual, socialite, healer, or artist. I will then spend a great deal of time agonizing over the proper name. Sometimes, this name will "arrive," just as the name Jeremiah popped into Josh's mind. Other times, I will pour over lists of baby names and read the meanings behind potential candidates. After the all-important name emerges, I begin to outline the background of the character, which often includes extensive research into the time period and culture from which the persona arises.

For example, I once spent weeks developing a character for a new *Vampire* LARP before I met the majority of the players in-person. I decided to create a five-hundred year old Toreador vampire from the Italian Renaissance named Eustacia Boccasavia. I had been fond of the first name Eustacia since I read Thomas Hardy's *The Return of the Native* in high school.[5] Searching through Italian-English dictionaries online, I then concocted the last name Boccasavia, which means "sensible mouth."[6] This surname encapsulated the character concept nicely: an expert courtier who gives sage advice and instruction. Then, I chose a physical representation, a famous person who not only looked "like" Eustacia, but also embodied the energy that I wanted the entity to possess. I downloaded hundreds of pictures of model/actress Monica Belluci. These photos exhibited a sense of grace, class, and sensuality, while retaining a hint of mystery.

I then wrote an elaborate, twenty-eight page short story detailing the events of her life from before her birth in 1510 to the year 1580. I inserted photos of Belluci throughout this narrative, offering visual augments. I drew her overall paradigm and manner of speaking from Baldassare Castiglione's *The Book of the Courtier* and even inserted a scene in the story that involved her obtaining and reading a copy of this manuscript.[7] I also read a history of the Italian Renaissance in order to better understand the political dynamics from which Eustacia originated, eventually deciding to establish her original location in the city-state of Milan. I then spent days accumulating costuming, which eventually included: extensive makeup; a long, black wig; dress pumps; costume jewelry; several corsets; bustle skirts; and ball gowns.

Though such character-building activities may seem excessive, each component added to my Gestalt of Eustacia. The costuming and pictorial representations enhanced my immersion in the persona and the back story aided my understanding of how the character spoke, moved, thought, and reacted. These aspects allowed me to present a unified concept of character, both as an avatar in the online role-playing forums and in-person at the LARP.

Though some role-players simply throw a concept together and "wing it" at the game, many of my respondents reported engaging in more complex character-building activities. Long-lived *Vampire* characters, in particular, require at least some conception of history and players try to fill in the gaps in their own knowledge through study. Chris states, "If I'm, for example, role-playing a character from 1920s Italy, I'm going to read about 1920s Italy, and that requires research. I [may] read some books from that era, some poetry, or maybe listen to some music, and the background writing comes last from that."[8] Matthew explains, "If I wanted a character to know about something, I made sure that I knew as much as

I could to ensure that the integrity of their answers were as accurate as possible." He describes the back story of one of his *Vampire* characters, William, which "focused on his life and times during the American Revolution, how his surrogate father was the one who started the Sons Of Liberty, to his abandonment and eventual embrace [into vampirism]."[9] Omega details an instance in which he heavily researched the cultural roots of satyrs in order to best perform one character concept:

> I actually spent two weeks researching satyrs: their pictures, their mentality, the lores that are from both the German background and also from the Greek background, ... the style of speech, ... the mannerisms, ... the campiness, ... and the shamelessness that they would have. I tried to find, through all of that background, a personality that would match the character that I was trying to create and the shape and the feel of the character.[10]

Unfortunately, Omega's satyr character died after two game sessions. Still, he insists, "I think the research itself and the going that deep into it was worth it. Because that was the deepest I've ever gone into building a character."[11] Indeed, for some role-players, part of the pleasure of developing characters lies in imagining life in a different time and culture and learning more about those aspects. The staid "facts" of history suddenly come alive when the player imagines what a facet of their consciousness would think or feel under alternate circumstances.

Players also often collaborate in the development of their characters. Some characters exist in a socially symbiotic relationship with others, as family members, allies, or even enemies. The players will co-create the details of their character back story, weaving their individual histories together. "Elton" describes this process in the following passage:

> We would, accidentally sometimes, and sometimes on purpose ... create these characters that have linked backgrounds. So, then that comes out in-game, where you may have allegiances between certain characters because, "Well, we were back in Paris during the French Revolution and so we went through that together and now we're here. So, we have this allegiance because we have the kinship of having gone through that experience together." Or enmity. You may have an enemy because of that.[12]

Sometimes, a character concept starts out weak, only blossoming when players combine creativity.

For example, I recently played an NPC in a *Vampire* LARP named Hortense Throckmorton. Because she was a "non-player character," meant as a tool for plot development, I created a persona that I knew I would not personally find appealing or emotionally engaging. Hortense hailed from nineteenth-century England and embodied many of the repressive elements of the Victorian paradigm, including sexual repression and an obsession with maintaining an air of bourgeois respectability. I intended to play her for only a couple of sessions, using her as a way to instruct new players on the "proper" etiquette of vampiric court life. However, Matthew entered the game, creating a character from the same a clan named Alastaire. The Storyteller placed us in the position of "sister" and "brother" from the same "sire," meaning that the same man turned both of our characters into vampires. Matthew and I then engaged in extensive, out-of-character AOL Instant Message conversations in which we detailed our collective background. From these conversations, I learned far more about Hortense than I initially thought I wanted to know. She developed into a three-dimensional character in my mind, rather than a flimsy "house of cards" construction based on a stereotype.

While preliminary character-building activities help the player understand the complexities of their persona before enactment, the character only fully "emerges" through actual role-play. Often, the original concept fails to stick and the character develops along other lines. I originally intended my Viviane character, for example, to be a streetwise graffiti artist. This concept quickly fell to the wayside, though, because her personality manifested in the game far more strongly as a snobby, hedonistic social climber. As Daniel MacKay explains, the character comes into fruition only when the player experiences an altered sense of self:

> The character comes to life in moments of alterity, where the player experiences the sensation of being another. The character concept is the point of origin for a character, but the words the player speaks in-character, in response to the constellation of addresses that occur during a session, become the inborn character concept that the player could not have identified when he first set himself upon the task of creating a character.[13]

Though writing a back story may produce a feeling of alterity in the player, the character "behaves" uniquely when forced into situations by the Storyteller and through interaction with other players. Thus, players may not fully understand what their character will come to represent with relation to their primary sense of self until after having played him or her for long periods of time. These meanings also shift over time, particularly with extensively-played characters.

The Realization Stage and Character Typologies

As characters experience events in role-playing situations, they grow and evolve. The in-game events mark them in ways unforeseen by even the Storyteller. Sometimes, the characters exhibit personality traits far different from the player's. Other times, the boundary between character and player seems more blurry. Experienced players, however, expect "good" role-players to attempt to maintain a strong sense of distinction between in-character and out-of-character thoughts, feelings, and actions. Players capable of strongly representing their alternate persona encourage others to immerse themselves in the game more deeply, enhancing the experience of the story.

Role-playing theorists attempt to create blanket explanations for the source of characters and for the reasons behind the player enjoyment. MacKay explains, "The roles that the players adopt allow them to delve into their emotional depths, their affective selves, and to express their feelings and ideas, but they do so through the creative distance the role provides."[14] Michelle Nephew claims that all role-playing characters represent an unconscious wish-fulfillment on the part of the players. She states, "The player's unconscious desires are allowed to become manifest in the role taken, since the persona of the character allows the player a disguise behind which to hide."[15] While these explanations may provide some indication of the impulse behind character enactment, they fail to fully explain the complexities of characterization.

To rectify this problem, this chapter details the various "types" of characters players enact. While chapter six focused on the age-old archetypes offered as concepts to players of games such as *Dungeons & Dragons*, this typology focuses more on the player's relationship to the character. When describing their various personas, many of my informants detail the similarities and differences between their primary personality traits and those of their character. They explain what functions they believe their characters serve and how closely their personas reflect their sense of ego-identity in the "real world." Classifications like these become difficult, though, because characters can often serve multiple functions for the players. I rely primarily on the language my respondents use when describing their characters for hints as to the relationship between the primary self and the persona.

The Doppelganger Self

Some role-players enact personas that closely resemble their primary sense of self. Players may construct a Doppelganger Self, who thinks and behaves as they would, despite discrepancies on the character sheet. I played in a *mirror* game, for example, in which we each imagined ourselves, in our current positions in life, suddenly turned into vampires. This interesting exercise forced us to think "as if" our primary selves were placed in the unique situation of suddenly becoming night-dwelling predators. In this case, the Doppelganger Self provided a heightened sense of self-awareness.

However, the majority of the time, experienced role-players dismiss the practice of enacting personas similar to the primary identity as amateurish. Many players create a Doppelganger Self when new to the game and still learning the world, as playing someone similar to one's self is far easier. As Fine suggests, "Some players admit that they or others play themselves. Younger, less-skilled players are particularly likely to adapt the traditional gaming posture of winning however they can."[16] However, Fine insists that the "hard-core, long-term, older gamers" believe "that what makes these games unique is that a player portrays a figure distinct from himself."[17]

For serious role-players, the game lies not only in the continued success and survival of the character, but in the successful enactment of an entity other than the self. Kirstyn explains, "You are the source. And unless you want to play yourself again and again, which some do and, subsequently, are not very fun to role-play with, you have to create a space for this separate entity."[18] She playfully refers to the "real world" identity as the "primary character" in the following passage:

> These are those who show up, throw a few concepts together ... and call it a day. That's about all the thought they give to the character. They will still dress the same way as their actual self, (primary character), talk the same way, and generally act the same way. And despite the persona they assume, their character's desires and general interests are remarkably similar to those of the primary character. These gamers essentially play themselves but with "*kewl powerz!*"[19]

Some players, then, only create surface-level characters, never fully immersing themselves into the game environment.

However, many of my respondents indicated a sense that certain characters they play possess inherent similarities to their primary sense of self. Though Matthew often engages in extensive character-building activities, he suggests, "There is a lot of them in me, as I generally take some aspect of myself to help make the character become more real for me."[20] Similarly, Carley intimates, "Moria has ... a similar energy to me. I really don't know how else to describe it. It's not a general demeanor even. But like, as I see her in my head, we share certain mannerisms and our general style of movement."[21] Alex, who often portrays female characters online, describes one of his only male personas in the following manner: "Adenauer was a drunkard, though wise, and a politician. I suppose I forget much about how I played him, though he was an exploration of myself in virtual form."[22]

John explains how one of his characters, Findo, exhibits similar personality traits to himself, despite Findo's fantastic existence as a gnome in an alternate world. He states, "[Findo's] given to sometimes unreasonable levels of debauchery. And if it's not fun, it's not worth doing with that character. He wants to see the positive in everything. He wants everybody to like him. He wants to just generally have a good life. Out of all the characters I play he's the only one like that. And I'm the most like that."[23] As I explained in chapter six, the gnome archetype in *Dungeons & Dragons* is often fun-loving and playful. Thus, Findo's archetype allows John to express aspects of his own primary personality in ways that other characters do not.

Thus, the Doppelganger Self need not necessarily be viewed as a shallow form of role-playing. The similarity between the primary self and the persona can also work to enhance self-esteem, offering an "ordinary" person the opportunity to do extraordinary things and make a difference in crisis situations.

The Devoid Self

One interesting role-playing exercise during character creation involves developing a persona that lacks an essential quality that the player possesses in the "real world." The Devoid Self may have a physical disability, a lack of empathy, or have been raised in more austere circumstances than the player experienced. A good way to think of the Devoid Self is the *Doppleganger Minus* some essential quality.

Guillermo's first tabletop character, Athaniel, was blind. He would request that the Storyteller explain to him everything the character could perceive through means other than vision and would even play blindfolded or with a hat over his eyes. This practice aided him in immersion and he believes that it enhanced the experiences of other players as well. He states, "I think it helped them get into the experience, because they were having to explain these things. Not take them for granted, but really say these things out loud."[24] Interestingly, the Devoid Self often behaves in radically different ways than a Doppleganger might. Removing, for example, one's empathy will severely change the way the character behaves within the universe of the game, even if the other personality qualities are essentially identical.

The Augmented Self

Likewise, some players enact personas that are similar to their primary identity, but have some form of Augmentation. The Augmented Self may have a super power, inexhaustible wealth, or immortality. Again, though the personality remains the same, the actions of the Augmented Self may veer wildly from those of the player based on these special abilities. The Augmented Self can be thought of as the *Doppleganger Plus* some other key quality.

In some ways, few characters ever evolve purely as Dopplegangers, or exact replicas of the primary ego identity. Almost all RPGs feature some form of supernatural augmentation for the characters. Possessing the ability to read minds, turn invisible, cast magic, or fly will change the way the character views reality, particularly in terms of his or her decision-making process. In the "real world," for example, a player would have to watch someone closely and interpret their body language to detect a lie, whereas a supernatural power in the game world might give them an "automatic success" in this sort of situation. Indeed, some players report replying on their supernatural powers or other mechanics in the game world to compensate for abilities that they feel their primary self lacks.

The Fragmented Self

In many cases, the persona enacted in RPGs emerges from a mere fragment of the player's personality. This fragment becomes accentuated, ballooned, or sometimes twisted. What may have originated as a subdued aspect of the player's self becomes the center of the character concept. Darren explains, "I think that for me playing a character is really more about picking an aspect of my own personality, no matter how dormant and how latent, and magnifying, and amplifying it to the forefront and making it the driving part of the character I play. So in this way, it does relate to my own personality, or at least a possible version."[25] This persona may come to represent the player's sensuality, their manipulativeness, their interest in a particular field of study, their dream of pursuing a specific profession — literally, anything from within them. John reflects, "Findo's probably got my sense of humor. Azul had my aggressiveness."[26] The freedom of the play space allows the individual to experience a small piece of themselves, expand it, magnify it, and ultimately, examine how it functions when carried to certain conclusions.

These elements may manifest as "positive" or "negative" traits. They may represent a tiny facet of the player's inner self or a large facet that is then isolated and amplified. Fine explains, "Some players argue that one plays a character as an *extension* of one's person — one's person in a more extreme fashion." One of Fine's informants, Andy, states, "You always kind of play your character in the way you think he might ... and they're usually traits that you have ... but you're playing them in a more exaggerated form."[27] However, this explanation fails to address the content of these personas and what functions they serve as tools for the primary consciousness to better experience and examine itself.

Therefore, the seed of these characters generally arises from a mental interest or perhaps psychological or spiritual need inherent to the individual at the moment of creation. These seeds may represent important aspects of self that need expression, such as a sense of grief, or of a mere passing fancy, such as an interest in a particular style of music. Guillermo describes the creation of his first character, Athaniel. He explains, "I imbued him with the things that I like to do, but on a larger scale. I try to consider myself a creative person, like, for instance, I enjoy writing. So, I made him a food critic who can describe, because he's blind, amazingly well all these sensations, the tastes and everything like that ... I also love to cook."[28]

Oftentimes, these aspects will play themselves out in specific archetypes. When a player enacts an archetype, certain aspects of self bubble to the surface and project outward, sublimating what socially defined roles the individual may have in the "real world." For instance, if a player enacts the archetype of "rogue," he or she must uncover aspects of sneakiness, greediness, or trickery within themselves and find the motivation for the actions of the character. In The World of Darkness, the Gangrel vampire clan and the various types of werewolves provide players the opportunity to explore their animalistic side, a process known as *anthropomorphic* role-play, or *anthro*. Desiree indicates that playing a Gangrel in *Vampire* has been her favorite role-playing experience to date. She describes,

> The passion, the fun ... It was very exciting for me to be animalistic and to be able to concentrate on my animalistic behaviors, instead of concentrating on the healing aspects of others. I could be irrational. I could be emotional. I could be a little bit crazed. And that was fun because it's very much unlike who I really am. It's a second part of me, but a very small second part of me. So it was nice to act out that part.[29]

The role-playing experience allowed Desiree a release from her daily social role as massage therapist, allowing her to explore more instinctive and "irrational" responses to situations.

One common archetype players enact involves overt sexuality and the manipulation of others through seduction. Because the remnants of Puritanism in American culture often discourage open displays of sexuality, especially among females, players utilize the safe space of the game to enact seduction archetypes, such as the *rake* or the *femme fatale. Vampire* particularly encourages such representations, as the drawing of another's blood is experienced as ecstatic by both parties, and the vampire often must use manipulation to convince humans to offer themselves. At one stage in her evolution, my character Viviane Morceau delighted in the seduction and manipulation of others. Years later, I realized that, unconsciously, I had chosen the French word for "piece" for Viviane's last name. I have often felt that the character represented a fragment of my personality amplified to an extreme degree.

Other of my respondents expressed a similar amplification of sexual expression through roleplaying. Haley admits, "With my characters, I can be much more sensual and sexual than I am in my own life because I'm very shy ... [in] the real world, there're real consequences whereas in game, no big deal."[30] Kirstyn describes her first role-playing character, a Toreador named Saffir, who used seduction as her art form:

> This is the first place in my psyche I explored, a strange choice for a chubby, low-self-esteem racked, barely-been-kissed, 17-year-old, gothic virgin, with a history of sexual abuse to go. I was slowly coming into my own but truly had no feeling of myself. I had always been a very sensual, if not sexual, creature. Some might say that I was obsessed with being desired, and I would often sit in front of my mirror when no one was home and act out various seductions in my head. Doing this in real life had always seemed folly.... With Saffir though I could be as sexually open as I pleased with ... relatively few consequences and judgments made by my peer group. They would see me as an actress.[31]

In Kirstyn's case, the game provided an outlet and safe space for her to explore her nascent sexual expression. Walter played his Elsbeth character while a corpsman in the Navy. He likens his military experience to "being in an emotional coma," and his Elsbeth character allowed him to access his deeper feminine self, as well as his sense of sensuality. He explains, "She was a powerhouse socially. She allowed me to be desirable. She allowed me to be elegant. She allowed me to be sensual even, in a time when those were all things that were denied to me in my real life. And if I hadn't had that escape ... I really think that there would have been even more damage done."[32] The emotional strain of the military experience was, in some part, alleviated by Walter's involvement with role-playing games and his enactment of Elsbeth.

Ultimately, these Fragmented Selves help provide a sense of introspection within the player. Alex explains, "Sometimes it helps me know about negative things like a tendency toward violence or my greed, and other times it helps me realize positive things like my ability to think abstractly or my loyalty. Each little revelation may not sound like much, but each has had their impact on how I think of myself and how I act because of it."[33] By "watching" Viviane's moral deterioration through events within the game, I can better curtail such negative behaviors in the "real world." Thus, while the game provides an outlet or release for subdued aspects of self, it can also function as source of self-reflection. The players can observe how aspects of the self would behave along alternate timelines, enhancing their overall sense of experience and awareness.

The Repressed Self

Related to the Fragmented Self, the Repressed Self also represents a subdued aspect of the player's personality. More specifically, I refer to the Repressed Self as another term for the Inner Child: the youthful, naïve self within each of us. Role-players sometimes use games as an outlet for younger, more carefree parts of themselves to emerge. The constraints of real world responsibilities and trials can weigh heavily upon people's shoulders. The game space provides an open expression for "childish" behaviors, an outlet for the Inner Child to emerge and play within the created confines of the game system. These entities often display a certain simplicity of spirit and desire, as well as a relative level of naivety about evil and pain in the world. These aspects also sometimes manifest as a temporary lack of comprehension of "proper" behavior, thus inspiring a demeanor of well-meaning mischievousness.

The Repressed Self also often reflects a desire on the part of the players to make other people laugh and to not have to be constantly taken seriously. As Alex describes, "Flarea was my first 'furry' character, being an anthro based off of the Pokemon she's named after. Basically, this character was made for the sole purpose of acting like an idiot. Hell, she could only say 'Flarea,' after all."[34] The Repressed Self is often enacted through the rogue, or Trickster, archetype. "Elton" explains his motivations for creating "a Prankster type Rogue in the *D&D* environment":

> I really, truly enjoyed that character because it was an excuse for me to cut loose, and I'm generally a pretty repressed individual, I'm generally very quiet ... this character was really my way of more being able to ... be that person that I wanted to be, and cut loose, and poke fun, and be that person. That was part of the reason he really stuck out. I could cause all the commotion I wanted and it didn't have any consequences.[35]

The desire to "cause commotion" is often trained out of us. Adult life demands a certain level of seriousness and of respect for the boundaries others. The boundaries become more permeable with role-playing characters, and players often enjoy when characters "cause commotion," as interesting story lines emerge as a result of the insertion of a chaotic element.

In a sense, the Repressed Self may be viewed as a conscious form of *regression* into a younger state of consciousness. According to the International Dictionary of Psychoanalysis, "The Latin equivalent of regression means 'return' or 'withdrawal'; it also signifies a retreat or a return to a less-evolved state."[36] Guillermo describes how one of his characters, Jinkari, reflects a younger side of himself. He admits, "Jin is twelve years old. A lot of times I honestly feel like a very immature person. I mean, ridiculously immature, and so it's easy for me to draw, for him, how would my character react. And I also try to imbue him with a great deal of innocence and humanity."[37] Kirstyn describes the activities of her *Vampire* character, Alicia:

> With the mentality of a very stubborn child and the appearance of a ten-year-old Snow White ... Alicia often found herself in the middle of conflict. [She was] sometimes openly manipulative, very often playing upon the little humanity left in her fellow vampires. She was known for running around the Prince's court complete with "blankee," slippers, and stuffed animals and could often be seen rolling on the ground while the Prince was speaking because it was "boring." The boring excuse was one that she regularly applied to get out of common task that other in her station would have to do.... While certainly capable of acting her age (approximately two hundred years old), because of her appearance, no one expected her to behave older and so she didn't.[38]

Kirstyn's Repressed Self was able to break social conventions and behave immaturely despite her age, and, in turn, Kirstyn was also able to do so, if only vicariously through the character.

My own Repressed Self has manifested as Hailee in a *Mage: The Ascension* tabletop campaign and as Blythe in a *Vampire: The Masquerade* LARP. Both characters shift in age, sometimes behaving like a young girl and, other times, like a precocious teenager. Both characters believe that love can solve all problems and possess an inherent incomprehension about "how people can be mean to each other." Of course, such entities are especially vulnerable in the World of Darkness, which attempts to portray a reality even darker than the "real world." However, their youthful zeal often inspires new levels of compassion and self-reflection in other characters. In one scenario, for example, Hailee's adventuring party encountered an extremely sad demon that had been separated from his original plane of existence. The other party members wished to kill the demon, but Hailee "solved the problem" by creating a magical cocoon of unconditional love and embracing the demon with it. Experiencing this compassion, the demon was able to depart. The Storyteller did not anticipate this solution, and other characters of mine would have solved the problem radically differently, but Hailee's unique, child-like perspective offered a consequently unique solution.

The Idealized Self

Role-playing games provide players the opportunity to perform amazing feats in extreme circumstances. Henry explains that RPGs offer "a sense of excitement and adventure that usually doesn't present itself to me in real life."[39] John states, "Sometimes, you do some pretty amazing things. I remember slaying dragons at the side of my companion, saving the world, and righting wrongs. It's like you're a hero and you get to be a hero with your friends."[40] Desiree enjoys role-playing for this reason as well, stating, "I want to save and I always want to give and I always want to be the hero."[41] For some players, the opportunity to portray the hero figure forms the basis behind their desire to play.

Regardless of whether or not the character acts heroically, role-playing characters often present an Idealized Self, a persona that possesses qualities the player wishes he or she had. As Fine explains, "Taking on a role helps one overcome deficiencies of one's 'real self.' The gaming community is described by participants as being protective for its members, and through the development of gaming competence coupled with the ability to enact idealized roles ... individuals claim to gain confidence."[42] This confidence arrives from playing out scenarios successfully, but also at developing characters that can perform the tasks necessary for success.

Several of my informants described how certain characters possessed physical attributes they felt they personally lacked. Haley developed severe C-spine scoliosis at a young age, which causes extreme amounts of daily pain. She explains, "Usually, [the characters] have what I don't. They have a physical ability. They're strong and they're healthy, and since I'm not, they get to have that."[43] Matthew, a two-time survivor of leukemia, always plays "warriors of some kind." He intimates, "Often times I felt powerless [as a child], and even to this day, I myself protect my friends with a furious rage if they are crossed. It sure takes a lot to even bring me to 'rage,' but if my friends are insulted, people won't hear the end of it until restitution is paid."[44] He enjoys having the physical strength he often lacked as a child and the characters provide him the opportunity to avenge wrongs done to his loved ones, even if enacted only within a game context.

Players report other qualities their character possess that they envy.

Carley, who often plays gay male characters, quips, "Damien gets all the sex I wish I could get, and I would be a lot more like Damien if I were hot enough."[45] Josh describes his character Hoodie as "more of an aspiration" of his. He explains, "He's always on top of the situation. He's always cool-headed even when there're a lot of problems. He's able to take care of it. He does what he needs [to do], but he always smiles and jokes. He's kind of something I want to be, so I base my decisions in general on what he would do."[46] Josh, like many players, uses his Idealized Self as a benchmark for proper or desirable behavior.

Some respondents attempt to play pacifistic characters, even though the game often necessitates some sort of mental or physical combat. These characters often embody the player's sense of spiritual idealism. One of my *Vampire* characters, Geneveve, represented a Mother Healer archetype. Her paradigm involved altruism and compassion at all costs and eventually, she decided to drop out of the cutthroat vampiric society completely in order to seek spiritual transcendence. Haley describes one of her characters, Illeana, as "a healer pacifist half-fey. She flies everywhere and won't hurt anybody, but she uses [the spell] Calm Emotions quite often to end battles."[47] Kirstyn details the thought process of her shaman character: "While passionate about her beliefs, she is ultimately a pacifist. [She] subsequently often finds herself either letting people continue down 'dark paths' after her warnings or she is forced to take action — if what one is doing will cause harm to others — and take life."[48] One of Omega's characters, Nightshine, jointly established his own city with other party, a place founded on tolerance for others regardless of race or class. Omega explains, "[Nightshine's] whole philosophy is 'Love your friends for they are your family.' And there's nothing that he wouldn't do for somebody else. He is a self-sacrificing fool, in some people's opinion, and he would stop the world from turning if it meant to save one single life."[49] These characters reflect a deeper understanding on the part of the players of the damage done by violence and a desire to embody a healing archetype rather than a destructive one.

Other players report constructing characters that embody idealized components, but have to adapt these aspects to the demands of the game world. Walter's character, Elsbeth, offered an interesting blend of manipulation and compassion:

> [Elsbeth] was manipulative, but she was, by definition, never self-serving. She always, always kept her eye on what she perceived as the greater good. So that was kind of interesting too to be playing a character who was motivated by basically noble things, like defending others and keeping stability

in the realm and helping people through their crises but could use these really underhanded vicious tactics at times to accomplish it.[50]

My character, Eustacia, manifests somewhat similarly to Elsbeth in that her primary concern is the safety of others, but she also understands the machinations of court politics and can navigate them to achieve these ends. Successful characters must find ways to manage the conflict between their inner beliefs and external pressures.

The Oppositional Self

Players sometimes find enjoyment in the creation of a character in complete opposition with their primary personality. These characters may embody behavior patterns that the player finds abhorrent, such as the desire to murder, betray, or otherwise destroy the lives of others. John describes his assassin character, Azul: "[Azul] was responsible for a lot of death in the game. I mean, he would seek out damage to do, contracts to find. He was proactive about finding people to go kill. I've never played a character like that." In addition, he exclaims, "I'm adventurous but I don't like to kill people while I'm about it!"[51] Erin describes her rogue character, who would steal from people, as "selfish." She states that the character was "dynamically different" from herself, explaining, "I always try and do stuff for anybody who needs help or if there's anything that I can do for somebody else, even above and beyond what I'm capable of, I'll try and help them."[52]

However, Oppositional Selves do not always behave in a reprehensible manner. Sometimes, these characters simply reflect attributes that the player would never normally association with him or herself. For instance, when I created Hortense, I imbued her with behaviors and preferences in direct contrast with my own. Hortense believes strongly in censorship and adopting the paradigm of the patriarchal status quo, whereas I have always rejected, or at least challenged, such values. Matthew would ask me questions such as, "What's Hortense's favorite scent?" I thought of the scent I find least appealing and responded, in this case, with "baby powder." Hortense adores authors such as Emily Dickinson, who I find trite; she detests the French, while I am a francophile. Hortense is not exceptionally evil. In fact, she cares deeply about the small number of people she allows into her inner sanctum. I describe her more as "me in negative."

As I explained in chapter three, sometimes exploration of an Oppositional Self aids players in better understanding both themselves and people with whom they would not normally relate. As Darren states, the "characters that we play represent a facet of our personalities, or maybe even the inverse. Somehow ... we reach out to try and understand a personality type or trait that we normally try to avoid in ourselves."[53] Henry explains, "I've played a few characters who were military personnel and/or very pious religious people, but I know I will never join the military, and though I have strong views about spirituality and the nature of the supernatural, I do not practice in any religion."[54] Chris also plays character diametrically oppositional from his belief system. He describes the logic behind the creation of his were-rat character, Burrito Supreme, which occurred after 9/11:

> There was a lot of patriotic fervor in the air ... I kinda saw for the first time how extreme people can get about their nationalistic tendencies. And I thought that it would be honest ... because I wanted Burrito Supreme to be a fanatic, I wanted him to really love Ratkin. I didn't relate to it, but ... I guess understanding helps really. I get the reason why people are so patriotic, are so "pro" something like that. I'm not that kind of person at all though ... I believe it to be a sin, because I believe it's ... a form of pride. And pride is a sin.[55]

In this case, playing the character allowed Chris to better understand the emotions people were experiencing in the "real world." In this sense, the character became a vehicle for exploration of other people's mentalities.

The Experimental Self

The next category of role-playing characters arises when a player attempts to create a character as an "experiment." These personas may exist as bizarre concepts, highlight interesting themes in the game, or may present difficult role-playing challenges. Some of my respondents detailed characters toward whom they seemed not to have an emotional attachment or affiliation, but who made the game itself more exciting or interesting. "Elton" describes one such character in the following passage:

> I remember one character in particular that I created who was ... a strongly evangelical preacher who was convinced that [he was] Jesus. And [he was] just psychotic enough to meld the religious with the rules of the vampire. And it was one of those experiments where I was just like, "Let's see what happens when I make this." And it was completely incompatible with the universe that this role-playing game existed in. But it was one of those experiments where I was just playing around with numbers and rules and character creation [and thought], "Let's throw this out, see if it floats." And it was a horribly fun character. Horribly, horribly fun.[56]

Experimental characters often function to test the bounds of the role-playing experience. Chris describes how he used the LARP format to enhance immersion into his Burrito Supreme character through costuming. Because Burrito Supreme was born a rat and later became human, Chris wanted to portray him as more animal than *homo sapiens*. He describes,

> My roommate had a rat for a pet and I played with the rat for three days.... And I finally got the personality down.... We went to the pet shop and she got me a leash. She got a little baggie of treats and stuff for pets that she could give me.... And I played him as animalistic as possible. I [blew] up little water balloons and kept them in my pockets ... I would never stand upright, I would always just kind of stand hunched over, because I was very uncomfortable with the idea of standing upright. I would pop a balloon so it would simulate me peeing my pants, right in front of somebody. Constantly, [my roommate] would feed me random food, and I would put it in my mouth and just keep chewing on it, but never swallow it, and when talking to people and trying to speak English, I would just spit this food out of my mouth and sometimes onto them, sometimes onto myself.[57]

Though playful and humorous, this type of forethought raises the bar for other players in terms of role-playing. It forces them to rethink many of their assumptions about both the process of role-playing itself, but also about the nature of the often supernatural, larger-than-life beings they portray.

The Taboo Self

Some characters allow players to explore taboo subjects through the safe space of the role-playing game, an environment which remains, for the most part, consequence-free. Common taboos explored with these personas include: incest, cannibalism, murder, rape, abuse, and transgenderism. While non-gamers may view the exploration of these topics shocking, the Taboo Self can often be used to create a space for in-character and out-of-character discussion about normally off-limits topics. Indeed, the Taboo Self often works to reaffirm the moral stance of the players, rather than to subvert it.

Integration

The experiences players have with characters deeply mark them, particularly if they enact one persona over a long stretch of time. Because the RPG creates a ritual space for players to inhabit, the moments they share within that space, both in-character and out-of-character, affect their understanding of themselves and others. MacKay claims,

After going through the process of creating a cohesive character from various fragments, players can then carry this experience over to their real life. I have observed this process in many of my role-player friends, many of whom confess to experiencing a sense of unity underlying the chaos and fragmentation of everyday reality because of the paradigms derived from role-playing.[58]

According to MacKay, for role-players, the experience of reality is more fragmented than the structured reality of the RPGs.

Many of my participants report relying on the judgment or personality strengths of their characters during times of "real life" struggle. I often "call upon" Viviane or Eustacia when I need to handle a delicate social situation. Omega explains that he relies on his favorite character in times of "crisis" because "she never panics. She would react quickly, quickly assigned a goal or a task to what she believed needed to be done, and she would just carry it through.... She would chose the best path for that instant. And afterward would look back and see if there were pieces she needed to pick up or if she actually did the right thing."[59] Haley explains that her "character," Xilliara, already existed in her mind before role-playing. Xilliara's personality developed more fully in the game space of role-playing. Haley explains, "I found that she had become stronger, more self-confident, and even more self realized. The biggest difference is that not only did playing Xillaira make her a more whole ego, it made me stronger and more sure of who I was. I know it sounds strange but the more I played her the better I knew myself."[60]

Indeed, many players report that enacting other entities helped them better understand their primary sense of self. Darren explains, "All my characters teach me something about myself because I get to externalize a part of me and really look at how it interacts and plays with other people."[61] Desiree believes that playing pretend actually enhances people's sense of honesty. She asserts, "[Role-playing] has allowed me to be more honest with myself and others. Because when you're pretending and you're participating in a fantasy world, there's more honesty than anyone ever wants to admit."[62]

This chapter responds to a need within gaming research to more fully delineate the types of roles that players enact and their relationship with those roles. Describing character-building activities, delineating the evolution of the character, and creating a basic typology aids in such a challenge. Ultimately, though, efforts to fully describe what a role-playing character "is" seems as elusive as defining the origins of imagination and creativity. However, when players create a character, they establish an internal space within their minds for that entity to inhabit and within which it can grow. Interactions both in-game and out-of-character contribute to the evolution of these entities, as do a myriad of other activities, such as drawing, writing, and reading. Long-played characters often exist beyond the life-span of the game, reappearing in the player's mind in the future. Players even report that they have even utilized the skills and personality traits developed through role-playing in "real life" situations. These situations strongly suggest that the experiences explored in role-playing games enhance the "reality" of mundane experience in surprising, meaningful ways.

Conclusion

Role-playing is rooted in essential aspects of human social behavior, and role-playing games in their current, systemized forms emerged as subcultural phenomena resulting from developments including culture-wide paradigm shifts regarding diversity; increased interest in the genres represented by the games; and the technological advances of the information age. Thus, the practice of role-playing arose from both specific cultural trends and more essential human behaviors. This volume has briefly examined these contributing threads, as well as explained the different types and categories of role-playing games.

Role-playing has manifested in a multitude of cultural contexts, from business to military training to health care and leisure. Role-playing lends to a heightened sense of community among players, encouraging interaction between people who might not normally socialize with one another. The practice of adopting an alternate persona, identity alteration, establishes a "theory of mind" within players. Role-played personas offer players the opportunity to shift paradigms and increase various interpersonal skills, from empathy to group cooperation. RPGs reflect a form of ritual performance in which group cohesion is established and maintained through the enactment of powerful archetypes and narratives.

Role-playing games encourage higher-level mental processing abilities, including scenario building and problem solving. Gaming provides the opportunity for participants to acquire personal, interpersonal, cultural, cognitive, and professional skills. RPGs establish an elaborate structure that encourages gamers to evaluate the world in terms of a set of rules. These games offer extensive scenarios that require puzzle-solving, as well as tactical and social maneuvering. Far from simply offering "mindless entertainment," role-playing games actually encourage the development and expansion of mental abilities.

The process of enacting a role involves, on some level, the creation of an alternate sense of self. While some RPGs encourage character development more than others, for a game to be considered "role-playing," I believe that some sort of suspension of one's primary identity and immersion into an alternate mental framework should transpire. This alteration of identity occurs while co-creating shared worlds and narratives in a structured environment. These practices arise from early forms of imaginative play, including the creation of paracosms, Imaginary Friends, and other forms of pretend play. As adults, people must enact a variety of different roles in order to succeed in daily life. Contained within each of us exists a multiplicity of identities, rather than a unitary ego-identity. The content of these identities often arises from cultural symbols and inherent psychological archetypes. Thus, we socially "role-play" on a daily basis, though this behavior remains largely unconscious and reflexive.

Role-playing games draw attention to the process of role development and enactment and often heighten the player's sense of self-awareness. Role-playing characters exist in a complicated relationship with the player's primary sense of self. The character concept is "born" and develops through various character-building activities, including back story writing, costuming, and co-creation with other players. In a theory arising from the responses of my participants and from my own experiences as a role-player, I establish nine types of role-playing characters; these character types relate less to the initial archetypal inspiration and more to the player's feeling of "sameness" or "difference" between their primary sense of ego-identity and the alternate persona. These characters often remain active mental formulations after the conclusion of game play, offering players experiences and personality traits that remain useful in "real world" situations. Thus, though role-players "escape" to a fantasy world, they return to their lives with a variety of useful skills and a stronger sense of self-awareness.

This volume has explored three major functions of role-playing in both "serious" and leisure contexts. Role-playing allows players to build community, problem-solve through the enactment of scenarios, and create and perform alternate identities. These aspects of the role-playing experience offer exceptional benefits to role-players of all ages. Contrary to media representations, participation in role-playing games is not merely an escapist or psychologically dangerous activity. Players overwhelmingly report positive experiences and state that these games offer them many opportunities for personal growth.

When examined together, these three psychological functions work to establish an overall theory of role-playing. This theory integrates description, interpretation, and analysis, providing a functional model for further research. Unfortunately, I could not address at length other fascinating aspects of role-playing, such as the relationship between gaming and gender/sexuality and the quality of immersion between in-person versus virtual gaming. However, the interviews I collected for this project provide ample material to explore such avenues in future work. Therefore, this volume is not intended to provide a comprehensive list of the various issues raised by participation in RPGs. Rather, I have selected what I believe to be the most important and universal aspects of role-playing, regardless of format.

This model establishes a functional theory for inclusion within the larger spectrum of game and leisure studies. Additionally, my overall goal for this project has been three-fold. I intend for readers familiar with RPGs to feel that gamers are fairly represented in this study, as all too often, media texts such as newspaper articles and documentaries ridicule and marginalize role-players. I also intend for readers unfamiliar with role-playing games to feel they have gained substantive insight into the fascinating potentialities offered by this practice. Finally, this work formulates a theory regarding the evolution of characters that will hopefully become useful not only to scholars in gaming studies, but also those interested in the nature of creativity and art. Like scholar Daniel MacKay, I strongly consider role-playing games a form of art, melding creative writing, gaming, and improvisational drama in a co-created Shared World. The ultimate goal of this volume, then, has been establish theoretical formulations that will work to validate the study and practice of role-playing as an emerging art form.

Appendix:
Interview Questionnaire

- What role-playing games have you played in the past?
- In how many role-playing groups have you participated?
- Do you have any background in theater and/or improvisation? How would you say role-playing is similar or different?
- Describe the role-playing groups in which you've participated. How would you describe the attitudes/personalities of the GMs? How large/small were these groups? How long did you participate?
- How did people interrelate in these groups?
- Did you feel that you were part of a community once getting involved with role-playing games?
- What were some of the memorable interactional dynamics you recall from these groups?
- How many major characters have you had? Minor?
- Describe each of your major characters.
- How would you define this character in terms of "type?" E.g. Warrior, Thief, etc. If you could describe this character's concept, what would it be? Did you delineate a Nature/Demeanor for this character?
- For each: Does this character relate to your personality? Why or why not?
- Do you feel this character represents a part of you?
- Why did you find this character interesting to play from the beginning?

- How did your character change over time?
- Did you participate in any out–of–game activities to build character, such as story-writing, backgrounding, drawing, etc.?
- What did you learn from playing this character?
- Describe some situations in which you've had to solve a problem in-game.
- Is this problem something you might have to deal with in the real world?
- If so, do you think gaming has helped you deal with such a problem in your "real life?"
- If not, do you think this scenario taught you any skills that help you in the real world?
- Can you think of any gaming situations that have helped you in real life situations?
- Can you think of gaming situations that have taught you any specific skills?
- Tell me about your social life growing up.
- How would you have classified yourself as a teenager? Later in life?
- How would you describe most gamers? Gamers you associate with? Do you identify with any of these characteristics?
- Do you participate in any fan behavior outside of gaming? What kind? What genre?
- What sort of relationships have you built with other gamers? Be specific?
- Do you feel gaming has had positive effects in your life? Why or why not?
- Negative effects? Why or why not?
- Do you think gaming is a positive practice for people in general? Why or why not?
- Negative practice? Why or why not?
- Has role-playing allowed you to explore relationships you would never had out of character?
- Has role-playing allowed you to explore sexual scenarios you never would have out of character?
- Has role-playing allowed you to explore alternative lifestyles or gender identifications IC?
- Has role-playing changed/enhanced/or become a detriment to your sex life?

Chapter Notes

Chapter 1

1. Gary Alan Fine, *Shared Fantasy: Role-Playing Games as Social Worlds* (Chicago, IL: University of Chicago Press, 1983), 195–196.

2. Joseph Campbell, *The Hero with a Thousand Faces* (Princeton, NJ: Princeton University Press, 1973), 3.

3. Joseph L. Henderson, "Ancient Myths and Modern Man," in *Man and His Symbols*, ed. Carl G. Jung and M.-L. von Franz (London, UK: Dell Publishing, 1964), 112.

4. Arnold Van Gennep, *The Rites of Passage*, trans. Monika Vizedom and Gabrielle Caffee (Chicago, IL: University of Chicago Press, 1960), 11.

5. Victor Turner, *The Ritual Process: Structure and Anti-Structure* (New York: Aldine De Gruyter, 1995), 96.

6. Daniel MacKay, *The Fantasy Role-Playing Game: A New Performing Art* (Jefferson, NC: McFarland, 2001), 111.

7. MacKay, 112.

8. MacKay, 15.

9. MacKay, 18.

10. MacKay, 15.

11. MacKay, 17.

12. Sandy Petersen and Lynn Willis, *Call of Cthulhu*. 5.6 Ed. (Oakland, CA: Chaosium, Inc., 1999).

13. Carrol Fry, "The Goddess Ascending: Feminist Neo-Pagan Witchcraft in Marion Zimmer Bradley's Novels," *Journal of Popular Culture* 27, no. 1 (Summer 1993): 67–80.

14. Mythopoeic Society, "Members," Mythopoeic Society, http://www.mythsoc.org/members/ (accessed May 1, 2008).

15. Tolkien Society, "About the Tolkien Society," the Tolkien Society, http://www.tolkiensociety.org/ts_info/index.html (accessed May 1, 2008).

16. Thomas M. Stallone, "Medieval Reenactments," in *Interactive and Improvisational Drama: Varieties of Applied Theatre and Performance*, ed. Adam Blatner (Lincoln, NE: iUniverse, 2007), 304–305.

17. Stallone, 303–304.

18. Stallone, 309–310.

19. David Pringle, *The Ultimate Encyclopedia of Fantasy: The Definitive Illustrated Guide* (Woodstock, NY: The Overlook Press, 1999), 222.

20. Pringle, 17.

21. Lawrence Schick, *Heroic Worlds: A History and Guide to Role-Playing Games* (Buffalo, NY: Prometheus Books, 1991), 18.

22. Kenneth Hite, "Narrative Structure and Creative Tension in *Call of Cthulhu*," *Second Person: Role-Playing and Story in Games and Playable Media* (Cambridge, MA: MIT Press, 2007), 31.

23. Garyn G. Roberts, "Introduction, Stories for the Millennium: Science Fiction and Fantasy as Contemporary Mythology," *The Prentice Hall Anthology of Science Fiction and Fantasy* (Upper Saddle River, NJ: Prentice-Hall, 2003), 3.

24. Quoted in Fine, 55.

25. Schick, 25.

26. Douglas Coupland, "Quit Your Job," in *Generation X: Tales for an Accelerated Culture* (New York: St. Martin's Press, 1991), 23.

27. Quoted in Michelle Nephew, "Playing with Identity," in *Gaming as Culture: Essays*

on *Reality, Identity and Experience in Fantasy Games*, ed. J. Patrick Williams, Sean Q. Hendricks and W. Keith Winkler (Jefferson, NC: McFarland, 2006), 125.

28. Graeme Davis, Tom Dowd, Mark Rein-Hagen, Lisa Stevens, and Stewart Wieck, *Vampire: The Masquerade*, 2nd Ed. (Stone Mountain, GA: White Wolf, 1992), front page.

29. Davis et al., 29.

30. Rebecca Huntley, *The World According to Generation Y: Inside the New Adult Generation* (Sydney, Australia: Allen & Unwin, 2006), 17.

31. *Uber Goober*, directed by Steve Metze, Scum Crew Pictures, 2004.

32. Sean Q. Hendricks, J. Patrick Williams, and W. Keith Winkler, "Introduction," *Gaming as Culture: Essays on Reality, Identity and Experience in Fantasy Games*, ed. J. Patrick Williams, Sean Q. Hendricks and W. Keith Winkler (Jefferson, NC: McFarland, 2006), 6.

33. Blizzard, "*World of Warcraft* Reaches New Milestone: 10 Million Subscribers," Blizzard Entertainment, 22 January 2008, http://www.blizzard.com /us/press/ 080122.html (accessed May 1, 2008).

34. I use *Vampire: The Masquerade* as an example, as the *Vampire* system is relatively simple to understand compared to mathematics-heavy games such as *Dungeons & Dragons, 3.5 Edition*. Part of the project of White Wolf's World of Darkness involved an attempt to strip down the complexity of its game system in order to access a wider variety of players and focus on Storytelling over mechanics.

35. Davis et al., 270.

36. Davis et al., 135.

37. Davis et al., 88.

38. Davis et al., 166.

39. Stallone, 307–308.

40. Amtgard, "Amtgard," Amtgard, Inc., http://www.amtgardinc.com/ (accessed May 1, 2008).

41. High Fantasy Society, "About HFS," HFS in Chaos, 2002, http://www .hfsinchaos. com/ (accessed May 1, 2008).

42. Amtgard, "Amtgard: The Rules of Play v7" Amtgard, Inc., 2005, http://amtgardinc. com/bldocs/AmtgardRoPv7_2.pdf (accessed May 1, 2008).

43. Society for Creative Anachronism, "SCA Kingdom and Principality Orders, Awards, and Honors," The Society for Creative Anachronism, Inc., 1997, http://www.p bm.com/~lindahl/jessa/kingdoms.html (accessed May 1, 2008).

44. Mark Rein-Hagen et al., *Mind's Eye Theatre: Laws of the Night* (Stone Mountain, GA: White Wolf Game Studio, 1997).

Chapter 2

1. Adam Blatner and Allee Blatner, "The Art of Play," in *Interactive and Improvisational Drama: Varieties of Applied Theatre and Performance*, ed. Adam Blatner with Daniel J. Wiener (Lincoln, NE: iUniverse, 2007), 272.

2. Blatner and Blatner, 272.

3. Blatner and Blatner, 275–276.

4. Lawrence Schick, "The History of Role-Playing Games," *Heroic Worlds: A History and Guide to Role-Playing Games* (Buffalo, NY: Prometheus Books, 1991), 17.

5. David L. Young, "Theatresports and Competitive Dramatic Improvisation," *Interactive and Improvisational Drama: Varieties of Applied Theatre and Performance*, ed. Adam Blatner with Daniel J. Wiener (Lincoln, NE: iUniverse, 2007), 284.

6. Young, 284.

7. Brian David Phillips, "Interactive Drama as Theatre Form," in *Journal of Interactive Drama: A Multi-Discipline Peer-Reviewed Journal of Scenario-Based Theatre-Style Interactive Drama* 1, no. 2 (October 2006), 53.

8. Phillips, 53.

9. Young, 284.

10. Martha Fletcher Bellinger [1927], "The Commedia Dell'Arte," TheatreHistory.com, http://www.theatrehistory.com/italian/com media_dell_arte_001.html (accessed May 1, 2007).

11. Phillips, 62–63.

12. Young, 284.

13. Young, 284.

14. Young, 284–285.

15. The Spolin Center, "Viola Spolin Biography," Intuitive Learning Systems, http://www.spolin.com/violabio.html (accessed May 1, 2007).

16. "Viola Spolin Biography."

17. Young, 284.

18. Adam Blatner, "Considering Moreno's Contributions," in Interactiveimprov.com, http://interactiveimprov.com/morenowb.html (accessed Nov. 4, 2007).

19. Adam Blatner, "Psychodrama, Sociodrama, Role Playing, and Action Methods," in *Interactive and Improvisational Drama: Varieties of Applied Theatre and Performance*, ed. Adam Blatner with Daniel J. Wiener (Lincoln, NE: iUniverse, Inc., 2007), 153.

20. Blatner, "Considering Moreno's Contributions."

21. Blatner, "Considering Moreno's Contributions."

22. Blatner, "Psychodrama, Sociodrama, Role Playing, and Action Methods," 154.

23. Daniel J. Weiner, "Rehearsals for

Growth," in *Interactive and Improvisational Drama: Varieties of Applied Theatre and Performance*, ed. Adam Blatner with Daniel J. Wiener (Lincoln, NE: iUniverse, 2007), 167.

24. Sally Bailey, "Drama Therapy," in *Interactive and Improvisational Drama: Varieties of Applied Theatre and Performance*, ed. Adam Blatner with Daniel J. Wiener (Lincoln, NE: iUniverse, 2007), 164.

25. Bailey, 166–167.

26. Bailey, 167.

27. Bailey, 167–168.

28. Bailey, 168.

29. Bailey, 169.

30. Wiener, 175.

31. Weiner, 174.

32. Weiner, 175.

33. Weiner, 175–176.

34. Hannah Fox, "Playback Theatre," in *Interactive and Improvisational Drama: Varieties of Applied Theatre and Performance*, ed. Adam Blatner with Daniel J. Wiener (Lincoln, NE: iUniverse, 2007), 3.

35. Fox, 4.

36. Fox, 5.

37. Fox, 5.

38. Fox, 5.

39. Mecca Burns, Doug Patterson, and John Sullivan, "Theatre of the Oppressed," in *Interactive and Improvisational Drama: Varieties of Applied Theatre and Performance*, ed. Adam Blatner with Daniel J. Wiener (Lincoln, NE: iUniverse, Inc., 2007), 218.

40. Burns, Patterson, and Sullivan, 219.

41. Burns, Patterson, and Sullivan, 222.

42. Ronald Miller and Armand Volkas, "Healing the Wounds of History,"in *Interactive and Improvisational Drama: Varieties of Applied Theatre and Performance*, ed. Adam Blatner with Daniel J. Wiener (Lincoln, NE: iUniverse, Inc., 2007), 34.

43. Ronald Miller and Armand Volkas, 34.

44. Ronald Miller and Armand Volkas, 35–36.

45. Ronald Miller and Armand Volkas, 36–37.

46. Ronald Miller and Armand Volkas, 39–40.

47. Ronald Miller and Armand Volkas, 36.

48. Ronald Miller and Armand Volkas, 40.

49. Ronald Miller and Armand Volkas, 42.

50. Rosilyn Wilder, "LifeDrama with Elders," in *Interactive and Improvisational Drama: Varieties of Applied Theatre and Performance*, ed. Adam Blatner with Daniel J. Wiener (Lincoln, NE: iUniverse, 2007), 23.

51. Kim Burden and Mario Cossa, "ActingOut: An Interactive Youth Drama Group," in *Interactive and Improvisational Drama: Vari-eties of Applied Theatre and Performance*, ed. Adam Blatner with Daniel J. Wiener (Lincoln, NE: iUniverse, Inc., 2007), 260.

52. Clark Baim, "Drama in Prisons," in *Interactive and Improvisational Drama: Varieties of Applied Theatre and Performance*, ed. Adam Blatner with Daniel J. Wiener (Lincoln, NE: iUniverse, Inc., 2007), 206.

53. Baim, 207–208.

54. Baim, 212–213.

55. Adam Blatner, "Creative Drama and Role Playing in Education," in *Interactive and Improvisational Drama: Varieties of Applied Theatre and Performance*, ed. Adam Blatner with Daniel J. Wiener (Lincoln, NE: iUniverse, Inc., 2007), 82.

56. Gustave J. Weltsek-Medina, "Process Drama in Education," in *Interactive and Improvisational Drama: Varieties of Applied Theatre and Performance*, ed. Adam Blatner with Daniel J. Wiener (Lincoln, NE: iUniverse, Inc., 2007), 91.

57. Weltsek-Medina, 90–91.

58. Weltsek-Medina, 93.

59. Blatner, "Creative Drama and Role Playing in Education," 79.

60. Blatner, "Creative Drama and Role Playing in Education," 83.

61. Joel Gluck and Ted Rubenstein, "Applied Drama in Business," *Interactive and Improvisational Drama: Varieties of Applied Theatre and Performance*, ed. Adam Blatner with Daniel J. Wiener (Lincoln, NE: iUniverse, Inc., 2007), 130.

62. Gluck and Rubenstein, 130.

63. Quoted in Jon Dovey and Helen W. Kennedy, *Game Cultures: Computer Games as New Media* (Berkshire, UK: Open University Press, 2006), 12.

64. Thomas M. Stallone, "Medieval Reenactments," in *Interactive and Improvisational Drama: Varieties of Applied Theatre and Performance*, ed. Adam Blatner with Daniel J. Wiener (Lincoln, NE: iUniverse, Inc., 2007), 311.

65. Stallone, 303.

66. Stallone, 304.

67. Stallone, 304.

68. Stallone, 305.

69. Stallone, 305.

70. Stallone, 306.

71. Stallone, 308.

72. Roy A. Rappaport, *Ritual and Religion in the Making of Humanity* (Cambridge, UK: Cambridge University Press, 1999), 14.

73. Emile Durkheim, *The Elementary Forms of Religious Life* (Oxford, UK: Oxford University Press, 2001), 6.

74. Arnold van Gennep, *The Rites of Pas-*

sage, trans. Monika B. Vizedom and Gabrielle L. Caffee (Chicago, IL: University of Chicago Press, 1969), 15.

75. van Gennep, 21.

76. Victor Turner, *The Ritual Process: Structure and Anti-Structure* (Chicago, IL: Aldine Publishing Co., 1969), 14.

77. Turner, 15.

78. J. Tuomas Harviainen, "Information, Immersion, Identity: The Interplay of Multiple Selves During Live-Action Role-Play," *Journal of Interactive Drama: A Multi-Discipline Peer-Reviewed Journal of Scenario-Based Theatre-Style Interactive Drama* 1, no. 2 (October 2006), 11.

79. Harviainen, 15.

80. Christopher I. Lehrich, "Ritual Discourse in Role-playing Games," The Forge, October 1, 2005, http://www.indie-rpgs.com/_articles/ritual_discourse_in_RPGs.html (accessed Nov. 3, 2007).

81. Lehrich.

82. Turner, 96–97, my emphasis.

83. Senior players may, in some cases, be given access to higher level characters if gained through gaming experience. Unfortunately, some level of nepotism can exist within gaming frameworks, as friends or family of the game organizers may be offered bonuses or advantages over the rest of the population. Such exceptions can work to undermine the ritual process, but are possible within any social framework and should not be singled out as exclusive to role-playing groups.

84. Adam Blatner, "Designing and Conducting Rituals, Ceremonies, and Celebrations," *Interactive and Improvisational Drama: Varieties of Applied Theatre and Performance*, ed. Adam Blatner with Daniel J. Wiener (Lincoln, NE: iUniverse, Inc., 2007), 46.

85. Large RPGs may require more than one GM, as the workload can be exorbitant. These individuals must be able to resolve conflict easily and sometimes rank each other based on duties or seniority in order to avoid future contests for authority.

86. The Tank designates the strongest or most powerful individual who will go first in battle, serving as a shield for weaker characters.

87. Lehrich.

88. Stallone, 311.

89. Lehrich.

Chapter 3

1. Brian Stableford, "The Nineteenth Century, 1812–99," *Fantasy Literature: A Reader's Guide*, ed. Neil Barron, (New York: Garland Publishing, 1990), 64–65.

2. Stableford, 65.

3. Stableford, 64–65.

4. Sean Q. Hendricks, J. Patrick Williams, and W. Keith Winkler, "Introduction: Fantasy Games, Gaming Cultures, and Social Life," in *Gaming as Culture: Essays on Reality, Identity and Experience in Fantasy Games*, ed. Sean Q. Hendricks, J. Patrick Williams, and W. Keith Winkler (Jefferson, NC: McFarland, 2006), 2.

5. Barbel Inhelder and Jean Piaget, *The Psychology of the Child*, trans. Helen Weaver (New York: Basic Books, 1972), 22.

6. Mike Eslea, "Theory of Mind: PS2200 Virtual Lecture," Uclan, http://www.uclan.ac.uk/psychology/bully/tom.htm (accessed February 22, 2008).

7. Tim Marsh, "Vicarious Experience: Staying There Connected With and Through Our Own and Other Characters," in *Gaming as Culture: Essays on Reality, Identity and Experience in Fantasy Games*, ed. Sean Q. Hendricks, J. Patrick Williams, and W. Keith Winkler (Jefferson, NC: McFarland, 2006), 202.

8. Marsh, 203.

9. Gary Alan Fine, *Shared Fantasy: Role-Playing Games as Social Worlds* (Chicago, IL: University of Chicago Press, 1983), 46.

10. Darren, interview by author, e-mail message, December 22, 2007.

11. Kirstyn, interview by author, e-mail message, February 1, 2008.

12. Kevin, interview by author, Dallas, TX, January 8, 2008.

13. Walter, interview by author, Austin, TX, January 13, 2008.

14. Omega, interview by author, Austin, TX, January, 27, 2008.

15. Omega, interview.

16. Fine, 206.

17. Walter, interview.

18. Desiree, interview by author, Ft. Worth, TX, January 26, 2008.

19. Omega, interview.

20. Kevin, interview.

21. Alex, interview by author, e-mail message, December 5, 2007.

22. John, interview.

23. Walter, interview.

24. Walter, interview.

25. "Elton," interview by author, Ft. Worth, TX, January 28, 2008.

26. Haley, interview by author, Austin, TX, December 9, 2007.

27. Matthew, interview by author, e-mail message, January 7, 2008.

28. Omega, interview.

29. Rachael Barth, Deird're Brooks, John Chambers et al. *Mage: the Ascension Revised Edition.* (Clarkston, GA: White Wolf Game Studio, 2000).

30. Chris, interview by author, Austin, TX, December 7, 2007.

31. Desiree, interview.

32. Guillermo, interview by author, Austin, TX, December 7, 2007.

33. Omega, interview.

34. Josh T., interview by author, Dallas, TX, January 8, 2008.

35. Matthew, interview.

36. "Elton," interview.

37. Henry, interview.

38. Chris, interview.

39. Josh T., interview.

40. Erin, interview.

41. Guillermo, interview.

42. Omega, interview.

43. Chris, interview.

44. Josh S., interview.

45. "Elton," interview.

46. Guillermo, interview.

47. Fine. 28.

48. Daniel MacKay, *The Fantasy Role-Playing Game: A New Performance Art* (Jefferson, NC: McFarland, 2001), 74.

49. Matthew J. Smith and Andrew F. Wood, *Online Communication: Linking Technology, Identity, & Culture*, 2nd Ed., (Mahwah, NJ: Lawrence Erlbaum Associates, Inc., 2005), 107.

50. Chris, interview.

51. Guillermo, interview.

52. Walter, interview.

53. Chris, interview.

54. Chris, interview.

55. Henry, interview.

56. John, interview.

57. Kevin, interview.

58. Chris, interview.

59. John, interview.

60. Walter, interview.

61. Walter, interview.

62. Aristotle [350 B.C.E.], "Section II Part XIV," *Poetics,* trans. S.H. Butcher, (Internet Classics Archive, Cambridge, MA: MIT, n.d.) http://classics.mit.edu/ Aristotle/poetics.2.2. html, (last accessed 2/26/2008).

63. Aristotle.

64. Aristotle [350 B.C.E.], "Section I Part VII,"*Poetics,* Trans. S.H. Butcher, (Internet Classics Archive, Cambridge, MA: MIT, n.d.) http://classics.mit.edu /Aristotle/poetics.1.1. html, (last accessed 2/26/2008).

65. *The Coriolis Effect: Adventure no. 5 for Champions Role Playing Game,* (Charlottesville, VA: Iron Crown Enterprises, Inc., 1986).

66. Cassady, Marshall and Pat, "The Be-ginnings of Theatre," *An Introduction to Theatre and Drama,* (Lincolnwood, IL: National Textbook Co., 1988), 3.

67. Victor Turner, *The Ritual Process: Structure and Anti-Structure* (Chicago, IL: Aldine Publushing Co., 1969), 96.

68. Arnold van Gennep, *The Rites of Passage,* trans. Monika B. Vizedom and Gabrielle L. Caffee (Chicago, IL: University of Chicago Press, 1969), 21.

69. Kirstyn, interview.

70. Walter, interview.

71. Walter, interview.

72. Graeme Davis, Tom Dowd, Mark Rein-Hagen, Lisa Stevens, and Stewart Wieck, *Vampire: The Masquerade,* 2nd Ed., (Stone Mountain, GA: White Wolf, 1992), 140.

73. Bill Bridges, Robert Hatch, and Mark Rein-Hagen, *Werewolf: The Apocalypse,* (Clarkston, GA: White Wolf Game Studio, 2000), 62.

74. Bridges, Hatch, and Rein-Hagen, 63–67.

75. Bridges, Hatch, and Rein-Hagen, 62.

76. Bridges, Hatch, and Rein-Hagen, 59.

77. Bridges, Hatch, and Rein-Hagen, 42.

78. Davis et al., 269.

79. Omega, interview.

80. "Community," Dictionary.com Unabridged v 1.1, http://dictionary.reference.com/browse/community, (last accessed 2/26/2008).

81. "Elton," interview.

82. Kevin, interview.

83. Chris, interview.

84. Chris, interview.

Chapter 4

1. Sean Q. Hendricks, J. Patrick Williams, and W. Keith Winkler, "Introduction: Fantasy Games, Gaming Cultures, and Social Life," *Gaming as Culture: Essays on Reality, Identity and Experience in Fantasy Games,* ed. Sean Q. Hendricks, J. Patrick Williams, and W. Keith Winkler (Jefferson, NC: McFarland, 2006), 8.

2. Sande Chen and David Michael, *Serious Games: Games that Educate, Train, and Inform* (Boston, MA: Thompson Course Technology, 2006), xvi.

3. Peter Schwartz, *The Art of the Long View: Planning for the Future in an Uncertain World* (New York: Currency Doubleday, 1991), back cover.

4. Uri P. Avin and Jane L. Debner, "Getting Scenario Building Right," *Planning* 67, no. 11 (November 2001): 22.

5. Avin and Debner, 23.

6. Beres Joyner and Louise Young, "Teaching Medical Students Using Role Play: Twelve Tips for Successful Role Play," *Medical Teacher* 28, no. 3 (2006): 225.

7. Mitchel Resnick and Uri Wilensky, "Diving into Complexity: Developing Probabilistic Decentralized Thinking Through Role-playing Activities," *The Journal of the Learning Sciences* 7.2 (1998): 154.

8. Joyner and Young, 225.

9. Howard Witt, "Researchers Say Video Games May Be Key to Teaching Youngsters," *Chicago Tribune*, February 9, 2007.

10. John Brickell and Robert Wubbolding, "Role Play and the Art of Teaching Choice Theory, Reality Therapy, and Lead Management," *International Journal of Reality Therapy* XXIII, no. 2 (Spring 2004): 42.

11. P. Dieckmann et al., "Role-playing for More Realistic Technical Skills Training," *Medical Teacher* 27, no. 1 (2005): 124.

12. Pamela D. Couture, "Ritualized Play: Using Role Play to Teach Pastoral Care and Counseling," *Teaching Theology and Religion* 2, no. 2 (1999): 97.

13. Boreum Choi et al. "Collaborate and Share: An Experimental Study of the Effects of Task and Reward Interdependencies in Online Games," *CyberPsychology and Behavior* 10, no. 4 (2007): 591–595.

14. Robert M. Fulmer, J. Bernard Keys and Stephan A. Stumpe, "Microworlds and Simuworlds: Practice Fields for the Learning Organization" *Organizational Dynamics* (Spring 1996): 37.

15. Mary T. Nguyen, "Mind Games: With No Aversions to Diversions, Columbia's Adult Gamers Come Together for Social Fun and Mental Challenges," *Columbia Daily Tribune*, March 9, 2007.

16. Nguyen.

17. Choi et al., 594.

18. Linda Naimi, "Strategies for Teaching Research Ethics in Business, Management and Organisational Studies," *The Electronic Journal of Business Research Methods* 5, no. 1 (2007): 33.

19. Bill MacKenty, "All Play and No Work: Computer Games are Invading the Classroom — and Not a Moment Too Soon," *School Library Journal* (September 2006): 47.

20. MacKenty, 48.

21. MacKenty, 48.

22. Brickell and Wubbolding, 41.

23. Couture, 96.

24. Brickell and Wubbolding, 41.

25. Andrea L. Foster, "Where Worlds are Born," *Chronicle of Higher Education* 53, no. 44 (June 7, 2007): 26.

26. Couture, 96.

27. MacKenty, 48.

28. Couture, 96.

29. Lynnette Hoffman, "Virtual Life Delivers Tools for a Real Life," *The Australian* (October 20, 2007): 30.

30. Naimi, 33.

31. Dal M. Herring, "Role Playing Shows Pitfalls of Quick Decision," *Journalism Educator* 40, no. 2 (Summer 1985): 27.

32. Anthony Breznican, "U.S. Army Recruiters Create Military-Life Video Games," *Toronto Star,* May 25, 2002.

33. Breznican.

34. Chen and Michael, 87.

35. William James Stover, "Teaching and Learning Empathy: An Interactive, Online Diplomatic Simulation of Middle East Conflict," *Journal of Political Science Education* 1, no. 2 (May-Aug 2005): 209.

36. Hoffman.

37. Stover, 217.

38. Elena Bodrova and Deborah J. Leong, "The Importance of Play: Why Children Need to Play," *Early Childhood Today* 2, no. 1 (September 2005)

39. Joyner and Young, 229.

40. Rob Foels and Thomas J. Tomcho, "Teaching Acculturation: Developing Multiple 'Cultures' in the Classroom and Role-Playing the Acculturation Process," *Teaching of Psychology* 29, no. 3 (July 2002): 226–229.

41. Valerie Schneider, "Role Playing and Your Local Newspaper," *Speech Teacher* 21.3 (Sept 1972), 227.

42. Naimi, 29.

43. Joyner and Young, 229.

44. Jack Arbuthnot, "Modification of Moral Judgment Through Role Playing," *Developmental Psychology* 11, no. 3 (May 1975), 323.

45. Foster.

46. Joyner and Young, 225.

47. Resnick and Wilensky, 154.

48. Bodrova and Leong.

49. Joyner and Young, 229.

50. Schneider, 227.

51. Stover, 211.

52. Teng-Wen Chang and Jessica H. Huang, "A Pilot Study of Role-Interplay in a Web-Based Learning Environment," *Educational Media International* 39, no.1 (March 2002):84.

53. Choi et al., 592.

54. Stover, 211.

55. Elizabeth Quill, "Course Uses an Online Game to Teach Leadership," *Chronicle of Higher Education* 54, no. 2 (September 7, 2007).

56. Janice Podsada, "A Path to Employment: Firm's Software Program Helps People With Cognitive Problems Gain Job Skills," *The Hartford Courant* (April 25, 2007).

57. Podsada.

58. Timothy Gifford and Howard S. Muscott, "Virtual Reality and Social Skills Training for Students with Behavioral Disorders: Applications, Challenges and Promising Practices," *Education and Treatment of Children* 17, no. 4 (November 1994).

59. "Virtual Life Delivers Tools for a Real Life," EBSCO Search, *The Australian* (20 Oct 2007).

60. James Amos, "In Case of Emergency: Actors Give Cops a Taste of Handling Crisis Situations," *The Pueblo Chieftan* (September 23, 2006).

61. Staff writers, "A Role for Role-play in Prisons," *People Management*, 12, no. 22 (November 9, 2006).

62. Foels and Tomcho, 226.

63. Stover, 209.

64. Foels and Tomcho, 226–227.

65. Ruth Davidhizar and Ruth Shearer, "Using Role Play to Develop Cultural Competence," *Journal of Nursing Education* 42, no.. 6 (Jun 2003), 273.

66. Steve Arney, "Role-playing Helps Students Understand Religion, Violence," *The Pentagraph* (June 15, 2007).

67. John J. Ratey, *A User's Guide to the Brain: Perception, Attention, and the Four Theaters of the Brain* (New York: Vintage Books, 2002), 38.

68. Ratey, 36–37.

69. MacKenty, 47.

70. Bodrova and Leong.

71. Chen and Michael, 117.

72. Schneider, 227.

73. Alec Luhn, "Young Students Become Urban Planners," *The Wisconsin State Journal* (June 27, 2007).

74. Luhn.

75. Resnick and Wilensky, 155.

76. Resnick and Wilensky, 154.

77. Resnick and Wilensky, 156.

78. Resnick and Wilensky, 166.

79. Resnick and Wilensky, 167.

80. Resnick and Wilensky, 167.

81. Fulmer, Keys, and Stump, 37.

82. Fulmer, Keys, and Stump, 48.

83. Fulmer, Keys, and Stump, 45.

84. Bodrova and Leong.

85. Bodrova and Leong.

86. Bodrova and Leong.

87. Bodrova and Leong.

88. Bodrova and Leong.

89. Stephanie A. Owens and Francis F. Steen., "Evolution's Pedagogy: An Adaptionist Model of Pretense and Entertainment," *Journal of Cognition and Culture* 1, no. 4 (2001), 289.

90. Owens and Steen, 316.

91. McKenty, 47.

92. Witt.

93. Staff writers, "Role-playing to Understand Resource Scarcity," *Curriculum Review*, 45 no. 6 (February 2006).

94. Joyner and Young, 229.

95. Aline Mendelsohn, "Real Men Play Soldier in Fake Battle," *The Orlando Sentinel* (Mar 06, 2006).

96. Staff writers, "U.S. Army Recruiters Create Military-Life Video Games," *Toronto Star* (May 25, 2002).

97. Janese Heavin, "Mock Gunman Teaches Police: Skills at School," *Columbia Daily Tribune* (July 26, 2007).

98. Rick Rothacker, "Session Ponders ID-Theft Scenario," *Charlotte Observer* (March 31, 2006).

99. Mark Davis, "Game Gives Teens New View of Family Finances: Role-playing Exercise Gives New View of What Really Goes On," *Kansas City Star* (Oct 29, 2006).

100. Barbara Rose, "Improve Yourself at Work with Acting Skills," *The Chicago Tribune* (Mar 16, 2006).

101. Rose.

102. Rose.

103. Chen and Michael, 49.

104. Chen and Michael, 49.

105. Chen and Michael, 49.

106. Chen and Michael, 53.

107. Chen and Michael, 58–59.

108. Chen and Michael, 55.

109. Chen and Michael, 56.

110. Chen and Michael, 55.

111. Chen and Michael, 61.

112. Chen and Michael, 62.

113. Gifford and Muscott.

114. James Mayse, "Players Match Wits, Command Armies in Gaming Convention" *Messenger-Inquirer* (January 7, 2007).

115. Mendelsohn.

116. Chen and Michael, 83.

117. Stover, 210.

118. Chen and Michael, 86.

119. Chen and Michael, 85.

120. Chen and Michael, 86.

121. Chen and Michael, 89.

122. Chen and Michael, 88.

123. Owens and Michael, 87.

124. Chen and Michael, 87.

125. Chen and Michael, 93.

126. Chen and Michael, 112.

127. Chen and Michael, 117.

128. Chen and Michael, 112.
129. Chen and Michael, 117.
130. Chen and Michael, 118.
131. Chen and Michael, 120.
132. MacKenty, 47–48.
133. Ray Braswell and Marcus D. Childress, "Using Massively Multiplayer Online Role-Playing Games for Online Learning," *Distance Education* 27, no. 2 (August 2006): 188.
134. Chen and Michael, 146.
135. Chen and Michael, 148.
136. Chen and Michael, 149.
137. Chen and Michael, 191.
138. Chen and Michael, 193.
139. Chen and Michael, 180.
140. Chen and Michael, 181–182.
141. Chen and Michael, 183.
142. Chen and Michael, 193.
143. Chen and Michael, 181.
144. Chen and Michael, 193.
145. Chen and Michael, 195.
146. Chen and Michael, 184.
147. Chen and Michael, 184.
148. Owens and Steen, 289.

Chapter 5

1. "Elton," interview by author, Ft. Worth, TX, January 28, 2008.
2. Gary Alan Fine, *Shared Fantasy: Role-Playing Games as Social Worlds* (Chicago, IL: University of Chicago Press, 1983), 57.
3. Fine, 73. Fine uses the masculine pronoun throughout his study because, by 1983, the fantasy gamers were almost exclusively male. While males still make up the majority of role-players, a far larger number of females participate in contemporary RPGs.
4. Chris, interview by author, Austin, TX, December 7, 2007.
5. Alex, interview by author, e-mail message, December 5, 2007.
6. Haley, interview by author, Austin, TX, December 9, 2007.
7. Chris, interview.
8. John, interview by author, Austin, TX, December 7, 2007.
9. Ron Edwards, "Chapter Four: The Basics of Role-Playing Design," *GNS and Other Matters of Role-playing Theory*, The Forge, http://www.indie-rpgs.com/articles/8/ (last accessed 2/19/2008).
10. John, interview.
11. Walter, interview by author, Austin, TX, January 13, 2008.
12. Matthew, interview by author, e-mail message, January 7, 2008.
13. Graeme Davis, Tom Dowd, Mark Rein-Hagen, Lisa Stevens, and Stewart Wieck, *Vampire: The Masquerade*, 2nd Ed. (Stone Mountain, GA: White Wolf. 1992), 104.
14. Davis et al., 23.
15. Josh S., interview by author, Austin, TX, December 9, 2007.
16. Heather L. Mello, "Invoking the Avatar," in *Gaming as Culture: Essays on Reality, Identity and Experience in Fantasy Games*, ed. Sean Q. Hendricks, J. Patrick Williams, and W. Keith Winkler (Jefferson, NC: McFarland, 2006), 189.
17. Walter, interview.
18. Desiree, interview by author, Ft. Worth, TX, January 26, 2008.
19. Darren, interview by author, e-mail message, December 22, 2007.
20. "Elton," interview.
21. Erin, interview by author, Dallas, TX, January 10, 2008.
22. Chris, interview.
23. Kevin, interview by author, Dallas, TX, January 8, 2008.
24. Fine, 42.
25. Fine, 78.
26. Fine, 79.
27. Josh T., interview by author, Dallas, TX, January 8, 2008.
28. John, interview.
29. Kevin, interview.
30. John, interview.
31. Monte Cook, Jonathan Tweet, and Skip Williams, *Dungeons & Dragons Player's Handbook: Core Rulebook I* (Renton, WA: Wizards of the Coast, 2000), 89–90.
32. Guillermo, interview by author, Austin, TX, December 7, 2007.
33. Walter, interview.
34. Guillermo, interview.
35. Davis et al., 222.
36. Maxine Schnall and Maxine Steinberg, *The Stranger in the Mirror: Dissociation, the Hidden Epidemic*, (New York: Cliff Street Books, HarperCollins, 2000), 11.
37. Schnall and Steinberg, 31.
38. Schnall and Steinberg, 32.
39. Bill Bridges, Robert Hatch, and Mark Rein-Hagen, *Werewolf: The Apocalypse*, (Clarkston, GA: White Wolf Game Studio, 2000), 55.
40. Davis et al., 55.
41. John, interview.
42. Desiree, interview.
43. Josh S., interview.
44. Guillermo, interview.
45. Erin, interview.
46. Omega, interview by author, Austin, TX, January, 27, 2008.

47. "Elton," interview.
48. "Elton," interview.
49. Chris, interview.
50. Davis et al., 38.
51. Chris, interview.
52. Davis et al., 32–35.
53. Richard E. Dansky, *Laws of the Night* (Stone Mountain, WA: White Wolf, 1997), 124.
54. Walter, interview.
55. Walter, interview.
56. Darren, interview.
57. "Elton," interview.
58. Davis et al., 187–188.
59. "Elton," interview.
60. Henry, interview.
61. Henry, interview.
62. Mello, 191.
63. Mello, 192.
64. Chris, interview.
65. Omega, interview.
66. Desiree, interview.
67. Omega, interview.
68. Desiree, interview.
69. Chris, interview.
70. John, interview.

Chapter 6

1. Sook-Yi Kim, "The Effects of Storytelling and Pretend Play on Cognitive Processes, Short-Term and Long-Term Narrative Recall," *Child Study Journal* 29, no. 3 (1999): 175–192.
2. Kim.
3. Kim.
4. Sigmund Freud, *Freud: Dictionary of Psychoanalysis,* ed. Nandor Fodor and Frank Gaynor (New York: Barnes and Noble Books, 2004), 143.
5. Freud, 153.
6. David Cohen and Stephen A. MacKeith, *The Development of Imagination: The Private Worlds of Childhood,* (London, UK: Routledge, 1991), 14.
7. Cohen and MacKeith, 77.
8. Cohen and MacKeith, 14.
9. Cohen and MacKeith, 22.
10. Gary Alan Fine, *Shared Fantasy: Role-Playing Games as Social Worlds* (Chicago, IL: University of Chicago Press, 1983), 130.
11. Fine, 131–132.
12. Alain de Mijolla, ed., "Family Romance," *International Dictionary of Psychoanalysis,* Enotes.com, http://soc.enotes.com/psychoanalysis-encyclopedia/family-romance (accessed January 9, 2007).
13. Mijolla.

14. Stephanie M. Carlson et al., "The Characteristics and Correlates of Fantasy in School-Age Children: Imaginary Companions, Impersonation, and Social Understanding," *Developmental Psychology* 40, no. 6 (2004), 1173.
15. Carlson et al., 1178.
16. Carlson et al., 1174.
17. Carlson et al., 1175.
18. Erik H. Erikson*, Identity: Youth and Crisis* (New York: W. W. Norton and Company, Inc., 1968), 87.
19. Erikson, 87.
20. Erikson, 87.
21. Erikson, 94.
22. Peter R. Wright, "Drama Education and Development of Self: Myth or Reality?" *Social Psychology of Education* 9 (2006): 47.
23. Wright, 47.
24. Wright, 48.
25. Erving Goffman, *The Presentation of Self in Everyday Life* (New York: Anchor Books, 1959), 23–24.
26. Turkle, Sherry, "Identity Crisis," in *CyberReader,* ed. Victor J. Vitanza. Upper Saddle River, NJ: Pearson Longman, 2005), 57–58.
27. Turkle, 63.
28. Marlene Steinberg and Maxine Schnall, *The Stranger in the Mirror, Dissociation: The Hidden Epidemic* (New York: HarperCollins, 2000).
29. Erikson, 21.
30. Erikson, 21.
31. Erikson, 134.
32. Daniel MacKay, *The Fantasy Role-Playing Game: A New Performance Art* (Jefferson, NC: McFarland, 2001), 157.
33. Turkle, 60–61.
34. Robert Assagioli, "Some Suggested Lines of Research," *Psychosynthesis: Individual and Social* (New York: Viking, 1965), 1.
35. Carl G. Jung, *Man and His Symbols,* ed. by Carl G. Jung and M.-L. von Franz (London, UK: Dell Publishing, 1964), 58.
36. Vladimir Propp, *Morphology of the Folktale* (Austin, TX: University of Texas Press, 1998), 26–35.
37. Propp, 79–80.
38. Joseph Campbell, *The Hero With a Thousand Faces* (Princeton, NJ: Princeton University Press, 1973), 19–20.
39. M. J. Young, "First Edition Advanced Dungeons & Dragons Charac-ter Creation," http://www.mjyoung.net/dungeon/char/step 002.html (accessed January 26, 2008).
40. Young.
41. Young.
42. Gary Gygax, *Official Advanced Dun-*

geons & Dragons Players Handbook (Lake Geneva, WI: TSR, Inc., 1978), 20–21.

43. Gygax, 21.

44. J. R. R. Tolkien, *The Lord of the Rings* (Boston, MA: Houghton Mifflin Co., 1994).

45. Young.

46. Young.

47. David Day, *The World of Tolkien: Mythological Sources of* The Lord of the Rings (New York: Gramercy Books, 2003), 120.

48. Day, 120.

49. Day, 120.

50. Young.

51. Louis Hyde, *Trickster Makes This World* (New York: North Point Press, Farrar, Straus and Giroux, 1999).

52. Hyde, 6.

53. Hyde, 7.

54. Young.

55. Young.

56. Day, 110.

57. "Gnome (Dungeons & Dragons)," Wikipedia.com, http://en .wikipedia.org/ wiki/Gnome_(Dungeons_&_Dragons) (accessed January 26, 2008).

58. "Gnome," Wikipedia.com, http://en. wikipedia.org/wiki/Gnome (accessed January 26, 2008).

59. Aardy R. DeVarque, "Literary Sources of D&D," Geocities.com, http://www.geoci ties .com/rgfdfaq/sources.htm (accessed January 26, 2008).

60. "Gnome."

61. DeVarque.

62. Young.

63. Young.

64. "Elf (Dungeons & Dragons)," Wiki pedia.com, http://en.wikipedia.org/wiki/Elf _(Dungeons_&_Dragons) (accessed January 26, 2008).

65. Young.

66. Day, 44.

67. Graeme Davis, Tom Dowd, Mark Rein-Hagen, Lisa Stevens, and Stewart Wieck, *Vampire: The Masquerade*, 2nd Ed. (Stone Mountain, GA: White Wolf, 1992), 132–139.

68. Davis et al., 88.

Chapter 7

1. Gary Alan Fine, *Shared Fantasy: Role-Playing Games as Social Worlds* (Chicago, IL: University of Chicago Press, 1983), 215.

2. Fine, 216.

3. "Elton," interview by author, Ft. Worth, TX, January 28, 2008.

4. Josh S., interview by author, Austin, TX, December 9, 2007.

5. Thomas Hardy, *The Return of the Native*, ed. John William Cunliffe (New York: C. Scribner Sons, 1917).

6. "Italian Surnames: Etymology and Origin, Surnames Starting with B," Italy World Club, http://www.italyworldclub.com/ genealogy/surnames/b.htm (accessed June 1, 2008).

7. Baldassare Castiglione, *The Book of the Courtier*, trans. Sir Thomas Hoby (London, UK: David Nutt, 1900).

8. Chris, interview by author, Austin, TX, December 7, 2007.

9. Matthew, interview by author, e-mail message, January 7, 2008.

10. Omega, interview by author, Austin, TX, January, 27, 2008.

11. Omega, interview.

12. "Elton," interview.

13. Daniel MacKay, *The Fantasy Role-Playing Game: A New Performance Art* (Jefferson, NC: McFarland, 2001), 86.

14. MacKay, 122.

15. Michelle Nephew, "Playing with identity: Unconscious Desire and Role-Playing Games," *Gaming as Culture: Essays on Reality, Identity and Experience in Fantasy Games*, ed. Sean Q. Hendricks, J. Patrick Williams, and W. Keith Winkler (Jefferson, NC: McFarland, 2006), 122.

16. Fine, 207.

17. Fine, 211.

18. Kirstyn, interview by author, e-mail message, February 1, 2008.

19. Kirstyn, interview.

20. Matthew, interview.

21. Carley, interview by author, e-mail message, February 10, 2008.

22. Alex, interview by author, e-mail message, December 5, 2007.

23. John, interview by author, Austin, TX, December 7, 2007.

24. Guillermo, interview.

25. Darren, interview by author, e-mail message, December 22, 2007.

26. John, interview.

27. Fine, 208.

28. Guillermo, interview by author, Austin, TX, December 7, 2007.

29. Desiree, interview by author, Ft. Worth, TX, January 26, 2008.

30. Kirstyn, interview.

31. Kirstyn, interview.

32. Walter, interview by author, Austin, TX, January 13, 2008.

33. Alex, interview.

34. Alex, interview.

35. "Elton," interview.

36. Alain de Mijolla, ed., "Regression," *In-*

ternational Dictionary of Psychoanalysis, Enotes.com, http://www.enotes.com/psycho analysis-encyclopedia /regression (accessed June 1, 2008).

37. Guillermo, interview.

38. Kirstyn, interview.

39. Henry, interview by author, e-mail message, December 22, 2007.

40. John, interview.

41. Desiree, interview.

42. Fine, 61.

43. Haley, interview.

44. Matthew, interview.

45. Carley, interview.

46. Josh S., interview.

47. Haley, interview.

48. Kirstyn, interview.

49. Omega, interview.

50. Walter, interview.

51. John, interview.

52. Erin, interview.

53. Darren, interview.

54. Henry, interview.

55. Chris, interview.

56. Elton, interview.

57. Chris, interview.

58. MacKay, 68.

59. Omega, interview.

60. Henry, interview.

61. Darren, interview.

62. Desiree, interview.

Bibliography

Abt, Clark C. *Serious Games*. New York: Viking Press, 1970.

Amos, James. "In Case of Emergency: Actors Give Cops a Taste of Handling Crisis Situations." *The Pueblo Chieftan* (September 23, 2006).

Amtgard. "Amtgard." Amtgard, Inc. http://www.amtgardinc.com/ (accessed May 1, 2008).

_____. "Amgtard: The Rules of Play v7." Amtgard, Inc. http://amtgardinc.com/bl docs/AmtgardRoPv7_2.pdf (accessed May 1, 2008).

Arbuthnot, Jack. "Modification of Moral Judgment Through Role Playing." *Developmental Psychology* 11, no. 3 (May 1975), 319–324.

Aristotle. "Section I Part VII." *Poetics*. Trans. S.H. Butcher. Internet Classics Archive, Cambridge, MA: MIT, n.d. http://classics.mit.edu/Aristotle/poetics.1.1.html, (last accessed 2/26/2008).

_____. "Section II Part XIV." *Poetics*. Trans. S.H. Butcher. Internet Classics Archive, Cambridge, MA: MIT, n.d. http://classics.mit.edu/Aristotle/poetics.2.2.html (accessed February 26, 2008).

Arney, Steve. "Role-playing Helps Students Understand Religion, Violence." *The Penatagraph* (June 15, 2007).

Assagioli, Robert. "Some Suggested Lines of Research." *Psychosynthesis: Individual and Social*. New York: Viking Press, 1965.

Avin, Uri P., and Jane L. Debner. "Getting Scenario Building Right." *Planning* 67, no. 11 (November 2001): 22–27.

Bailey, Sally. "Drama Therapy." In *Interactive and Improvisational Drama: Varieties of Applied Theatre and Performance*, ed. Adam Blatner with Daniel J. Wiener, 164–173. Lincoln, NE: iUniverse, Inc., 2007.

Baim, Clark. "Drama in Prisons." In *Interactive and Improvisational Drama: Varieties of Applied Theatre and Performance*, edited by Adam Blatner with Daniel J. Wiener, 205–216. Lincoln, NE: iUniverse, Inc., 2007.

Barth, Rachael, Deird're Brooks, John Chambers et al. *Mage: The Ascension, Revised Edition*. Clarkston, GA: White Wolf Game Studio, 2000.

Bellinger, Martha Fletcher. "The Commedia Dell'Arte." TheatreHistory.com, http://www.theatrehistory.com/italian/comme dia_dell_arte_001.html (accessed May 1, 2007).

Blatner, Adam. "Considering Moreno's Contributions." Interactiveimprov.com. http://interactiveimprov.com/morenowb.html (accessed Nov. 4, 2007).

_____. "Creative Drama and Role Playing in Education." In *Interactive and Improvisational Drama: Varieties of Applied Theatre and Performance*, edited by Adam Blatner with Daniel J. Wiener, 79–89. Lincoln, NE: iUniverse, Inc., 2007.

_____. "Designing and Conducting Rituals, Ceremonies, and Celebrations." In *Interactive and Improvisational Drama: Varieties of Applied Theatre and Performance*, edited by Adam Blatner with Daniel J. Wiener, 45–55. Lincoln, NE: iUniverse, Inc., 2007.

_____. "Psychodrama, Sociodrama, Role Playing, and Action Methods." In *Interactive and Improvisational Drama: Varieties*

of Applied Theatre and Performance, edited
by Adam Blatner with Daniel J. Wiener,
153–163. Lincoln, NE: iUniverse, Inc.,
2007.

_____, and Allee Blatner. "The Art of Play."
In Interactive and Improvisational Drama:
Varieties of Applied Theatre and Performance,
edited b y Adam Blatner with Daniel J.
Wiener, 272–282. Lincoln, NE: iUniverse,
Inc., 2007.

Bodrova, Elena, and Deborah J. Leong. "The
Importance of Play: Why Children Need
to Play." Early Childhood Today 2, no. 1
(September 2005).

Bogost, Ian. Persuasive Games: The Expressive
Power of Videogames. Cambridge, MA:
MIT Press, 2007.

Brackin, Adam Lloyd. "Tracking the Emergent Properties of the Collaborative Online
Story Deus City for Testing the Standard
Model of Alternate Reality Games." Ph.D.
diss., University of Texas at Dallas, 2008.

Braswell, Ray, and Marcus D. Childress,
"Using Massively Multiplayer Online Role-
Playing Games for Online Learning." Distance Education 27, no. 2 (August 2006):
187–196.

Breznican, Anthony. "U.S. Army Recruiters
Create Military-Life Video Games."
Toronto Star, May 25, 2002.

Brickell, John, and Robert Wubbolding.
"Role Play and the Art of Teaching Choice
Theory, Reality Therapy, and Lead Man-
agement." International Journal of Reality
Therapy XXIII, no. 2 (Spring 2004): 41–
43.

Bridges, Bill, Robert Hatch, and Mark Rein-
Hagen. Werewolf: The Apocalypse. Clarkston, GA: White Wolf Game Studio, 2000.

Burden, Kim, and Mario Cossa. "ActingOut:
An Interactive Youth Drama Group." In Interactive and Improvisational Drama: Varieties of Applied Theatre and Performance, edited by Adam Blatner with Daniel J. Wiener
260–270. Lincoln, NE: iUniverse, Inc.,
2007.

Burns, Mecca, Doug Patterson, and John Sullivan. "Theatre of the Oppressed." Interactive and Improvisational Drama: Varieties of
Applied Theatre and Performance, edited by
Adam Blatner with Daniel J. Wiener, 218–
229. Lincoln, NE: iUniverse, Inc., 2007.

Campbell, Joseph. The Hero with a Thousand
Faces. Princeton, NJ: Princeton University
Press, 1973.

Carlson, Stephanie M., Carolyn Charley,
Lynne Gerow, Mayta Maring, and Marjorie
Taylor. "The Characteristics and Correlates
of Fantasy in School-Age Children: Imag-

inary Companions, Impersonation, and Social Understanding." Developmental Psychology 40, no. 6 (2004), 1173–1187.

Cassady, Marshall and Pat Cassady. "The Be-
ginnings of Theatre." An Introduction to
Theatre and Drama. Lincolnwood, IL: National Textbook Co., 1988. 1–9.

Castiglione, Baldassare. The Book of the
Courtier. Translated by Sir Thomas Hoby.
London, UK: David Nutt, 1900.

Chang, Teng-Wen, and Jessica H. Huang. "A
Pilot Study of Role-Interplay in a Web-
Based Learning Environment," Educational
Media International 39, no.1 (March 2002):
75–85.

Chen, Sande and David Michael. Serious
Games: Games that Educate, Train, and In-
form. Boston, MA: Thompson Course
Technology, 2006.

Choi, Boreum, Dongseong Choi, Jinwoo
Kim, and Inseong Lee. "Collaborate and
Share: An Experimental Study of the Ef-
fects of Task and Reward Interdependen-
cies in OnlineGames." CyberPsychology and
Behavior 10, no. 4 (2007): 591–595.

Cohen, David and Stephen A. MacKeith. The
Development of Imagination: The Private
Worlds of Childhood. London, UK: Rout-
ledge, 1991.

"Community," Dictionary.com Unabridged v
1.1. http://dictionary.reference.com/bro
wse/community (accessed February 26,
2008).

Cook, Monte, Jonathan Tweet, and Skip
Williams. Dungeons & Dragons Player's
Handbook: Core Rulebook I. Renton, WA:
Wizards of the Coast, 2000.

The Coriolis Effect: Adventure no. 5 for Champions Role-Playing Game. Charlottesville,
VA: Iron Crown Enterprises, Inc., 1986.

Coupland, Douglas. "Quit Your Job." In Generation X: Tales for an Accelerated Culture.
New York: St. Martin's Press, 1991.

Couture, Pamela D. "Ritualized Play: Using
Role Play to Teach Pastoral Care and Counseling." Teaching Theology and Religion 2,
no. 2 (1999): 96–102.

Davidhizar, Ruth, and Ruth Shearer. "Using
Role Play to Develop Cultural Competence." Journal of Nursing Education 42, no.
6 (Jun 2003), 273–276.

Davis, Graeme, Tom Dowd, Mark Rein-
Hagen, Lisa Stevens, and Stewart Wieck,
Vampire: The Masquerade, 2nd Ed. Stone
Mountain, GA: White Wolf, 1992.

Davis, Mark. "Game Gives Teens New View
of Family Finances: Role-playing Exercise
Gives New View of What Really Goes On,"
Kansas City Star (Oct 29, 2006).

Day, David. *The World of Tolkien: Mythological Sources of* The Lord of the Rings. New York: Gramercy Books, 2003.

Deloria, Philip Joseph. *Playing Indian.* New Haven, CT: Yale University Press, 1998.

de Mijolla, Alain, ed, "Family Romance." *International Dictionary of Psychoanalysis.* Enotes.com. http://soc.enotes.com/psychoanalysis-encyclopedia/family-romance (accessed January 9, 2007).

_____, ed. "Regression," *International Dictionary of Psychoanalysis,* Enotes.com, http://www.enotes.com/psychoanalysis-encyclopedia/regression (accessed June 1, 2008).

DeVarque, Aardy R. "Literary Sources of D&D." Geocities.com. http://www.geocities.com/rgfdfaq/sources.htm (accessed January 26, 2008).

Dieckmann, P., W. Herzog, J. Junger, C. Nikendei, C. Roth, S. Schafer, D. Schellberg, M. Volkl, and A. Zeuch. "Role-playing for More Realistic Technical Skills Training." *Medical Teacher* 27, no. 1 (2005): 122–126.

Dovey, Jon, and Helen W. Kennedy. *Game Cultures: Computer Games as New Media.* Berkshire, UK: Open University Press, 2006.

Durkheim, Emile. *The Elementary Forms of Religious Life.* Oxford, UK: Oxford University Press, 2001.

Edwards, Ron. "Chapter Four: The Basics of Role-Playing Design." *GNS and Other Matters of Role-playing Theory. The Forge.* http://www.indie-rpgs.com/articles/8/ (accessed February 19, 2008).

"Elf (Dungeons & Dragons)." Wikipedia.com.http://en.wikipedia.org/wiki/Elf_(Dungeons_&_Dragons) (accessed January 26, 2008).

Erikson, Erik H. *Identity: Youth and Crisis.* New York: W. W. Norton and Company, Inc., 1968.

Eslea, Mike. "Theory of Mind: PS2200 Virtual Lecture." *Uclan.* http://www.uclan.ac.uk /psychology/bully/tom.htm (accessed February 22, 2008).

Evans, Monica Joyce. "Computer Games and Interactive Narrative: A Structural Analysis." Ph.D. diss., University of Texas at Dallas, 2007.

Fine, Gary Alan. *Shared Fantasy: Role-Playing Games as Social Worlds.* Chicago, IL: University of Chicago Press, 1983.

Foels, Rob, and Thomas J. Tomcho. "Teaching Acculturation: Developing Multiple 'Cultures' in the Classroom and Role-Playing the Acculturation Process" *Teaching of Psychology* 29, no. 3 (July 2002): 226–229.

Foster, Andrea L. "Where Worlds are Born." *Chronicle of Higher Education* 53, no. 44 (June 7, 2007): 26.

Fox, Hannah. "Playback Theatre." In *Interactive and Improvisational Drama: Varieties of Applied Theatre and Performance,* edited by Adam Blatner with Daniel J. Wiener, 3–12. Lincoln, NE: iUniverse, Inc., 2007.

Freud, Sigmund. *Freud: Dictionary of Psychoanalysis.* Ed. Nandor Fodor and Frank Gaynor. New York: Barnes and Noble Books, 2004.

Fry, Carrol. "The Goddess Ascending: Feminist Neo-Pagan Witchcraft in Marion Zimmer Bradley's Novels." *Journal of Popular Culture* 27, no. 1 (Summer 1993): 67–80.

Fulmer, Robert M., J. Bernard Keys and Stephan A. Stumpe. "Microworlds and Simuworlds: Practice Fields for the Learning Organization" *Organizational Dynamics* (Spring 1996): 36–49.

Gee, James Paul. "Learning by Design: Games as Learning Machines" *Interactive Educational Multimedia* 8 (April 2004): 15–23.

_____. *What Video Games Have to Teach Us About Learning and Literacy.* New York: Palgrave/Macmillan, 2003.

Gifford, Timothy, and Howard S. Muscott. "Virtual Reality and Social Skills Training for Students with Behavioral Disorders: Applications, Challenges and Promising Practices." *Education and Treatment of Children* 17, no. 4 (November 1994).

Gluck, Joel, and Ted Rubenstein. "Applied Drama in Business." In *Interactive and Improvisational Drama: Varieties of Applied Theatre and Performance,* edited by Adam Blatner with Daniel J. Wiener, 130–140. Lincoln, NE: iUniverse, Inc., 2007.

"Gnome." Wikipedia.com. http://en.wikipedia.org/wiki/Gnome (accessed January 26, 2008).

"Gnome (Dungeons & Dragons)." Wikipedia.com. http://en.wikipedia.org/wiki/Gnome_(Dungeons_&_Dragons) (accessed January 26, 2008).

Goffman, Erving. *The Presentation of Self in Everyday Life.* New York: Anchor Books, 1959.

Gygax, E. Gary. *Official Advanced Dungeons & Dragons Players Handbook.* Lake Geneva, WI: TSR, Inc., 1978.

Hardy, Thomas. *The Return of the Native.* Ed. John William Cunliffe (New York: C. Scribner Sons, 1917).

Harviainen, J. Tuomas. "Information, Immersion, Identity: The Interplay of Multiple Selves During Live-Action Role-Play." *Journal of Interactive Drama: A Multi-Dis-*

cipline *Peer-Reviewed Journal of Scenario-Based Theatre-Style Interactive Drama* 1, no. 2 (October 2006): 9–52.

Heavin, Janese. "Mock Gunman Teaches Police: Skills at School." *Columbia Daily Tribune* (July 26, 2007).

Henderson, Joseph L. "Ancient Myths and Modern Man." In *Man and His Symbols.* Edited by Carl G. Jung and M.-L. von Franz. London, UK: Dell Publishing, 1964.

Hendricks, Sean Q., J. Patrick Williams, and W. Keith Winkler. "Introduction." In *Gaming as Culture: Essays on Reality, Identity and Experience in Fantasy Games,* edited by J. Patrick Williams, Sean Q. Hendricks and W. Keith Winkler, 1–18. Jefferson, NC: McFarland, 2006.

Herring, Dal M. "Role Playing Shows Pitfalls of Quick Decision." *Journalism Educator* 40, no. 2 (Summer 1985): 27–30.

High Fantasy Society. "About HFS." HFS in Chaos. http://www.hfsinchaos.com/ (accessed May 1, 2008).

Hite, Kenneth. "Narrative Structure and Creative Tension in *Call of Cthulhu.*" In *Second Person: Role-Playing and Story in Games and Playable Media,* edited by Pat Harrigan and Noah Wardrip-Fruin, 31–40. Cambridge, MA: MIT Press, 2007.

Hoffman, Lynnette. "Virtual Life Delivers Tools for a Real Life." *The Australian* (October 20, 2007): 30.

Huntley, Rebecca. *The World According to Generation Y: Inside the New Adult Generation.* Sydney, Australia: Allen & Unwin, 2006.

Hyde, Louis. *Trickster Makes This World.* New York: North Point Press, Farrar, Straus and Giroux, 1999.

Inhelder, Barbel, and Jean Piaget. *The Psychology of the Child,* trans. Helen Weaver. New York: Basic Books, 1972.

"Italian Surnames: Etymology and Origin, Surnames Starting with B," Italy World Club, http://www.italyworldclub.com/genealogy/surnames/b.htm (accessed June 1, 2008).

Joyner, Beres, and Louise Young. "Teaching Medical Students Using Role Play: Twelve Tips for Successful Role Play." *Medical Teacher* 28, no. 3 (2006): 225–229.

Jung, Carl G. *Man and His Symbols.* Edited by Carl G. Jung and M.-L. von Franz. London, UK: Dell Publishing, 1964.

Kim, Sook-Yi. "The Effects of Storytelling and Pretend Play on Cognitive Processes, Short-Term and Long-Term Narrative Recall." *Child Study Journal* 29, no. 3 (1999): 175–192.

Lehrich, Christopher I. "Ritual Discourse in Role-playing Games." *The Forge,* October 1, 2005, http://www.indie-rpgs.com/_articles/ritual_discourse_in_RPGs.html (accessed Nov. 3, 2007).

Luhn, Alec. "Young Students Become Urban Planners" *The Wisconsin State Journal* (June 27, 2007).

MacKay, Daniel. *The Fantasy Role-playing Game: A New Performing Art.* Jefferson, NC: McFarland & Company, Inc., 2001.

MacKenty, Bill. "All Play and No Work: Computer Games are Invading the Classroom — and Not a Moment Too Soon" *School Library Journal* (September 2006): 46–48.

Marsh, Tim. "Vicarious Experience: Staying There Connected With and Through Our Own and Other Characters." In *Gaming as Culture: Essays on Reality, Identity and Experience in Fantasy Games,* edited by Sean Q. Hendricks, J. Patrick Williams, and W. Keith Winkler, 196–214. Jefferson, NC: McFarland, 2006.

Mayse, James. "Players Match Wits, Command Armies in Gaming Convention" *Messenger-Inquirer* (January 7, 2007).

Mello, Heather L. "Invoking the Avatar." In *Gaming as Culture: Essays on Reality, Identity and Experience in Fantasy Games,* ed. Sean Q. Hendricks, J. Patrick Williams, and W. Keith Winkler, 175–195. Jefferson, NC: McFarland, 2006.

Mendelsohn, Aline. "Real Men Play Soldier in Fake Battle." *The Orlando Sentinel* (Mar 6, 2006).

Miller, Ronald, and Armand Volkas. "Healing the Wounds of History." In *Interactive and Improvisational Drama: Varieties of Applied Theatre and Performance,* edited by Adam Blatner with Daniel J. Wiener, 34–44. Lincoln, NE: iUniverse, Inc., 2007.

Mythopoeic Society. "Members." Mythopoeic Society. http://www.mythsoc.org/members/ (accessed May 1, 2008).

Naimi, Linda. "Strategies for Teaching Research Ethics in Business, Management and Organisational Studies" *The Electronic Journal of Business Research Methods* 5, no. 1 (2007): 29–36.

Nephew, Michelle. "Playing with Identity." In *Gaming as Culture: Essays on Reality, Identity and Experience in Fantasy Games,* edited by J. Patrick Williams, Sean Q. Hendricks and W. Keith Winkler, 120–139. Jefferson, NC: McFarland, 2006.

Nguyen, Mary T. "Mind Games: With No Aversions to Diversions, Columbia's Adult Gamers Come Together for Social Fun and

Mental Challenges." *Columbia Daily Tribune*, March 9, 2007.

Owens, Stephanie A. and Francis F. Steen., "Evolution's Pedagogy: An Adaptionist Model of Pretense and Entertainment" *Journal of Cognition and Culture* 1, no. 4 (2001), 289–321.

Petersen, Sandy and Lynn Willis. *Call of Cthulhu*. 5.6th Ed. Oakland, CA: Chaosium, Inc., 1999.

Phillips, Brian David. "Interactive Drama as Theatre Form." *Journal of Interactive Drama: A Multi-Discipline Peer-Reviewed Journal of Scenario-Based Theatre-Style Interactive Drama* 1, no. 2 (October 2006):

Podsada, Janice. "A Path To Employment: Firm's Software Program Helps People With Cognitive Problems Gain Job Skills." *The Hartford Courant* (April 25, 2007).

Pringle, David. *The Ultimate Encyclopedia of Fantasy: The Definitive Illustrated Guide*. Woodstock, NY: The Overlook Press, 1999.

Propp, Vladimir. *Morphology of the Folktale*. Austin, TX: University of Texas Press, 1998.

Quill, Elizabeth. "Course Uses an Online Game to Teach Leadership." *Chronicle of Higher Education* 54, no. 2 (September 7, 2007).

Rappaport, Roy A. *Ritual and Religion in the Making of Humanity*. Cambridge, UK: Cambridge University Press, 1999.

Ratey, John J. *A User's Guide to the Brain: Perception, Attention, and the Four Theaters of the Brain*. New York: Vintage Books, 2002.

Rein-Hagen, Mark et al. *Mind's Eye Theatre: Laws of the Night*. Stone Mountain, GA: White Wolf Game Studio, 1997.

Resnick, Mitchel and Uri Wilensky. "Diving into Complexity: Developing Probabilistic Decentralized Thinking Through Role-playing Activities." *The Journal of the Learning Sciences* 7.2 (1998): 153–172.

Roberts, Garyn G. "Introduction, Stories for the Millennium: Science Fiction and Fantasy as Contemporary Mythology." In *The Prentice Hall Anthology of Science Fiction and Fantasy*, edited by Garyn G. Roberts, 1–3. Upper Saddle River, NJ: Prentice Hall, 2003.

"A Role for Role-play in Prisons." *People Management* 12, no. 22 (November 9, 2006).

"Role-playing to Understand Resource Scarcity." *Curriculum Review* 45, no. 6 (February 2006).

Rose, Barbara. "Improve Yourself at Work with Acting Skills." *The Chicago Tribune* (Mar 16, 2006).

Rothacker, Rick "Session Ponders ID-Theft Scenario." *Charlotte Observer* (March 31, 2006).

Schick, Lawrence. *Heroic Worlds: A History and Guide to Role-playing Games*. Buffalo, NY: Prometheus Books, 1991.

Schnall, Maxine, and Maxine Steinberg. *The Stranger in the Mirror: Dissociation, the Hidden Epidemic*. New York: Cliff Street Books, HarperCollins, 2000.

Schneider, Valerie. "Role Playing and Your Local Newspaper." *Speech Teacher* 21.3 (Sept 1972), 227.

Schwartz, Peter. *The Art of the Long View: Planning for the Future in an Uncertain World*. New York: Currency Doubleday, 1991.

Society for Creative Anachronism. "SCA Kingdom and Principality Orders, Awards, and Honors." The Society for Creative Anachronism, Inc. http://www.pbm.com/~lindahl/jessa/kingdoms.html (accessed May 1, 2008).

Smith, Matthew J., and Andrew F. Wood. *Online Communication: Linking Technology, Identity, & Culture*. 2nd Ed. Mahwah, NJ: Lawrence Erlbaum Associates, Inc., 2005.

Spolin Center. "Viola Spolin Biography." Intuitive Learning Systems. http://www.spolin.com/violabio.html (accessed May 1, 2007).

Stableford, Brian. "The Nineteenth Century, 1812–99." *Fantasy Literature: A Reader's Guide*, edited by Neil Barron, 62–115. New York: Garland Publishing, 1990.

Stallone, Thomas M. "Medieval Re-enactments." In *Interactive and Improvisational Drama: Varieties of Applied Theatre and Performance*, edited by Adam Blatner, 303–312. Lincoln, NE: iUniverse, Inc., 2007.

Stover, William James. "Teaching and Learning Empathy: An Interactive, Online Diplomatic Simulation of Middle East Conflict." *Journal of Political Science Education* 1, no. 2 (May–Aug 2005): 207–219.

Tolkien, J.R.R. *The Lord of the Rings*. Boston, MA: Houghton Mifflin Co., 1994.

Tolkien Society. "About the Tolkien Society." The Tolkien Society. http://www.tolkiensociety.org/ts_info/index.html. (accessed May 1, 2008).

Turkle, Sherry. "Identity Crisis." In *Cyber-Reader*, edited by Victor J. Vitanza. Upper Saddle River, NJ: Pearson Longman, 2005. 57–76.

Turner, Victor. *The Ritual Process: Structure and Anti-Structure*. New York: Aldine De Gruyter, 1995.

Uber Goober. Directed by Steve Metze. Scum Crew Pictures, 2004.

"U.S. Army Recruiters Create Military-Life Video Games." *Toronto Star* (May 25, 2002).

van Gennep, Arnold. *The Rites of Passage.* Translated by Monika Vizedom and Gabrielle Caffee. Chicago, IL: University of Chicago Press, 1960.

"Virtual Life Delivers Tools for a Real Life," *The Australian* (Oct 20, 2007).

Weiner, Daniel J. "Rehearsals for Growth." In *Interactive and Improvisational Drama: Varieties of Applied Theatre and Performance*, edited by Adam Blatner with Daniel J. Wiener, 174–183. Lincoln, NE: iUniverse, Inc., 2007.

Weltsek-Medina, Gustave J. "Process Drama in Education." In *Interactive and Improvisational Drama: Varieties of Applied Theatre and Performance*, edited by Adam Blatner with Daniel J. Wiener, 90–98. Lincoln, NE: iUniverse, Inc., 2007.

Wilder, Rosilyn. "LifeDrama with Elders." In *Interactive and Improvisational Drama: Varieties of Applied Theatre and Performance*,

edited by Adam Blatner with Daniel J. Wiener, 23–33. Lincoln, NE: iUniverse, Inc., 2007.

Witt, Howard. "Researchers Say Video Games May Be Key to Teaching Youngsters." *Chicago Tribune*, February 9, 2007.

"*World of Warcraft* Reaches New Milestone: 10 Million Subscribers." *Blizzard Entertainment.* January 22, 2008. http://www. blizzard.com/us/press /080122 .html (accessed May 1, 2008).

Wright, Peter R. "Drama Education and Development of Self: Myth or Reality?" *Social Psychology of Education* 9 (2006): 43–65.

Young, David L. "Theatresports and Competitive Dramatic Improvisation." In *Interactive and Improvisational Drama: Varieties of Applied Theatre and Performance*, edited by Adam Blatner with Daniel J. Wiener, 283–293. Lincoln, NE: iUniverse, Inc., 2007.

Young, M. J. "First Edition Advanced Dungeons & Dragons Character Creation." http://www.mjyoung.net/dungeon/char/step002.html (accessed January 26, 2008).

Index

203